RETHINKING
TRAUMA TREATMENT

A Norton Professional Book

RETHINKING TRAUMA TREATMENT

Attachment, Memory Reconsolidation, and Resilience

Courtney Armstrong

W. W. NORTON & COMPANY
Independent Publishers Since 1923
New York   London

Note to Readers: Standards of clinical practice and protocol change over time, and no technique or recommendation is guaranteed to be safe or effective in all circumstances. This volume is intended as a general information resource for professionals practicing in the field of psychotherapy and mental health; it is not a substitute for appropriate training, peer review, and/or clinical supervision. Neither the publisher nor the author(s) can guarantee the complete accuracy, efficacy, or appropriateness of any particular recommendation in every respect. All case examples presented in this book are either composites of several client stories or have had names and identifying information changed to protect client confidentiality.

As of press time, the URLs displayed in this book link or refer to existing Internet sites. The publisher and the author are not responsible for any content that appears on third-party sites.

For information about permission to reproduce selections from this book, write to Permissions, W. W. Norton & Company, Inc., 500 Fifth Avenue, New York, NY 10110

For information about special discounts for bulk purchases, please contact W. W. Norton Special Sales at specialsales@wwnorton.com or 800-233-4830

Manufacturing by Sheridan Books
Production manager: Katelyn MacKenzie

Library of Congress Cataloging-in-Publication Data

Names: Armstrong, Courtney, author.
Title: Rethinking trauma treatment : attachment, memory reconsolidation, and
    resilience / Courtney Armstrong.
Description: First edition. | New York : W.W. Norton & Company, [2019] |
    "A Norton professional book." | Includes bibliographical references and index.
Identifiers: LCCN 2018050514 | ISBN 9780393712551 (hardcover)
Subjects: | MESH: Stress Disorders, Traumatic--therapy | Stress Disorders,
    Traumatic—psychology | Psychotherapy--methods | Psychotherapeutic Processes
Classification: LCC RC552.T7 | NLM WM 172.5 | DDC 616.85/21—dc23
LC record available at https://lccn.loc.gov/2018050514

W. W. Norton & Company, Inc., 500 Fifth Avenue, New York, N.Y. 10110
www.wwnorton.com

W. W. Norton & Company Ltd., 15 Carlisle Street, London W1D 3BS

1 2 3 4 5 6 7 8 9 0

To all trauma survivors and the helpers who serve them. You are living examples of triumph and courage in the face of adversity. Thank you for your strength, wisdom, and compassion.

Contents

Phase I: Create Safety, Hope, and Therapeutic Alliance

Phase II: Transform Traumatic Memories

Phase III: Facilitate
Post-Traumatic Growth

Acknowledgments

Books are like children and it takes a whole village to raise them! First I must thank my editor Deborah Malmud. Your extraordinary patience and tenacious encouragement breathed life into this project when my self-doubt was attempting to smother it. I am also grateful to Ben Yarling who initiated the project; Sara McBride for her editorial assistance; Mariah Eppes for coordinating the project; Bill Bowers's sharp editing eye; and Norton's designers, who found the perfect symbol to represent the blooms of resilience contained in all trauma survivors.

Again, thanks to my husband Joel for your unwavering love and support. To Jon Connelly and Bill O'Hanlon—magical mentors who taught me to believe in possibilities. To my assistant Susan for her mind-blowing organization skills. To my dear friends Allyson Bowman, Tiffany Warner, Denise Powell, Tara Dickherber, and Nancy Gershman for cheering me on. To Penny Randolph for her lovely brain illustration. To Pat Ogden for permission to use the Window of Tolerance illustration that has helped both me and my clients understand and comfort a traumatized nervous system.

Finally, I want to thank all the pioneering clinicians and researchers who have ushered in more compassionate, positive approaches to trauma treatment. Though there are hundreds of you, I want to thank the following clinicians who have greatly influenced my perspective and the material in this book: Bessel van der Kolk, Bruce Ecker, Sara Bridges, Laurel Hulley, Robin Ticic, Dan Siegel, Bonnie Badenoch, Pat Ogden,

Janina Fisher, Francine Shapiro, Deany Laliotis Lisa Ferentz, Linda Graham, Richard Schwartz, Robin Shapiro, Peter Levine, Diane Poole Heller, Diana Fosha, Sue Johnson, Mary Jo Barrett, Martin Seligman, Marylene Cloitre, Christine Courtois, Bruce Perry, Stephen Porges, Allan Schore, Lou Cozolino, and Joe LeDoux.

Introduction

The Brain Changes Through the Heart

Neuroscience discoveries over the last 20 years have given us new insight and hope for healing trauma. We've learned how trauma disrupts healthy attachment and impacts the brain's ability to regulate itself, but we've also learned interventions that can help the brain heal and repair attachment wounds. Scientists once thought traumatic memories were indelible, but now they've shown the brain actually has an innate process for assuaging painful memories, called memory reconsolidation. We've learned that trauma can have positive effects on people, too. Research has shown a large number of people developed increased inner strength, greater appreciation for life, closer relationships, spiritual growth, and an openness to new possibilities after trauma.

While all these discoveries are promising, it's hard to know how to translate these scientific revelations into practical applications we can use in our sessions. Hundreds of new trauma therapy methods have emerged, leaving therapists encouraged, but confused. Which trauma therapy method do I use? Do I need to get trained in all these various approaches to be effective? How do I do this with the limited time and resources I have?

I've written this book to offer answers to these questions for you. Over the past 20 years I've trained in a variety of trauma therapy approaches, attempted to keep up with all the neuroscience, and learned what works best from my clients' experiences. This book gets you up to date on the brain science, provides you with practical strategies, and focuses on what the best trauma therapy methods have in common. You don't need to go get any more specialized training to help your clients right now. You've got the essentials right here and can use them as stand-alone interventions, or integrate them into therapy approaches you already use.

Rethinking Trauma Treatment is divided into three sections that parallel the three phases of trauma-informed therapy. Phase I: Create Safety, Hope, and Therapeutic Alliance gives you the foundation for understanding the neurobiology of trauma, establishing a strong therapeutic alliance, and tools for helping clients access hope and regulate strong emotions. Chapter 1, Trauma and the Brain, highlights the areas of the brain that are impacted during traumatic experiences and explains why resolving implicit memories is the key to reducing post-traumatic stress symptoms and triggers. Chapter 2, Attachment and the Brain, discusses how childhood trauma impacts brain development and explains why survivors of complex trauma have difficulty regulating their emotions and forming healthy relationships.

If you find brain science boring and want to jump into techniques and interventions, you can start with Chapter 3, Relationships Change the Brain. This chapter will give you the confidence of knowing that offering skills of empathy, authenticity, and positive regard influence your client's emotional well-being more than any specific technique. In addition, I review the four basic attachment styles and encourage you to assess your own attachment style so you can better understand the interactions between yourself and your clients. In Chapter 4, How to Engage Insecure Attachment Styles, I explain why your empathic presence may not be enough to connect with traumatized clients and discuss how to secure an alliance with people who have avoidant-dismissive, anxious-preoccupied, and disorganized-unresolved attachment styles.

If you're looking for techniques to help clients regulate emotions, go to Chapter 5, Tools for Grounding, Calming, and Soothing. For tips on how to help clients manage dissociation or dissociative identity disorder, go to Chapter 6, How to Work with Dissociation. Although we rarely think of uplifting clients as part of trauma treatment, I find it absolutely essential. Chapter 7, Instill Hope and Empowerment, gives you techniques and guided imagery scripts for helping clients recognize their strengths, access positive emotions, and create their desired futures.

Phase II of the book, Transform Traumatic Memories, gives you the nuts and bolts of reprocessing traumatic memories. Chapter 8, Memory Reconsolidation, gives you the science behind this revolutionary discovery and a five-step protocol you can use to resolve traumatic memories and reverse negative core beliefs. Chapter 9, Sexual Trauma, addresses the common issues clients experience after sexual assault or abuse. I demonstrate how to use memory reconsolidation to heal different types of sexual trauma, and interventions that help survivors shed shame, repair attachment wounds, and reclaim their identities.

Chapter 10, Childhood Physical Abuse, discusses how to use the memory reconsolidation process with clients who suffered extreme abuse and exhibit disorganized attachment. You'll get ideas for addressing suicidal ideation, updating beliefs of worthlessness, working with inner conflicts about change, and handling flashbacks in a session. Chapter 11, Relational and Attachment Trauma, addresses how to work with attachment breaches that weren't necessarily caused by direct physical abuse, but by experiences of growing up in chaotic, neglectful, or critical family environments. Chapter 12, Traumatic Grief and Loss, gives you tools for working with clients who struggle with guilt, nightmares, and complicated grief after a loved one dies suddenly or violently. In addition, I illustrate how to help a client with dissociative amnesia recover her memories. Chapter 13, Combat Trauma, addresses how to work with the war memories, flashbacks, and survivor's guilt that often plague soldiers and veterans.

Phase III, Facilitate Post-Traumatic Growth, discusses how to help clients thrive beyond trauma. Chapter 14, Post-Traumatic Growth, discusses the five areas where positive change and growth often occur for trauma survivors and how to facilitate them. Chapter 15, Healthy Relationship Skills, addresses how to help clients develop healthy relationships after trauma. Last but not least, Chapter 16, Counter Compassion Fatigue, gives you tools for managing your own vitality and stamina, so you can continue offering the world your gifts.

Choosing to be a trauma therapist takes courage and compassion. It's challenging, but it's also the most meaningful and rewarding work you'll do. I am hopeful this will be a supportive and useful resource to you. Think of it as your on-the-fly guide to trauma therapy that you can refer to when you need ideas, techniques, reassurance, and encouragement. More important, you'll learn why *you* are your most valuable tool when it comes to treating trauma. Research has shown the therapeutic relationship supersedes any single technique. In other words, neuroscience has validated what we've intuitively known as therapists: the brain changes through the heart.

RETHINKING TRAUMA TREATMENT

PHASE I

Create Safety, Hope, and Therapeutic Alliance

1

Trauma and the Brain

I t was 8 o'clock in the evening and I was packing up my things to go home after a long day of back-to-back sessions, when the phone rang. My heart sank. Although I wanted to go home, I knew I'd better answer it. On the other end of the line, a young woman named Katie cried in a panicked voice, "I'm sorry. I know it's late, but I'm calling to beg you to help my husband with his road rage," she sniffled. "He just threw a Frosty and a cup of hot chili at another driver as we were pulling out of Wendy's. He's been like this since he was in an accident 11 years ago, and he's not getting any better. I'm afraid he's going to get himself arrested or killed if he doesn't do something soon. Is there any way you could see us this week?"

Usually I would've asked to speak directly to the person a family member was referring to me before scheduling an appointment. But the desperation in Katie's voice called to my compassion. I did have an opening the next day and knew the sooner we could intervene, the better. So, I agreed to see Katie and her husband Dixon the next morning at 10 a.m.

When I walked into the waiting room that bright sunny morning, Katie greeted me warmly and thanked me for scheduling them on such short notice. Dixon rolled his eyes as he reluctantly strolled into my office behind Katie. As he plopped down on the couch next to her, he folded his arms across his chest and sulked. Before I could even ask the first question, he quipped, "Listen, I tried therapy 10 years ago right after my car accident and it didn't help. All the guy did was teach me some stupid breathing exercises and insist I talk about watching my sister burn to death in a flaming vehicle over and over again. So, if that's what you're planning on doing, forget it! The accident was bad enough the first time, I don't want to relive it."

Nodding vigorously, I replied, "I completely agree with you, Dixon. Reliving a horrible memory like that doesn't fix it, and I'm so sorry you had that experience. Fortunately, we've learned much better ways to deal with trauma over the last 10 years. So, I think you'll have a completely different experience this time. But before we get into that, I need to understand what you think makes you angry while driving. Do *you* think it's a problem?"

Although I was sure Dixon's road rage was a problem given Katie's pleas for help, I knew Dixon wouldn't trust me if I wasn't willing to hear him out and understand his side of the story. I listened compassionately as he told me how infuriated he felt any time he thought a driver was being careless or inattentive. He disclosed, "Just about anything could set me off—someone gabbing on their cell phone, or following me too close, driving too fast, meandering into my lane, or cutting me off in traffic—it doesn't matter. If they're not paying attention or putting me and my family in danger, I'm going after them!" He admitted that he regularly hurled expletives at other drivers, usually punctuated by the liberal use of his middle finger. Worse, at times he tailgated drivers who upset him, blowing his horn and screaming at them until they pulled off the road.

Dixon agreed that his road rage began after a horrible car accident 11 years earlier. He and his older sister were driving to a family gathering when a teenaged drunk driver swerved onto their side of the highway and hit them head-on. The collision had killed his sister instantly and ignited the car into flames, scorching his body with third-degree burns. His injuries had kept him in the hospital for a month, undergoing excruciating debriding treatments, skin grafts, and physical therapy.

He didn't have any obvious physical scars on his angular, clean-cut face, but when he wore open-collar shirts, I could see the swaths of salmon-colored scars that trailed down his neck toward his chest and smoldered across both arms. Dixon said he hadn't been able to sleep more than three hours consecutively since the incident. In addition to recurring nightmares, he said he'd frequently wake up startled by the slightest noise and tossed and turned so much his wife Katie wasn't getting much sleep either. Katie had tried to be supportive, but after 11 years, she was frustrated.

Katie lamented, "It's like a part of your mind is frozen in time replaying this accident, Dixon. You've got to let it go and move on." Then her eyes welled up with tears as she bit her lip and mumbled, "Or I'm afraid I'll have to move on from this marriage."

Suggesting that Dixon was "frozen in time" is actually a pretty accurate way to describe post-traumatic stress disorder (PTSD). Although PTSD was initially classified as an anxiety disorder when it was first introduced in the third edition of the *Diagnostic and Statistical Manual of Mental Disorders* (DSM-III) in 1980, advances in neuroscience suggest that it's more accurate to say PTSD is a disorder of memory integration between the three levels of our triune brain.

THE TRIUNE BRAIN

As Yale neuroscientist Paul MacLean (1990) described in his theory of the triune brain, the human brain is essentially "three brains in one" that develops in stages from the inside out and bottom up in this order: (1) the reptilian brain; (2) the mammalian brain; and (3) the cerebral cortex. When we're in a calm state of mind, these three regions of the brain communicate quite nicely with each other and we're able to comfortably control our impulses and thoughts. Yet when we're in a highly aroused emotional state, the reptilian and mammalian brains have the capacity to "hijack" the cerebral cortex in order to mobilize a survival response. At this point, all our logic goes out the window—just like the cup of chili that Dixon threw at the other driver. It wasn't that Dixon consciously decided to throw the chili—and his logic—out the window.

His reptilian and mammalian brains commanded it! Before I describe why and how that happens, let me briefly review the regions of your triune brain that are of particular interest when it comes to treating trauma. Figure 1.1 (page 13) provides an illustration you can reference as you read about these following brain regions.

Reptilian Brain (Brain Stem, Cerebellum, & Basal Ganglia)

Sitting at the base of the skull, the reptilian brain supports our most basic survival needs and includes the brain stem, cerebellum, and basal ganglia. You can think of this region as the "body-brain" because it connects the brain to the spinal cord and controls functions in the body.

- *Brain stem.* The brain stem regulates basic bodily functions such as sleep, respiratory rate, heart rate, digestion, and reflexes we are born knowing how to do, such as grasping and sucking.
- *Cerebellum.* The cerebellum coordinates posture, balance, and voluntary movements. Research by Teicher (2000) also suggests that activating the cerebellum through rhythmic movement helps to calm and balance the nervous system.
- *Basal ganglia.* The basal ganglia are a collection of structures that link up to midbrain regions to encode procedural memories. Housing the reward centers of the brain, this region also encodes habitual behaviors and learns through operational and classical conditioning.

Mammalian Brain (Emotional Brain/Limbic System)

Unlike their reptilian ancestors, mammals evolved to be warm-blooded, social creatures that live in packs. Likewise, the mammalian brain came equipped with social and emotional networks that endowed mammals with the ability to experience joy, play, and caring connections with fellow pack members (Panksepp & Biven, 2012). This "emotional brain" lies in the midbrain between the brainstem and the cerebral cortex. In addition to being the seat of our emotional responses and attachment instincts, this area of the brain is also involved in procedural learning, motivation, and memory. The following section lists the areas of the emotional brain that are involved in post-traumatic stress responses that are of most interest to therapists.

- *Thalamus.* The thalamus sits at the top of the brain stem and receives sensory input from both the external world and within our bodies. The thalamus acts kind of like a gatekeeper, determining which sensory information is relevant and needs our conscious attention versus sensory information we can let fade into the background. It is unique in that it has connections to all three levels of the brain and can communicate directly to the brain stem, limbic system, and middle prefrontal cortex. However, the thalamus transmits and receives information more quickly to and from the emotional brain than it does to and from higher cortical areas. So, our thinking brain is always a half second behind when it comes to processing emotional responses (Cozolino, 2015).
- *Hypothalamus.* The hypothalamus sits under the thalamus. Although it's a small structure about the size of a peanut, it controls our autonomic nervous system and regulates body temperature, sleep/wake cycles, food intake, and thirst.
- *Amygdala.* The amygdala is involved in emotional learning and is most known for its role in processing and activating the emotion of fear. You have an amygdala in both the right and left hemispheres of your brain that receive sensory information from the thalamus. The amygdala assesses the emotional significance of a stimulus and prompts the hypothalamus to tell the nervous system whether we should approach or avoid a stimulus based on past experiences. If the amygdala determines a stimulus is safe to move toward, like a loving caregiver, it signals the hypothalamus to release oxytocin, a stress-reducing hormone that promotes bonding. If the amygdala

tags a stimulus as dangerous, it signals the hypothalamus to activate hormones that cause the release of neurochemicals like adrenaline and cortisol to mobilize a fight-flight-freeze response.

- *Hippocampus.* The hippocampus is shaped like a seahorse and sits directly behind the amygdala on each side of the brain. The hippocampus organizes emotional experiences into time, context, and space and transfers this information up to the medial prefrontal cortex to form explicit, conscious memories. While the amygdala generalizes the meaning of a stimulus, the hippocampus helps to differentiate the nuances. For example, if you burn your hand after touching a stove, your amygdala may initially tag the stove as dangerous, but your hippocampus clarifies that the stove is only dangerous when the burner is hot, helping your amygdala refine its learning.

The Cerebral Cortex or "Thinking Brain"

The cerebral cortex refers to the frontal lobes and topmost outer layer of the human brain that's involved in higher-order thinking, language, consciousness, and emotion regulation. The cerebral cortex is divided into right and left hemispheres. The right hemisphere is more directly connected to the emotional brain and specializes in spatial reasoning, metaphorical thinking, nonverbal communication, and processing negative emotions. The left hemisphere has more connections to the prefrontal cortex (PFC) and specializes in logical analysis, verbal communication, integrating positive emotions, and organizing our experiences into a coherent narrative of our lives.

Although many mammals have a cerebral cortex, humans have the most well-developed PFC, which sits right behind your forehead. The PFC is the area of the human brain that gives us the ability to use abstract thought, plan, make conscious decisions, regulate emotions, and use verbal reasoning. We can divide the PFC into the dorsolateral regions (tops and sides) and the medial (bottom and middle) regions, which specialize in different functions as described below:

- *Dorsolateral PFC (DLPFC).* Located at the tops and sides of the frontal lobes, this region of the cerebral cortex is involved in working memory, planning, decision making, intellectual insight, and your relationship to your external surroundings. However, the DLPFC doesn't have direct connections to the amygdala, so it can't promptly regulate emotional responses. Instead it sends input to the medial prefrontal cortex (MPFC).
- *Medial PFC (MPFC).* Sitting right behind your eye sockets, the MPFC is the primary region of the cortex we use to regulate our emotions and impulses. Because of its midline location, the MPFC is able to receive input from both the emotional brain and the rational brain to predict outcomes, guide decision making, and direct adaptive responses. The MPFC also works directly with the hippocampus to form explicit memories, and stores cognitive schemas based on our past experiences. However, emotion and reasoning processes compete for resources in the MPFC (Pessoa, 2013). When emotional arousal is high, massive neurochemical signals from the emotional brain flood the MPFC with affective inputs and temporarily hinder its ability to access the brain's executive centers in the DLPFC. This is why we may lash out initially when we're stressed, only to realize more adaptive responses we could've taken after we've calmed down. I describe how and why this happens in the following section.

YOUR TRIUNE BRAIN ON TRAUMA

When the amygdala detects a threat to your survival, it signals the hypothalamus to release hormones that activate the fight-flight-freeze response via the hypothalamic-pituitary-adrenal (HPA) axis. More specifically, the pituitary gland releases endogenous opioids to help dull pain and prompt the adrenal glands to release epinephrine (adrenaline), norepinephrine, and cortisol. Adrenaline and norepinephrine elevate heart rate and mobilize increased blood flow to the brain and body to make us more alert, fuel us with energy, and strengthen our muscles. The combination of these powerful neurochemicals helped Dixon react quickly, gather the strength to pull his sister from a burning vehicle, and tolerate the painful heat from the scorching flames.

Meanwhile, cortisol promotes the release of glucose into the blood-stream and inhibits body activities—such as reproduction, growth, and immune system functions—that aren't necessary during an immediate threat. Cortisol also inhibits activity in the hippocampus and prefrontal cortex. Cortisol isn't suppressing our "thinking" brain to make us less intelligent. It's helping us conserve energy and ensure all our attention and resources go toward immediate survival. If cortisol didn't do this, we may be tempted to pause and analyze the situation before taking action, which could get us killed. For example, if Dixon had stopped to contemplate why the other driver wandered onto his side of the road instead of quickly getting himself and his sister out of their conflagrant car, he would've died.

If the fight-flight-freeze response becomes exhausted or fails to protect us from threat, the brain and body activate a "submit-collapse" response through the parasympathetic nervous system. During the submit-collapse response, the dorsal vagus nerve initially immobilizes our muscles and then causes them to become limp. Although this inability to move or fight back feels frightening, it's another way the mammalian brain learned to survive predatory threats. Like a possum, our bodies "play dead" in hopes the predatory animal will move on and leave us alone. Going limp is also a way the body conserves energy and limits injury. Additionally, the pituitary gland releases even larger doses of endogenous opioids during the submit-collapse response. Not only do these internal painkillers mitigate physical pain, but they're also intended to shield us from mental pain by causing us to dissociate, faint, or have little conscious recollection of the details of a traumatic event when it overwhelms our resources to cope.

TRAUMA IS A DISORDER OF MEMORY

You may be thinking, "Okay, I understand why the emotional brain might want to suppress the thinking brain during a life-threatening event. But, why does it seem to keep doing this after the event is over or cause us to overreact to things that aren't actually life-threatening?" I'm glad you asked. It has to do with the way the brain forms implicit and explicit memories.

During emotionally stressful encounters, the amygdala encodes all the sensory information associated with the event into what is called an implicit memory. Implicit memory is a network of neurons that contains the felt, experiential part of a memory and has four components: 1) emotional, 2) perceptual, 3) physical, and 4) procedural. Dixon's implicit memory of the accident consisted of the 1) the emotions of fear and rage; 2) the sense of another car moving too close to his car, the smell of smoke, and sight of flames; 3) the feeling of being out of control of his car; and 4) the impulse to fight the scorching flames, scream for help, and pull his sister and himself toward safety.

Together these four components of implicit memory made up a mental model or schema in Dixon's emotional brain. Anytime his amygdala detected anything similar to the original traumatic event, it was primed to activate this encoded programming instantly. Dixon's amygdala was engaging a full fight-flight-freeze response at the slightest hint another car may be inching over into his lane, or generating feelings of terror and flashbacks if he saw flames or smelled smoke.

Under less extreme emotional conditions, the thalamus, hippocampus and medial prefrontal cortex (MPFC) can stay online during the event and modify learning in the amygdala by adding contextual details to form an explicit memory. Explicit memory includes 1) the factual details of the event; 2) episodic memory—where the memory occurs in the timeline of your life; and 3) autobiographical memory—the cognitive context and meaning of the event. But cortisol and endogenous opioids can interfere with the brain's ability to form explicit memories during extreme stress responses. Thus, the sensory cues associated with the traumatic experience stay locked in implicit memory and fail to be integrated with the context and knowledge contained in higher cortical regions.

Of course, a person might be able to reflect on the event at a later time when they are calm and seem to form an explicit memory of the event. For example, when Dixon was calm, he could describe factual details of the accident and demonstrate insight into his reactions. But this explicit memory was not formed during the accident. It was formed after the accident, when he was in a calmer state and hadn't been fully integrated with the implicit memory formed while he was in a terrified state. Thus, anytime he encountered any sensory cues similar to the original event, his emotional brain activated the same extreme emotional responses that saved his life the first time, regardless of what his rational brain was telling him to do.

When I explained this to Dixon and Katie, Dixon poked Katie, and teased, "See honey, I can't help it when I yell at other drivers. My amygdala made me do it!"

Katie rolled her eyes and winced, "You mean there's nothing we can do? He'll be like this forever?"

"Fortunately, there is something we can do," I said reassuringly. "It has to do with a new discovery called memory reconsolidation that is changing the way we treat trauma."

MEMORY RECONSOLIDATION

When PTSD was first established as a diagnosis in the 1980s, it was considered an anxiety disorder and the target of treatment was to help patients desensitize themselves to trauma triggers through cognitive-behavioral therapies like prolonged exposure therapy. Foa and Kozak (1986) developed a prolonged exposure therapy protocol for PTSD and substantiated it with a plethora of empirical studies. Unfortunately, exposure therapy not only runs the risk of retraumatizing the client, but research has also shown that it may only yield temporary results. Often the client's fears can return under extreme stress or over long periods of time (LeDoux, 2015).

Affective neuroscientists like Joe LeDoux at New York University were racking their brains to determine if there was a way to get the brain to permanently unlearn a fear. Finally, in the year 2000, scientists in LeDoux's lab identified a process called memory reconsolidation in rats that appeared to reveal the brain's own mechanisms for updating fear-based memories. By 2010, neuroscientists had discovered ways this new discovery could be applied to updating implicit, emotional memories in humans. The key lies in recalling the implicit memory while simultaneously evoking a *new experience* that changes the meaning of the memory and invalidates negative beliefs attached to the traumatic event. Neuroscientists call these new experiences "mismatch experiences," because the new experience has to create a "mismatch" or prediction error that causes the emotional brain to update its prior learning.

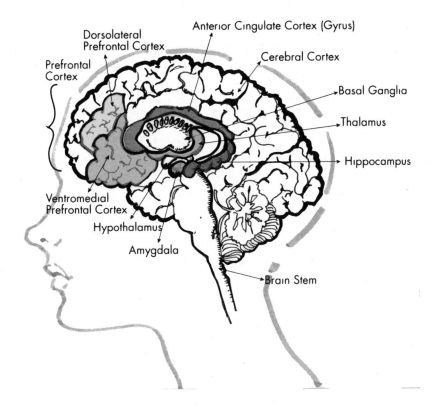

FIGURE 1.1: Regions of the emotional brain
Source: Copyright © 2014 Penelope Randolph/Randolph Design Group

Merely talking about the event or attempting to tame the emotional brain with verbal reasoning doesn't work. The mammalian and reptilian parts of the brain where implicit memories are stored don't understand words. These regions process information like an animal and can only learn through *experience, association,* and *repetition*. I'll discuss how to create effective mismatch experiences in Phase II of this book, Transform Traumatic Memories.

First, it's important to understand the conditions that need to be in place before you attempt to reconsolidate traumatic memories so the client doesn't get retraumatized. This is especially relevant when a person has experienced complex, developmental trauma and didn't experience secure attachment with a caregiver as a child. As you'll learn in Chapter 2, secure attachment is what buffers the impact of trauma. Without this, the brain doesn't develop the neural networks needed to regulate emotions, integrate traumatic memories, and cultivate resilience. For these clients, healing from trauma isn't so much about creating a mismatch experience to rewire a memory, it's about filling in the *missing experience* of secure attachment first in the form of a trusting, attuned, therapeutic relationship.

2

Attachment and the Brain

As discussed in Chapter 1, reminders of a traumatic experience can rev a person's emotional brain into high gear and commandeer the thinking brain. Worse, when traumatic stressors are chronic and occur during critical stages of development, additional changes happen in the brain that interfere with a person's ability to cope in general. For years, numerous studies have shown that people who experience chronic abuse or neglect in childhood have problems 1) identifying and regulating emotions; 2) controlling behavioral impulses; 3) focusing attention; 4) making decisions and planning for the future; and 5) getting along with themselves and others. Moreover, Felitti's Adverse Childhood Events study (Felitti et al., 1998) linked a history of adverse childhood experiences to the development of health problems such as obesity, heart disease, substance abuse, irritable bowel syndrome, fibromyalgia, and chronic pain.

HOW CHILDHOOD TRAUMA AFFECTS BRAIN DEVELOPMENT

When I began practicing in psychiatric hospitals and medical settings 20 years ago, physicians and staff often labeled children who exhibited these behaviors with learning disabilities and diagnoses like attention deficit and hyperactivity disorder, oppositional defiant disorder, somatoform disorders, or even bipolar disorder. Similarly, adults with these issues were labeled with treatment-resistant depression, generalized anxiety disorder, hypochondriasis, eating disorders, or worse—a personality disorder. Extreme emotional outbursts and behaviors were viewed as willful attempts to resist treatment and manipulate staff. Chronic health complaints were interpreted to be psychosomatic cries for attention or malingering attempts to get drugs. The medical model's solution was to medicate these patients' symptoms into submission and set firm boundaries with their behaviors. If these patients didn't comply with these demands or dropped out of treatment, they were viewed as noncompliant.

Granted, it's difficult to stay calm and therapeutic when a client is cutting on herself, raging at you for being two minutes late for a session, or insisting she has chronic pain even though the doctors can't find anything physically wrong with her body. But when we understand how chronic stress, trauma, and abuse reorganize the developing brain, these behaviors and somatic complaints begin to make sense. The brains of these patients aren't trying to sabotage treatment or give you a hard time. They're simply responding to the way they've been programmed to survive in a chaotic environment. In the following sections, I'll highlight brain areas that appear to be altered by childhood trauma and how that translates into the symptoms and behaviors we see in these survivors.

Alterations in the HPA axis, thalamus, and amygdala

As discussed in Chapter 1, the amygdala signals the hypothalamic-pituitary-adrenal (HPA) axis to release powerful hormones and neurochemicals like adrenaline, norepinephrine, and cortisol to fight off a threat. Unfortunately, the same stress hormones that help us survive during short-term stress are harmful—and even toxic—when they are chronically released. Elevated levels of norepinephrine lead to feelings of generalized anxiety, irritability, aggression, and hypervigilance. Persistent surges of these excitatory neurochemicals increase blood pressure, damage blood vessels, and contribute to cardiovascular disease. High cortisol levels interfere with cognition and memory, suppress the immune system, and alter insulin responses, contributing to health conditions like diabetes, obesity, and even alcoholism.

Childhood trauma researchers DeBellis and Zisk (2014) have shown that chronic maltreatment in childhood interferes with normal brain development as the brain begins to adapt to the onslaught of stress hormones flooding its neurons. Neurons in the amygdala become enhanced for sensing danger. Meanwhile, neurons in the hippocampus and prefrontal cortex (PFC) begin to atrophy, shrink, and even die off. The thalamus has trouble filtering out irrelevant stimuli, leading to sensory overload and feelings of overwhelm from even routine activities like going to the grocery store. In an effort to prevent further damage, the brain starts pruning away receptors for norepinephrine, cortisol, and endogenous opioids. Unfortunately, this leads to more problems with mood, memory, motivation, and pain control.

Decreased volume in the hippocampus

Smaller hippocampal volume is a hallmark of patients who've experienced post-traumatic stress disorder (PTSD). If you recall from Chapter 1, the hippocampus is involved in learning and memory. While some studies suggest individuals vulnerable to developing PTSD could have been born with a smaller hippocampus, other studies suggest exposure to high levels of cortisol cause the hippocampus to shrink. For example, animal studies have shown that repeated exposure to high levels of glucocorticoids, like cortisol, inhibit neuronal growth, stymie neural connections, and even kill off neurons in the hippocampus. (Diamond et al., 1996; Charney et al., 1993).

Although we can't fully prove the same effect in human brains without doing autopsies, several studies suggest cortisol has the same effect on the hippocampus in the human brain. For instance, a longitudinal study by Carrion, Weems, and Reiss (2007) demonstrated that maltreated children had higher levels of cortisol in their saliva, which also seemed to correlate with reductions in the size of their hippocampus during the 18 months of the study. Similarly, a study by Andersen et al. (2008) found young adult women who had experienced sexual abuse between the ages of three and five had smaller hippocampal areas. Because the hippocampus is rapidly maturing between the ages of three and five, damage during these years is the most critical. Yet, chronic stress at any age can impact hippocampal functioning—resulting in problems with learning, short-term memory, mood regulation, and fear inhibition. Fortunately, studies in neuroplasticity suggest we can reverse these effects in the hippocampus with regular exercise, good nutrition, positive life experiences, and even antidepressant medication. (Doidge, 2016; O'Hanlon, 2014).

Decreased volume and activity in the prefrontal cortex

Numerous neuroimaging studies have demonstrated that when adults with PTSD are exposed to reminders of traumatic events, there is significant deactivation of activity in the frontal lobes, particularly in Broca's area, the left dorsolateral prefrontal cortex (DLPFC), and the medial prefrontal cortex (MPFC). (Bremner et al., 2008; Sherrin et al., 2011; van der Kolk, 2015). Broca's area is responsible for expressive speech, which helps us understand why traumatized clients have difficulty putting their feelings into words. As discussed in Chapter 1, the DLPFC is involved in working memory, planning, and intellectual insight, while the MPFC is involved in emotional regulation, decision making, and forming contextual, explicit memory.

DeBellis and Zisk (2014) cite multiple studies that demonstrated children impacted by abuse and neglect have decreased volume in the cerebral cortex associated with deficits in language, working memory, inhibition, auditory attention, and processing speed tasks. Although the prefrontal cortex is slow growing during early childhood and doesn't fully mature until we're about 25 years old, it engages in a phase of rapid development between the ages of 8 and 14. Consequently, trauma during this age range has the most impact on the PFC's ability to develop strong neural connections.

Cozolino (2015) provides a plethora of research that shows the brains of adults diagnosed with borderline personality disorder (BPD) have similar impairments in the PFC. Neuroimaging studies show people with BPD don't just have high amygdala activity and abnormal PFC activity when recalling traumatic memories: Their brains appear stressed even when looking at emotionally neutral facial expressions or social interactions. It's as if their brains are wired to perceive any social interaction as dangerous, so the amygdala stays on high alert ready to deploy a survival response, with little protest from the PFC.

Similarly, in his book *The Body Keeps the Score* trauma expert Bessel van der Kolk (2015) reports that survivors of developmental trauma have impairments in regions of the prefrontal cortex that are involved in perceiving ourselves in relation to the world. He refers to these regions as the "Mohawk of self-awareness" because they take the shape of a narrow Mohawk that begins right behind the eye sockets, trails through the center of the brain, and connects back to the parietal areas. The brain regions of this "Mohawk" include the:

- Orbitofrontal cortex (OFC): involved in social learning and capacity for empathy.
- Ventral medial prefrontal cortex (vMPFC) we discussed in Chapter 1.
- Insular cortex: where we derive our interoceptive state of awareness and subjective feeling states.
- Anterior cingulate cortex, which is involved in attention and coordinating cognition and emotion.
- Posterior cingulate cortex, which gives us our physical sense of where we are.

Dr. van der Kolk speculates that survivors of childhood trauma learned to shut down these integrative regions in the brain in order to blunt the overwhelming sensations of terror and confusion they were experiencing as kids. Consequently, he opines, this "shutdown" interferes with a person's ability to "feel fully alive" and maintain a coherent sense of self.

Diminished right-left hemisphere integration

Trauma not only affects top-down processing in the brain, but it also interferes with lateral processing between the right and left hemispheres. Studies cited by Martin Teicher (2000) found the corpus callosum to be much smaller in maltreated children than in children who had not experienced neglect or abuse, suggesting fewer connections between the left and right brain. Additionally, Teicher conducted several electroencephalogram (EEG) studies that found alterations in brain wave activity in the left frontal lobes of maltreated children. Dysregulation of the left hemisphere has been associated with temporal lobe epilepsy, feelings of dissociation, mood swings, and aggressive behavior.

Neuroimaging scans of adults with PTSD also suggest integration problems between the left and right hemispheres when it comes to recalling traumatic memories. Researchers at the University of Minnesota (Engdahl et al., 2010) found military veterans who suffered flashbacks had dramatic increases in right hemisphere activity and little to no activity in the left hemisphere when recalling memories of war. In contrast, veterans without PTSD showed more activity in the left hemisphere when reflecting on the war.

Similarly, a study by Lanius et al. (2004) observed these differences in bilateral processing among 24 subjects who had experienced a sexual assault or a motor vehicle accident. Of the 24 subjects, 11 met the criteria for PTSD and 13 did not. Results showed that the 13 subjects without PTSD showed greater left-prefrontal activity while verbally recalling a traumatic memory. Conversely, the 11 subjects with PTSD had significantly increased activity in the right hemisphere and less activity in the left hemisphere. Moreover, upon recalling their traumatic experiences, these subjects with high right hemisphere activity and low left hemisphere activity reported feeling like they were dissociated from the present moment and right "back at the scene of the incident," vividly re-experiencing the memory as if it were still happening. This suggests symptoms of PTSD are not only due to integration problems between the limbic system and prefrontal cortex but also due to integration problems between the left and right hemisphere. To address this issue, we can use interventions that promote integration between the hemispheres, like eye movement desensitization and reprocessing (EMDR). But researchers like UCLA's Allan Schore suggest therapists already come equipped with a powerful way to spark healthy brain development and integration within their clients' brains—our ability to compassionately respond and attune to others.

SECURE ATTACHMENT IS THE ANTIDOTE

Allan Schore (2012) has made a compelling argument that secure attachment between mother and child is what fosters healthy brain development. Because the left hemisphere and verbal centers don't begin rapid development until after the first two years of a baby's life, Schore has theorized that the neural pathways that shape our attachment schemas are stored in the nonverbal right hemisphere and form through the sensory and physical interactions we experience with our caregivers. It's not so much what the mother says that calms the baby down, it's the soft gaze of her eyes, the warm cradle of her arms, and the soothing sound of her voice that reassures her baby that she is safe, wanted, and loved.

Schore suggests the baby's brain imprints these caregiving experiences into neural networks in the right hemisphere that serve as a template for developing her sense of self, perceptions of others, and emotional regulation skills. As the prefrontal cortex develops, these repeated relational experiences are registered in the orbitofrontal cortex (OFC), which is included in van der Kolk's "Mohawk of self-awareness" described earlier in this chapter. The OFC is not only associated with emotional regulation, it is also associated with empathy and our ability to interpret the emotional states of others.

Recent neuroimaging studies bear Schore's theory out. A review of the literature by Lenzi et al. (2015) reported PET scans of mothers with secure attachment showed they had bilateral symmetry between the right and left hemispheres when they responded to their baby's cues. In addition, securely attached mothers demonstrated increased activation of the OFC and reward centers in the brain and increased levels of the bonding hormone oxytocin in the bloodstream. In contrast, when mothers with insecure attachment styles responded to their baby's cues, they demonstrated dysregulated activity in the amygdala and prefrontal cortex, with little activation of oxytocin and reward centers. In other words, these mothers felt stressed when their baby cried or reached out to them. Holding their babies didn't feel calming or rewarding, but left them reeling with more insecurity and self-doubt.

The results of this study may explain how developmental trauma and insecure attachment are inadvertently transmitted from generation to generation. If secure attachment was not modeled for you, it's hard to know how to give it to someone else. Then again, as mammals we come hardwired for secure attachment. It is instinctive. Perhaps we don't have to *learn* it, we just have to have more experiences that make it safe to trust and access what is already inherent in our biology.

THE POLYVAGAL HIERARCHY

Allan Schore's attachment theory correlates with the polyvagal theory of the nervous system proposed by Stephen Porges (2011). As most of us learned in graduate school, our autonomic nervous system is divided into two branches: the sympathetic nervous system and the parasympathetic nervous system. The sympathetic nervous system (SNS) connects to muscles in our limbs and is associated with arousal, alertness, and fight-or-flight states. On the other end is the parasympathetic nervous system, which is associated with relaxation, recovery, and "rest and digest" states. The parasympathetic nervous system is triggered by a large cranial nerve called the vagus nerve that originates in the brain stem and connects to internal organs like our intestines.

In 1994, Stephen Porges, then a neuroscientist at the University of Maryland, discovered that in mammals (including humans) the vagus nerve appeared to branch off into two separate channels that activate the parasympathetic nervous system in two very different ways. Like reptiles, mammals have a dorsal (back) branch of the vagus nerve that connects to the organs below the diaphragm like the stomach, pancreas, and intestines. But, unlike reptiles, mammals also have a ventral (front) branch of the vagus nerve that connects to the heart, bronchi, and muscles in the face, eyes, middle ear, and areas of the throat.

Because many mammals are pack animals, it occurred to Porges that the ventral branch of the vagus nerve evolved so mammals could bond and communicate safety to one another through expressions of the face, a soft gaze of the eyes, melodic prosody of speech, and the ability to hear one another's pitch of voice through the middle ear. He calls this the *social engagement system* and explains this is why we feel calmer when we connect with another human who feels safe. Porges further surmised that when faced with a threat, rather than fight or flee, the first thing mammals and humans do is look for their pack or a safe other they can turn to for help and protection. There's safety in numbers, especially for vulnerable little mammals like chipmunks and rabbits.

Imagine a scared little chipmunk separated from his mother in the woods. His ventral vagal system prompts him to cry out in a high-pitched squeak that is undetectable to reptiles, but the chipmunk's mother can hear him. When she finds him, she looks at him with soft eyes and a warm facial expression, letting him know everything is okay, and may even return her own rhythmic squeak to calm and soothe him as she ushers him back to the safety of their burrow.

If the chipmunk couldn't find his mother and saw a cat approaching, his brain would shut off the ventral vagal system and activate the sympathetic nervous system so he could run and hide, or if caught, bite the daylights out of that cat in an effort to escape danger! If the fight-or-flight response didn't deter the ferocious feline, the chipmunk's dorsal vagus nerve would cause the parasympathetic nervous system to shift to energy conservation mode. The chipmunk's dorsal vagus nerve would cause it to freeze or collapse, and shut down his digestive system. In addition, his heart and respiratory rate would slow down and his endocrine system would release a cascade of endogenous opiates to kill pain.

Why would the chipmunk's sympathetic nervous system shut down while he's being chased by a hungry cat? Because in the wild, the next best way to survive is to freeze and play dead. A predatory animal is reluctant to eat an animal that has already died because it could be unsanitary. In addition, when the body goes limp, it is less prone to injury. So, if the cat was just playing with the chipmunk with no intention of eating it, the chipmunk would fare better if his body was loose and limp. Moreover, the submit-collapse response could cause the chipmunk to feel dissociated from his body, or lose consciousness, so he wouldn't have to feel the excruciating pain and terror of this life-threatening experience.

Porges's polyvagal theory has significant implications for how we think about and treat trauma. First, understanding how the ventral vagal system works suggests that one of the best ways we can calm hyperaroused states in our clients is to modulate our voices and facial expressions to create a sense of safety and comfort. It harkens back to Daniel Siegel's (2010) theory of interpersonal neurobiology, which posits we can regulate emotion just by being an attuned presence with our clients. Second, understanding the function of the dorsal vagal system explains why many people who suffer from PTSD had the experience of dissociating, collapsing, or feeling completely paralyzed. Clients who have experienced this extreme dorsal vagal response often feel ashamed that they submitted or collapsed, believing that they were somehow complicit, weak, or "broken" because they didn't fight back. They are usually very relieved when you explain that this "submit and collapse response" is activated unconsciously and is the body's way of buffering them from pain during a traumatic incident. I'll talk more about how to help clients who experience extreme dorsal vagal responses under stress in Chapter 6, How to Work with Dissociation.

For now, I think it's useful to let Porges's theory guide us as we co-regulate the nervous system through the therapeutic relationship.

Taking a cue from Allan Schore's (2012) work, creating a safe, trusting relationship is not just something we do in therapy because it feels good, it's the first step in rewiring the traumatized brain. However, when a client has never experienced the feeling of secure attachment, they are not likely to believe it's possible to trust another human being. Showing up with a warm Rogerian stance of empathy, congruence, and unconditional positive regard is not enough. You have to adapt to your client's attachment style. I'll discuss the four primary attachment styles, and how to connect with each of them, in Chapters 3 and 4.

3

Relationships Change the Brain

No matter what you hear from managed care companies or see in advertisements for the latest "evidence-based" treatment— the *evidence* says a strong therapeutic relationship is the key to effective therapy, regardless of the treatment method you use (Murphy & Joseph, 2013; Norcross & Wampold, 2011). Remember this on those days when you are doubting yourself, thinking you need more training, or gulp . . . wondering if you should look for another line of work. Your willingness to show up, be present, and listen compassionately to your clients is the best medicine you can give them. I realize empathic listening isn't going to fix everything, but it is the basis for everything else we do.

Bonnie Badenoch (2017) states, " . . . trauma is also a relational experience in that the embedding of trauma may arise not primarily from the nature of events, but from who is with us before, during, and after the overwhelming happening." (p. 12).

I agree. Clients who have been sexually or physically abused consistently tell me the wounds from the violence weren't nearly as devastating as the feeling that no one cared about them. Being in the room with you is the first step in helping traumatized clients feel like they are important, cared for, and valued.

Research by Marylene Cloitre (2004, 2010) director of the Institute for Trauma and Stress at the New York University Child Study Center, has shown that the quality of the therapeutic relationship considerably impacts treatment outcomes for trauma survivors. In fact, her groundbreaking research changed the guidelines for treating complex trauma. Namely, Cloitre asserts that trauma therapy must be done in phases. Phase I is focused on creating a safe, secure therapeutic alliance and helping clients develop skills for managing emotions and relationships. Phase II focuses on revisiting traumatic memories and revising trauma narratives. Phase III focuses on helping the client apply new knowledge and coping skills to current life stressors and get more satisfaction out of life.

Cloitre's assertion that we return to a three-phase model that puts the therapeutic relationship at the center of trauma treatment is significant. Interestingly, pioneering psychiatrist Pierre Janet recommended a similar three-phase model in the 19th century. But, the medical model took precedence in the 20th century and pushed psychotherapy to become more symptom focused than interpersonally focused. Trauma treatment was driven toward cognitive-behavioral therapies aimed at reducing hyperarousal symptoms and avoidance behavior, while interpersonal therapy took a backseat. Exposure therapy may still have a place in PTSD treatment, but if you don't take the time to cultivate a safe, trusting relationship and help clients understand their emotional responses, you risk retraumatizing them. Clients must feel empowered and have choices about how their treatment is paced in order reclaim their identities.

SAFE RELATIONSHIPS REGULATE EMOTIONS

We're taught we need to teach clients emotional regulation skills, but the best way to regulate emotions is through a relationship with a safe person. Neuroscience studies suggest that human contact calms us down because it signals the hypothalamus to release oxytocin—a powerful hormone that inhibits fear responses, lifts our mood, and promotes trust and bonding with others. (Bryant, 2016; Charuvastra & Cloitre, 2008). Simply holding the hand of a spouse, or even a total stranger during a stressful experience has been shown to attenuate emotional responses in the brain. (Coan et al., 2006).

Coan's hand-holding studies lend support to Allan Schore's theory that humans co-regulate one another right brain to right brain through nonverbal attunement and responsiveness. Schore (2012) asserts this attuned responsiveness from another person is what helps our brains and nervous systems develop the neuropathways for emotional regulation and resilience. In other words, your attuned presence isn't just a kind thing to offer, it's a powerful brain-changing tool.

FOUR ATTACHMENT STYLES

Schore's theory elaborates on John Bowlby's theory that we are biologically wired to attach and seek proximity with caregivers (or a safe other) because it helps us survive. Bowlby theorized that our brains form an Internal Working Model (IWM) for relationships based on the type of relationship (or lack of relationship) we had with early caregivers (Bowlby, 1988). One of Bowlby's associates, Mary Ainsworth (2015) classified these attachment styles in her longitudinal study of 26 mother-child pairs in Baltimore during the years 1963–1967.

For the experiment, Ainsworth designed the Strange Situation Procedure to study how attachment responses may vary when a child is under stress. In the Strange Situation Procedure, a child between one and two years old is invited to play together with his mother in a pleasant room stocked with toys. After one minute, a stranger to the child enters the room and makes the child's acquaintance. The mother leaves the child in the room with the stranger for three minutes and returns. The researchers were not so much interested in the child's behavior while the mother was out of the room as they were in the child's reaction to being reunited with his mother. They hypothesized the child's reaction to the mother's return was indicative of the type of attachment bond the child had with the mother.

Twenty-one years later, they interviewed the children from this study, who had now become young adults. As hypothesized, the attachment style the children demonstrated as infants was consistent with the attachment style they reported as adults. Furthermore, the study has been replicated many times with similar results, making attachment researchers fairly confident in these findings.

Ainsworth identified three primary attachment styles: 1) secure, 2) anxious-avoidant, and 3) anxious-ambivalent. Securely attached children were more upset when their mothers left the room, but when she returned they reached for her and were quickly calmed when their mothers held and comforted them. Children with anxious-avoidant attachment styles showed little outward distress when their mothers left the room and ignored or turned away from the mother when she attempted to pick them up to comfort them. Researchers theorized that these children had learned to shut down their attachment needs because their parents had been emotionally unavailable, critical, or rejecting when they'd expressed their emotions.

In contrast, children with anxious-ambivalent styles showed distress even when their mothers returned to the room. Although they reached and clung to their mothers when held, these infants didn't seem soothed by their mothers' attempts to comfort them. Worse, these children often responded with resentment and anger toward their mothers by hitting or shouting at them. Researchers theorized this attachment style develops when attuned responsiveness from the caregiver is inconsistent. Ainsworth theorized these children learned to cope with perceived rejection or distance from their parents by acting out and exaggerating their feelings in order to get their parents to pay attention to them.

In addition to these three primary styles, Mary Main and her colleague Judith Solomon (1990) identified a fourth type of attachment style they labeled "disorganized." Children who fit into this category seemed to seek both proximity and distance from their caregivers during the Strange Situation. Upon the mother's return, these children appeared dazed, frightened, or disoriented. They seemed interested in approaching their caregivers, but cautious. Main and Solomon (1990) proposed that disorganized attachment occurs when the child is frightened by her caregiver. The child's feelings of disorientation and confusion result from two competing urges: the instinct to seek proximity to the mother vs. the urge to protect oneself from a mother who may inflict harm.

Bowlby opined that a child's attachment style and Internal Working Model of relationships is formed by the time she is three years old and continues to influence her relationships as an adult. Of course, a child can have more than one attachment figure and experience different attachment styles with different caregivers. Many of your clients won't fit neatly into one category. For example, a child may develop a secure relationship with his consistent, responsive father, yet develop an avoidant style with his depressed, alcoholic mother. As an adult, he may find it relatively easy to trust and get along with other men, but feels guarded and distant with women.

New relationship experiences can also modify a person's inherent attachment style. For example, an adult who had secure attachment as a child could develop avoidant, anxious, or disorganized traits after being in an abusive relationship. Likewise, an adult with an insecure attachment style could develop more secure relationship behaviors upon experiencing a healthy, caring, long-term relationship with a partner, friend, or therapist. But, we all have a tendency to revert back to the attachment styles we formed as infants under times of extreme stress, or when forming a relationship with a new person.

TOOLS FOR ASSESSING ATTACHMENT STYLES

The gold standard for assessing adult attachment styles is the Adult Attachment Interview (AAI) protocol developed by George, Kaplan, and Main (1985). The interview consists of 20 open-ended questions that invite the client to explore and discuss his relationships with his family of origin. The questions start out a bit factually, asking the client to describe where he or she grew up and what their family members did for a living. Then the questions dive into deeper discussion of the client's relationships with caregivers, asking the client to name five adjectives that would describe his relationship with each parent, which parent the client was closer to, and how the client would cope with emotional upsets as a child.

The full AAI interview takes at least 90 minutes and can bring up very intense feelings for clients. Thus, it is not recommended to dive into such a deep look at the client's attachment relationships until you feel like you've got a secure enough relationship with the client yourself. I usually work the questions in over time when I sense the client is ready to talk about these early relationships, or when the client is attempting to understand where she learned a particular relationship pattern.

The AAI is a qualitative, rather than quantitative assessment. The way the client answers the questions is as revealing of one's attachment style as the answers themselves. For example, clients with an avoidant attachment style tend to be very dry, brief, or factual in their responses. They may idealize their parents or say they have few clear childhood memories. Clients with an anxious attachment style may be very demonstrative, emotional, and loquacious as they answer the questions. They are usually insightful regarding family dysfunction, but admit most of their family issues are still unresolved or ongoing. Clients with a disorganized attachment style tend to give fragmented, incoherent narratives, and may even dissociate as they are answering the questions. Therefore, the AAI authors recommend attending a two-week training institute to learn how to fully administer and score the AAI (see https://attachment-training.com).

There are also briefer attachment assessment scales you can give to clients to complete. Fraley, Waller, & Brennan's (2000) Experiences in Close Relationships-Revised (ECR-R) Questionnaire is a 36-item scale that measures relationship behaviors in regard to anxious or avoidant patterns. Diane Poole-Heller, psychologist and developer of the Dynamic Attachment Repatterning Experience program has an online attachment style assessment that consists of 45 items and ranks responses according to secure, avoidant, anxious, or disorganized attachment styles. You can find Poole-Heller's assessment at https://dianepooleheller.com/attachment-test/.

Last, Nancy Collins (1996), a psychology professor at the University of California Santa Barbara, developed a Revised Adult Attachment Scale that has been reliably used in attachment research studies. Collins created a version that examines how a person feels in romantic relationships, and a version that evaluates how a person feels in any close relationship. I like using this version for people who are not currently in romantic relationships. Additionally, I *strongly recommend* you take these assessments yourself so you can understand your own attachment style and behaviors. It's critical for you to have this self-awareness so you can develop more secure attachment in your own relationships, be a more secure presence in the therapeutic relationship, and manage transference/countertransference issues as they arise.

CONNECTING WITH SECURELY ATTACHED CLIENTS

For the most part, it's fairly easy to establish rapport with clients who have secure attachment histories. They are able to reflect on their childhoods and describe them with a coherent narrative that makes sense. They may describe their parents as "good" and "loving," but don't necessarily idealize their parents and can recognize their flaws. They may have picked up a few negative beliefs from their parents that they want to work on in therapy. For example, they may have gotten the implicit message that they needed to be hardworking, good-looking, perfect, or wealthy to succeed in the world. Their parents may not have meant for their children to internalize those messages or think that they weren't "good enough" children. But, kids learn by watching the adults around them and adapt to the parents' version of reality.

For example, my client Natalie developed an eating disorder in spite of secure attachment with her parents. Natalie explained that her grandmother was obese, which caused her mother to be terrified of gaining weight. Natalie grew up watching her mother obsessively exercise, restrict her food intake, and talk with her friends about the horrors of being fat. Natalie recalled becoming self-conscious about food and her appearance as early as age seven. Her mother didn't intend for Natalie to feel like she was worthless if she gained weight or develop an eating disorder. But Natalie internalized her mother's fears and patterns.

Clients who have secure attachment are very responsive to the social support we offer, and it doesn't take long to develop a strong working alliance with them. If you make a mistake, securely attached people are generally forgiving once you apologize or explain yourself. In addition, they usually have a support system outside the therapy room that is helpful to them.

Securely attached people can also experience rape, combat trauma, and abusive relationships that challenge their assumptive beliefs about themselves and other people. They may say, "I'm scared of people now. I don't think I can ever trust anyone again. I feel damaged and like no one will want me." But, if they have a secure attachment history, they usually recognize that there was a time when they didn't feel that way, so they can overcome the negative impact of trauma more quickly. In contrast, someone with insecure attachment will say they've never felt like they were lovable or could trust others. This makes it difficult for them to believe healthy relationships are possible, even with their therapists.

CONNECTING WITH INSECURELY ATTACHED CLIENTS

When a client's attachment figures were also the source of their trauma and pain, it's not so easy to establish rapport. As discussed in Chapter 2, childhood abuse and neglect can alter a person's neurocircuitry for social bonding. Neuroimaging shows that people impacted by childhood maltreatment have diminished activation in reward centers and heightened activity in fear centers associated with social contact. In other words, it's not comforting to interact with other people, it's anxiety provoking. With these clients, it will take more than the Rogerian traits of congruence, empathy, and unconditional positive regard to earn trust. In Chapter 4, I describe how insecurely attached clients tend to present in therapy and how to effectively connect with each attachment style to build trust and rapport.

4

How to Engage
Insecure Attachment
Styles

What's going on when your best efforts to establish a secure therapeutic alliance aren't working? Do you label the client as resistant? Do you assume you're a "bad fit" and refer the client out to another therapist? Do you need more training? Not necessarily. When you understand how to connect with various attachment styles, you can more easily develop rapport and avoid unnecessary frustration. For instance, clients with an avoidant style are going to be reserved and will pull back if you push them to reveal deep emotions too quickly. Anxiously attached clients may idealize you in the first few sessions, then suddenly become angry if you have to reschedule an appointment or challenge their thinking. Disorganized clients may dissociate in your sessions, seem frightened of you, or suddenly become enraged with you.

In this chapter, I'll share tips for how to navigate these emotional defenses, and securely connect with these insecure attachment styles. It helps to remember these attachment styles were adaptive responses that helped these clients survive complex trauma. Their behaviors may seem self-defeating to our rational brains, but for our clients' emotional brains, they still seem necessary for their survival.

ENGAGING AVOIDANT-DISMISSIVE ATTACHMENT STYLES

A child can develop an avoidant attachment style when she experiences her parents as critical, rejecting, or indifferent to her emotional needs. In adults, we call this style of attachment "dismissive" because the person copes by being dismissive of his emotional and relationship needs. He also tends to dismiss or minimize the feelings of others. In the therapy room, these clients intellectualize their feelings and may present as aloof, guarded, or controlling. When you ask him about his childhood, he'll tend to describe it as "great," or unremarkable or use vague descriptions such as "fine," or "normal." He could also say he doesn't have many childhood memories, but he won't really seem troubled by this ancestral amnesia.

Bowlby (1980) described these clients as "compulsively self-reliant" because they rarely turn to others for help and withdraw from relationships under stress. Though these individuals can look calm and detached on the surface, studies have shown that they have biomarkers of distress when their attachment needs are triggered, indicating they still desire intimate connections with others. But dismissive clients aren't sure how to form close relationships and doubt other people can adequately respond to their emotional needs.

Being self-reliant, dismissive clients don't eagerly come to therapy. If they do come voluntarily, they seem ambivalent about being there. What disturbs them most is their inability to function or get a handle on their feelings. They don't want to explore their emotions. They're more interested in how to get rid of their feelings and symptoms so they can get back to business as usual. Issues that usually bring them to therapy are depression or anxiety that has escalated to the point of interfering with their daily functioning; relationship breakups and losses; substance abuse or addictions; or stress-related somatic complaints.

In addition, dismissive clients can present with narcissistic, schizoid, and guarded personality traits that make it very hard to build rapport. Such traits can leave therapists feeling angry, frustrated, and insecure because these clients seem downright dismissive of you and the whole therapy process! Control is a big issue for these clients, and you can feel like you're in a constant power struggle with them. It's not unusual for them to question your recommendations, dismiss your insights, and cancel appointments when they start to feel vulnerable. In spite of these obstacles, the effort to get to know these clients is worthwhile. They're usually bright, humorous, and can be delightfully successful in therapy because they are motivated to be functional.

My client Craig is a great example of a client with a dismissive attachment style. Standing at 6 feet 4 inches tall, he was a broad-shouldered man with an authoritative presence and a booming voice that felt intimidating to me at times. He came to therapy because he had been having unusual bouts of nausea and abdominal pain that physicians could not explain. His primary care physician opined that Craig's gastrointestinal issues were related to extreme stress and urged him to call me for an appointment. He told Craig that I also offered hypnosis and biofeedback if he didn't want to do traditional therapy. Craig rolled his eyes and said to his doctor, "Seriously? You want me to see a shrink? I don't know. I'll have to think about it."

A few weeks later, Craig reluctantly called me to schedule his first appointment. He insisted he did not need "therapy," but was interested in learning "self-hypnosis" and pain management strategies. His use of the word "self-hypnosis" was not lost on me. Rather than explore his resistance to therapy in our first sessions, I aligned with his pride about being self-reliant. I told him I'd be happy to teach him self-hypnosis and normalized his symptoms by explaining how stress can wreak havoc with the gastrointestinal system. He seemed relieved that there was a scientific explanation of his symptoms. When I asked if he could tell me what kind of stress he'd been under, Craig shrugged his shoulders and admonished, "That's just it. I'm under no more stress than usual. In fact, I've been way more stressed out than this. That's why I'm not convinced my stomach pain is stress related."

"I hear you. Tell me what you think is going on. I want to understand." I offered.

Craig rubbed his hands along the tops of his legs, took a deep breath, and sighed, "My son died, okay? But he died five years ago. Why would I be feeling sick now?"

"Oh, my goodness, I am so sorry. What happened to your son?" I asked empathically.

"He died in a car crash. He and his friends were drinking when it happened. It sucks, but there's no sense in dwelling on it. I just have to move forward and live my life," Craig said very matter-of-factly.

I was struck by his nonchalant attitude, but also sensed cutting off from his emotions was the only way he knew how to cope with unbearable pain. Since it was our first session, I decided not to push him too hard emotionally and stuck with the factual sorts of questions he seemed comfortable answering.

When I asked if he had other children, he looked out the window and sighed, "Yep. I have a daughter who is estranged from me, and a younger son who has been missing since he attended a music festival two months ago."

At this point, Craig's nausea made a lot of sense to me, but he still wasn't making the connection. My empathy wouldn't let me pace with his emotional detachment any longer, so I exclaimed "Jesus, Craig! What the heck is going on with your kids? No wonder you feel sick to your stomach."

Craig threw up his hands and mirrored my expression of exasperated bewilderment.

"I don't know," he shrugged. "I had a crazy ex-wife. She made my kids crazy, and they all turned to drugs. I've resigned myself to accepting I'm probably going to lose all three of them." His words were stern. He clenched his jaw and gave me a cold look as I sat frozen in my chair, wondering what to do next.

I imagined Craig felt devastated after losing all three of his children, but I read his stern, dry responses as a warning for me to back off. Like a dog that snaps at you if get too close to an open wound, I knew I had to earn Craig's trust and respect before he'd let me examine his sore spots. Aligning with Craig's feelings of frustration and appealing to his desire to function in spite of these tragedies worked better, at least in the beginning of our therapy. As he requested, I began teaching him pain management strategies using mindfulness meditation and self-hypnosis tools. He liked the idea of observing his thoughts and pain sensations from a detached, nonjudgmental point of view, and even practiced the techniques at home. Though I worried I might be reinforcing his tendency to detach from his feelings with mindfulness interventions, they were giving him relief and the hope he could feel better.

Over time, as Craig watched his thoughts, he began to recognize how critical he was of himself and other people. He admitted to me that he was disturbed to realize how angry and cynical he was. When I asked where he learned to be critical, he didn't know at first. But, as he kept with the meditation, memories of his childhood began to emerge and revealed deep feelings of rage toward his dismissive, controlling father. After months of struggling with how I could help Craig move beyond using our sessions for quasi-meditation and superficial conversation, it finally felt like we were getting somewhere. I'll elaborate on how I helped Craig deal with his childhood memories and process the overwhelming feelings of grief around the loss of his children in Chapter 11, Relational and Attachment Trauma.

Right now, I just want to give you the sense of how it feels to work with an avoidant-dismissive client in the initial stage of therapy. Even though it often feels like you're skating along the surface of real issues, they need to ease into deeper work. Helping them understand the physiological aspects of their stress responses and giving them tools they can use to "control" their symptoms works better in the beginning. They have to get comfortable with you first, and will only reveal deep feelings on their own terms. If you push them to address painful material or admit to vulnerability before they're ready, they'll cut and run. They'll convince themselves that therapy wasn't helping, or that you were too "touchy-feely," or that they can figure their problems out on their own. Don't take it personally.

Clients with dismissive styles often use humor and sarcasm to deflect from their feelings too. Again, you're better off joking around with them to build rapport, rather than challenging them on their deflections too soon. Play and humor are wonderful ways to connect with clients, and these are safer entryways into feelings of vulnerability. It's the same for adolescents who feel ambivalent about therapy. You have to play with them and align with their resistance in order for them to feel understood and trust you.

ENGAGING ANXIOUS-PREOCCUPIED ATTACHMENT STYLES

An anxious attachment style is characterized by fears of rejection and abandonment resulting from inconsistent parenting whereby the child sometimes felt understood and nurtured by her caregivers, followed by episodes of feeling rejected, abandoned, or abused by her parent(s). For adults, this attachment style is referred to as "preoccupied" because these individuals seem preoccupied with how to get attention and affection from other people. They are sensitive to the slightest hint of rejection or disapproval, and are prone to clinging behavior, obsessive worry, and jealousy in relationships. They fear they'll be abandoned if they don't stay in close proximity to their partners and can be quite intrusive and demanding in relationships.

Clients with a preoccupied attachment style may demonstrate classic traits of codependency and people-pleasing behaviors. Or they can seem self-centered, controlling, and manipulative as they protest perceived slights by becoming vengeful, self-destructive, promiscuous, or helpless.

The latter style of behavior often renders these clients a diagnosis of borderline or histrionic personality disorder. Classifying these patterns as a personality disorder can keep you stuck because it implies their ability to change is limited. But it's not. If you look at these behaviors through the broader lens of attachment trauma, their sensitivities and pleas for attention make sense.

You may not initially recognize a client with anxious-preoccupied attachment because they've become experts at reading people and will instinctively know how to please you and get you to like them. They are often friendly, charming, flattering, and even superficially compliant in the beginning. Your first inkling that a client may have this attachment style is when they idealize you with statements of praise like, "You're the best therapist I've ever had. Nobody understands me like you do. I wish I could talk to you every day!" Or they may call, text, or email between sessions for "quick questions" or to "check in."

Not surprisingly, what usually brings these clients to therapy is relationship issues and problems with self-esteem. They may have struggled with depression and anxiety throughout their lives, and will readily disclose that they've had a family history plagued by trauma, loss, substance abuse, or mental illness. Unlike avoidant-dismissive clients, preoccupied clients seem to recall everything about their childhoods and have no problem expressing disappointment and anger about their upbringing. Deep down, part of them is hoping that you will be the perfect therapist who will rescue them from their internal angst and provide them with the unconditional love they've been longing for. Yet, another part of them suspects you'll let them down like everybody else, grow tired of them, and find a way to get rid of them. They'll be watching your every move for any hint of incongruence, frustration, or judgment and will be quick to either act out—or call you out—in an effort to defend against disconnection.

For you to successfully connect with preoccupied clients, they need to feel like you sincerely understand the pain of their predicament. Warm, empathic responses are like honey to them. You'll sense that they are most satisfied with therapy when you take the role of compassionate

listener as they stay in the role of angry or helpless victim. As a therapist, you could begin to feel drained and frustrated, wondering if you're
really a competent counselor or nothing more than a "rent-a-friend."
You recognize these clients need to learn relationship skills and more
effective ways to get their needs met. Yet, when you attempt to introduce
these concepts, they can react as if you're like all the other disapproving
people in their lives, blaming them for their problems.

The way around this dilemma is to validate these clients' feelings
and show compassion for their heartache as you also express fascination
with their insight, strengths, and resilience. Getting curious about how
they've survived tumultuous circumstances in their lives helps *them*
become interested in their strengths and capacity for self-sufficiency.
Mind you, transformation doesn't happen overnight. And, if you push
for self-sufficiency too quickly, they'll interpret it as your attempt to
push them out the door and react by becoming more symptomatic,
angry, or helpless. Recognize this as a sign to slow down and move
back to offering empathic support and encouragement until you sense
the relationship is strong enough for you to address their abandonment
fears more directly.

My client Mallory is a good example of a preoccupied client who was
hard to connect with initially. She was an attractive woman with dark,
wavy hair, emerald green eyes, and an infectious smile punctuated by
two delightful dimples in her cheeks. Those cute little dimples tugged
at my heartstrings, reminding me of her childlike innocence as she
recounted a history of inconsistent caregiving by her mother and sexual
abuse by her stepfather between the ages of 12 and 14. On other days,
her dimples seemed devilish as she expressed rage at her husband's inat-
tentiveness, and plotted revenge by pursuing affairs with other men—or
becoming physically sick and retreating to her bed for days.

Mallory also had three children. Even though she had affairs, she
said she'd never leave her husband because he was a good father. She
thought a divorce would be too hard on the kids. While she seemed
attentive to her children's needs, I was worried about the impact her

affairs and bedridden days could be having on them. I knew I needed to challenge her manipulative behavior with her husband. But I also knew she was in deep emotional pain and felt unwanted. She was trying to secure love and attention with the same behaviors that worked in her childhood—making herself sexually available or becoming sick and helpless.

If we think of it from a neuroscience perspective, Mallory's sexual abuse occurred between the ages of 12 and 14, when the prefrontal cortex (PFC) hits its growth spurt. But, as research has shown, trauma during this developmental stage interferes with the development of the PFC, particularly areas in the middle PFC that help us regulate emotions and engage in self-reflection. Before Mallory would be ready to reprocess traumatic memories, let alone handle confrontation from her therapist, we needed to focus on interventions that could help her 1) feel safe and understood by me; 2) manage strong emotions and impulses; and 3) engage more of her left hemisphere by thoughtfully reflecting on her feelings and behaviors.

Patiently pacing with anxious-preoccupied clients in this phase can be draining. They may not change their behavior right away, and you may feel like you are just letting them vent about their problems rather than doing "real" therapy. But, if you recall Allan Schore's theory that empathic right brain to right brain communication fosters secure attachment and the neural connections to regulate emotions, you're doing more work than you think. In addition to empathic listening, these clients are responsive to compassionate and curious questions that help them reflect on their emotions and behaviors. This engages their prefrontal cortex and begins to teach them emotional regulation skills.

For example, Mallory came to a session furious because her husband didn't take her side in an argument she had with her 12-year-old daughter. Her daughter wanted to go to a school dance, and Mallory insisted on being a chaperone. Her daughter said it would be humiliating to have her mother at the dance watching her, and her husband agreed.

Mallory said she'd been lying in her bed depressed for two days and felt like killing herself because nobody in her family loved her.

The hair on the back of my neck stood up upon hearing her suicidal ideation. Though we're taught to immediately start assessing whether clients have a plan when they drop the "S bomb," it's better to show empathy to anxiously attached clients and help them express their pain first. Otherwise, they are prone to assuming that you're trying to get rid of them by sending them to the hospital. Rather than probe for a suicide plan, I mirrored her sad affect, and softly said, "I'm so sorry. It sounds like your family didn't understand your desire to protect your daughter and share the experience of her first dance."

"Yes! You get it!" she exclaimed. "As somebody who has been sexually abused, isn't it normal for me to want to keep an eye on my daughter and make sure nothing happens to her?"

"Of course it is," I replied. "You want to keep her safe. Why do you suppose she is reluctant to have you attend?"

"Because she thinks I am controlling and neurotic," Mallory huffed.

"Well, most teenagers think their mothers are controlling and neurotic. I don't think you're alone in that camp. What else do you suppose is going through her mind?"

Mallory sat back and sighed, "I guess she thinks all the kids will make fun of her if mommy is there hovering over her. I'm not trying to cramp her style, but I don't want some guy to put the moves on her. She's naïve. She wouldn't know how to handle it."

"I see. Is there another way you could prepare her so she knows how to protect and take care of herself?"

"Yeah, I guess I need to talk to her, let her know what worries me, and teach her how to handle herself if a guy makes a pass at her. I know the principal. He's not going to let the kids make out in the corner or sneak outside. They'll be watching them. I guess it's okay."

Next, I wanted to give Mallory a way to manage her anxious feelings. I suggested, "Maybe it's not just the mom in you, but the sweet little 12-year-old girl in you that wants to look out for your daughter. What does that 12-year-old girl say about this situation, and what can you tell her to make it better?"

Mallory closed her eyes and imagined talking with her 12-year-old self. "She's scared. When she was in that situation, she just froze and didn't know what to do." Then her lip began to quiver as she cried and whispered to me, "She couldn't make it stop."

"I know. The 12-year-old you didn't know what to do when her stepfather made sexual advances toward her. What can you tell your 12-year-old self now? What do you know now that you didn't know then?"

"I want to tell her that it wasn't her fault. He was bigger than you. You didn't do anything wrong."

"That's right. And how did 12-year-old you feel around other boys her age? If a 12-year- old boy made a pass at her, how did she handle it?"

Mallory opened one eye and smirked at me, "I'd tell them to 'F' off!" She chuckled, "That's funny. Just then, I realized 12-year-old boys weren't that scary to me. They were goofy. I could handle them."

"Mm-hmm," I mused. "Now imagine your daughter going to a dance with a bunch of goofy kids and tell me if it still seems scary."

Mallory closed her eyes for a moment to visualize it, then shook her head and said, "No. My daughter is pretty assertive. She can handle kids her age. I still need to make sure she understands the difference between friendly touch and sexual touch. I should also talk to her about managing her own sexual impulses. But I'm not too good at that myself. That's what's got me into all these affairs. What do you do when someone comes on to you and it feels good? Maybe that's what I'm worried about."

I'll address how I worked with Mallory around this issue in Chapter 9, Sexual Trauma. For now, I hope this gave you a sense of how to pace with anxiously attached clients when you're still developing trust and rapport. They are more receptive when you compassionately ask questions that help them reflect on their feelings and explore less hurtful explanations for someone else's behavior. They do not do well with direct confrontation because it feels like you are rejecting and judging them. They long to be understood, supported, and compassionately guided toward solutions that improve their self-esteem and interpersonal relationships.

ENGAGING DISORGANIZED-
UNRESOLVED ATTACHMENT STYLES

A disorganized or unresolved attachment style results from parenting that is chaotic, extremely abusive, or exceedingly neglectful. People raised in these situations long for close, loving relationships, but are also terrified of them. Whereas the anxious-preoccupied client harbors the implicit belief *"I want to be close, but I'm afraid you'll leave or reject me,"* the disorganized-unresolved client believes, *"I want to get close, but I'm afraid you're going to kill me!"* They may not consciously express this terrifying belief, but deep down they expect that other people will harm, betray, or exploit them because that was their experience as a child.

Relationships feel scary and confusing to these clients, and as a therapist, you may feel scared and confused when you're with them. At times, they may seem open and interested in connecting with you, then suddenly shift into a hostile, suspicious stance, or collapse into a helpless, childlike state. While not all clients with disorganized styles have dissociative identity disorder, it can sometimes feel like they have several personalities. Each of these personas can respond to interventions very differently, leaving even the most skilled therapist befuddled. An intervention that worked in one session may upset or annoy the client the next session.

Technically these "personas" are neural networks that contain different survival strategies that worked at various times in the client's life. For instance, as a young child the client may have successfully coped with abuse by becoming withdrawn and hopeless. But as a teenager the client may have managed abuse by becoming angry and combative with their parents. Each of these responses is stored in separate neural networks that are not integrated into one coherent strategy. This is why it can look like you're seeing two (or more) entirely different personalities or feel confused when you're attempting to form a therapeutic alliance with them. The work is slow with clients who have disorganized attachment. It can take months or even years to see real progress. But it is probably the most rewarding work you will ever do.

My client Pamela is a good example. She was a successful 40-year-old engineer who initially called me for help with recurring depression. When I greeted her in the waiting room for our first session, she looked right through me with a wide-eyed stare and drew back as she tightly gripped her fingers around the arms of the chair. Sensing her trepidation, I smiled softly and said, "I'm glad you're here. I know it can be unnerving to meet someone for the first time. Do you still want to talk? Or is there anything I can do to make you feel more comfortable?"

She shook her head, took a deep breath, and cautiously rose to her feet, muttering, "Thanks. I'm okay."

As we walked back to my office, I felt the vibration of her stiff, heavy footsteps plodding along the floor like a fatigued soldier marching home from a long, bloody battle. Upon entering my office, she quickly darted her eyes around the room and sat in the chair closest to my office door. Her pallor quickly flushed from ghostly white to florid red as she leaned forward, and said, "Before I tell you anything about me, I need to ask you a few questions."

Nodding gently, I replied, "Yeah, sure."

Then she narrowed her eyes and proceeded to grill me with questions you'd expect to answer in a job interview, or worse—a deposition. She wanted to know all about my training and job experiences, my approach to therapy, my success rate, and most of all—why in the world did I become a therapist in the first place? Was I just a voyeur who liked peeking into other people's lives, or did I have a martyr complex, or was I just a naïve do-gooder who thought I could save the world?

The questions didn't rattle me as much as her harsh, accusatory tone. Vacillating between fear and frustration, my heart started racing and I imagined my amygdala was pinging all over the place looking for the nearest exit. But my compassionate side knew Pamela's suspicious demeanor was only a sign that she'd been through something harrowing and horrible. She needed to be sure she could trust me before she led me through the dark halls of her weary, wounded heart. I took a deep breath and did my best to maintain my composure and answer her questions as candidly as possible. She seemed satisfied with my answers and commented, "At least you seem honest. That's the most important thing. I think I can give you a try."

Pamela was softer and more open in our next session, but it took several sessions before she seemed even remotely relaxed with me—or I felt relaxed with her. She slowly began to tell me about her long history of physical abuse, which began with daily beatings from her parents. At 18, she joined the Navy to escape her abusive home, but was discharged after a superior officer raped her and she became pregnant. He gave her money to terminate the pregnancy and buy an airline ticket home. Instead of going back home, she fled to Alaska, where she met her first husband. Unfortunately, he committed suicide and she found herself in a series of violent relationships after that. At the time she came to see me, she'd decided against being in relationships altogether. She coped by focusing on her job and spent her weekends playing video games, binge eating, and crying herself to sleep.

Upon hearing her story, I felt so sad for all the cruelty she'd experienced and didn't blame her for hiding in her home away from other people. But, she recoiled at the thought of me pitying her. One side of Pamela was quite hardened and tough. On these occasions, she'd snap at me if I came across as overly sympathetic and responded better if I validated her anger, appealed to her strength, and helped her recognize her courage and fortitude in surviving such brutal circumstances. At other times Pamela would show up confused, helpless, and fragile. Although she was quite competent at solving engineering problems at work, relationships threw her into a tailspin. She'd lose all access to rational thinking and collapse into tears as she clung to the pillows on my sofa and contemplated suicide. On these occasions, she responded better if I took a softer, more nurturing tone and validated her pain and fears.

We danced like this for a several years, and I wondered if I was really helping her. But gradually, I began to notice her mood swings were not as erratic or intense as they used to be, she was getting better at comforting herself and recovering from setbacks faster than she used to. She began to make new friendships and was getting out more on the weekends. She was more receptive to humor in our sessions and could laugh when she made a mistake, instead of feeling like killing herself over it. Our work ended 10 years after our first meeting, when she took a new job in another state. During our last session, I asked her what was most helpful about our sessions. She thought for a moment then smiled, "You didn't try to make me change right away. You gave me suggestions and ideas, but let me decide when to change my own mind."

Her feedback was profound for me. I realized that when people have been through trauma they've usually felt coerced to do things they didn't want to do or weren't ready to do. Pamela was confirming the primary catalyst for her healing was being in a relationship where she felt respected, cared for, valued, and could go at her own pace. That doesn't mean I sat by passively as she moaned in misery. We had our conflicts, too. But she said my willingness to work through conflicts with her respectfully and to never give up on her was extremely meaningful. Before this, she'd never thought it was possible to work through a conflict with someone. She'd thought the only solution to conflict was to end the relationship.

I was surprised by Pamela's answers because she did some powerful work when we began reprocessing her traumatic memories. While I thought that phase of her treatment was most helpful, it obviously wasn't as meaningful to her as our therapeutic alliance. Never underestimate the value of showing up day after day for your clients, even when you think you're not helping them. Your genuine, attuned, consistent presence fills in the *missing experience* of secure attachment that helps their brains begin to rewire. Of course, clients also benefit from learning tools they can use to regulate intense emotions when you're not around. We'll address this in Chapter 5, Tools for Grounding, Calming, and Soothing.

5

Tools for Grounding, Calming, and Soothing

"Either I'm broken or bipolar!" Tracy sighed as she raised her arms into a surrender gesture above her head and waved her hands. "Since the rape, my emotions are all over the place! I feel like I'm swinging between two poles. One minute I'm a nervous wreck, anticipating danger around every corner, jumping anytime someone calls me, and trying to keep my heart from leaping out of my chest. The next minute, I feel like I'm walking in a stupor. I don't feel anything. I don't care about anything. It's like my mind wanders off to this hazy place where no one can reach me. Will I ever be normal again?"

People who have been through trauma are often confused and overwhelmed by their emotions. As Tracy described, their sensitized nervous systems can cause them to escalate quickly into hyperarousal states in which they feel anxious, agitated, hypervigilant, and enraged. Or they may find their bodies hijacked by hypoaroused states in which they feel immobilized, numb, disconnected, and dissociated.

Research has shown survivors of childhood trauma find it difficult to even name their emotions—a condition referred to as alexithymia (van der Kolk, 2015). They just know that they feel "bad" and often resort to unhealthy ways of managing strong feelings. Avoidant-dismissive clients tend to cope by shutting down and cutting off their feelings with drugs, workaholism, and other distractions. Disorganized-unresolved clients attempt to escape their emotions in similar ways, but could also discharge feelings through violence, or find themselves dissociating under extreme stress. Anxious-preoccupied clients frantically act out their emotions, desperately hoping others will comfort them, but their intense emotional expression pushes loved ones away. Likewise, when a client is really keyed up or shut down, it may feel like they're pushing *you* away. In both hyper- or hypoaroused states it's very difficult to access rational thinking skills, let alone engage in therapy. In this chapter, I'll discuss how to help your clients understand their emotions and regulate emotional arousal with grounding, movement, and self-soothing tools.

EMPOWER CLIENTS WITH EMOTION EDUCATION

Because clients impacted by trauma often feel confused or ashamed by their emotions, it's imperative to reassure them that their emotions serve an important purpose. Psychologist and author Lara Fielding (2015) asserts that the purpose of an emotion is to: 1) motivate an action that seems useful for your survival; 2) make you aware of a need that you have; and 3) communicate to your group or pack what you need. In the following table, I list six common emotions for trauma survivors and the survival needs they are attempting to meet:

Emotion	Action Request	Need
Fear	Run away! Avoid!	Safety
Anger	Stop! Get out of my way!	Protection/boundaries
Sadness	Withdraw, rest, take stock	Healing/respite/care
Disgust	Stay away—that's toxic!	Preserve well-being
Shame	Hide, cover up	Social approval
Panic/Grief*	Call the loved one home	Care/connection/belonging

I include panic and grief in the same category because neuroscientist Jaak Panksepp (Panksepp & Biven, 2012) found the same brain network activates both of these emotions. He opined that panic essentially results from the fear of being separated from your pack. Indeed, I've found that panic attacks resolve more quickly when you address underlying feelings of grief, loss, or disconnection.

What is your emotion asking you to do?

Before you attempt to help your client quell an emotion, invite her to explore what it's asking her to do or what need it's trying to meet. Cultivating the skill of compassionate curiosity toward her feelings not only calms the emotional brain, but also helps her develop caring attunement toward herself. Moreover, it engages and strengthen networks in the medial prefrontal cortex that facilitate regulation of the emotional brain (Ogden & Fisher, 2015). If your client is able, invite her to compassionately observe the emotional and physical sensations she is experiencing and ask herself:

- Where am I sensing this emotional energy in my body?
- What is this emotion asking me to do?
- What do I need right now?
- What do I want people to understand?

The point of emotional regulation is not to get rid of an emotion, but to help the client learn how to adjust the intensity of an emotional response within her "window of tolerance." Dan Siegel (1999) defines the window of tolerance as the state in which "various intensities of arousal can be processed without disrupting the functioning of the system" (p. 253). In other words, the window of tolerance is the optimal state of arousal where we can integrate the intuitive, sensory information from our emotional brains with the planning and reasoning skills from our prefrontal cortex. Marsha Linehan (1993), developer of dialectical behavioral therapy, refers to this state as "wise mind" (p. 214). Guiding your clients toward this balanced state helps them access "wise mind," reclaim their authentic selves, and take *effective* action instead of reacting impulsively. Figure 5.1 provides a chart to help you and your client recognize when he or she is in their window of tolerance versus a hyperaroused or hypoaroused state.

Hyperaroused states indicate the client's sympathetic nervous system is activating fight-or-flight states and are characterized by feeling anxious, agitated, hypervigilant, or unsafe. A client in a hyperaroused state may also experience intrusive images or obsessive, racing thoughts, increased heart rate, blood pressure, breathing rates, or shaking and sweating. In contrast, hypoaroused states indicate the client's parasympathetic/dorsovagal "freeze and collapse" response has been activated. Hypoaroused states are characterized by absence of sensation, numbness, apathy, low energy, inability to think clearly, or feeling weak, hopeless, or powerless. When someone is in a hyper- or hypoaroused state, his ability to socially engage is limited. If your client is too keyed up or shut down to identify and reflect on his emotional state, then movement, grounding, and orienting techniques can help bring him back into his emotional window of tolerance.

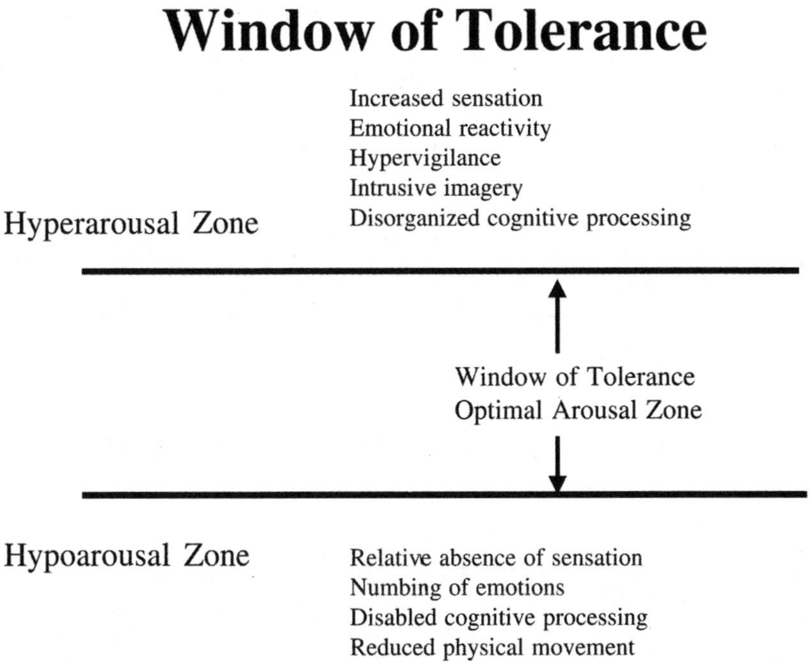
Window of Tolerance
Increased sensation
Emotional reactivity
Hypervigilance
Intrusive imagery
Disorganized cognitive processing
Hyperarousal Zone
Window of Tolerance
Optimal Arousal Zone
Hypoarousal Zone
Relative absence of sensation
Numbing of emotions
Disabled cognitive processing
Reduced physical movement

FIGURE 5.1: Window of Tolerance

From TRAUMA AND THE BODY: A SENSORIMOTOR APPROACH TO PSYCHOTHERAPY by Pat Ogden, Kenkuni Minton, Clare Pain. Copyright © 2006 by Pat Ogden. Copyright © 2006 by W. W. Norton & Company, Inc. Used by permission of W. W. Norton & Company, Inc.

TOOLS FOR ORIENTING
AND GROUNDING

Grounding and orienting techniques help clients return to the present moment and access a sense of external support beneath them. They can be helpful when a client feels spacey, fuzzy, foggy, numb, or cut off from her body. Grounding can also help clients focus attention when they are feeling scattered or overwhelmed. Additionally, I like to use these techniques to help clients *feel* what it is like "stand their ground" and cultivate an inner sense of power.

Orienting tools

Name Five Things: Notice what happens when you slowly turn your head from side-to-side to scan the room you are in right now. This helps your emotional brain register where you are physically located at this moment. Next, name: 1) five objects you can see; 2) four objects you can touch or feel against your skin; 3) three sounds you can hear; 4) two scents you can smell; and 5) one thing you can taste. When you guide clients through this exercise, it's best to do it slowly and encourage them to give you as many details as they can about the objects they notice. Activating the five senses redirects the emotional brain away from threatening sensory cues or memories. Naming the objects and describing the details engages the frontal lobes and brings a person more fully into the present moment.

Rhythm and play: Anything that engages the client's physical participation in the present moment can be orienting, grounding, and even fun! Tossing a beach ball back and forth, playing hand-clapping games, drumming, handling clay or stones, digging in dirt or sand, splashing cold or warm water on the face, sniffing aromatherapy scents, or taking mindful walks outside are all viable ways to bring your client into the present moment. You may suggest these activities to your client, then let her choose the activity that resonates most with her. Letting your client make choices about the activities she wants to do helps her reclaim her power and identity. You never want the client to feel coerced or forced into doing anything. This is why I frame everything as an *invitation*, not a directive.

Grounding tools

Feet on the Floor, Seated: This exercise helps to counter feeling weak, numb, spacey, or mentally overwhelmed. Invite the client to find a comfortable seated position that allows her to fully place both feet flat on the floor. From here, invite her to look at her feet or notice what it feels like to stomp her feet, or push her feet into floor, or slide her feet back and forth, and roll from her toes back to the heels of her feet, and so on. You can also invite her to notice how it feels to elongate her spine as her feet make contact with the floor. As she inhales, you could invite her to imagine her breath running down the length of her spine, down her legs, and through her feet to increase a sense of connection with the earth. She could also experiment with tensing and relaxing the muscles in her legs and feet. Guide your client to tap into sensations of support, strength, or power she can sense in her lower body. If the client is unable to focus on her feet, she can do similar motions with any other area of her body that can make contact and rest against a solid surface.

Feet on the Floor, Standing: If the client is able, invite her to stand up and notice the sensations in her feet as they make contact with the ground. You can invite her to notice if she feels more secure with her feet hip distance apart, shoulder distance apart, or closer together. You can bend your knees a little and invite the client to bend her knees along with you, noticing the strength in her legs. As described in the seated version of this exercise, you and the client can experiment with stomping your feet into the floor, pressing them into the floor, or moving them in various ways. Standing and leaning against a wall is another way to help the client feel grounded and supported by a solid surface. Again, the goal is to help the client find a way to fully engage in the present moment, feel an external sense of support, and develop greater awareness of the energy, strength, and power within her body.

Deep Muscle Pressure: Applying deep pressure to muscles modulates arousal and brings balance to the nervous system, too. Resting a weighted neck wrap/rice bag across the lap or feet is very comforting and grounding without being too intrusive. Weighted blankets, pressure foam rollers, and therapy balls are also great objects your clients can use to apply deep pressure.

MOVE THE BODY

Movement is often overlooked as a psychotherapeutic tool, but studies have shown that the way we hold and move our bodies has a profound effect on our mood. Each emotion triggers certain postures and action tendencies in the body. For example, feelings of sadness are characterized by a slouched posture, lowering the head down, wrapping one's arms around oneself, or resting one's head on the arms or hands. Studies have shown that asking a group of people to hold such postures for a few minutes caused them to feel lower in energy, recall more negative than positive memories, and focus on negative traits about themselves (Peper, Lin, Harvey, & Perez, 2017; Shafir, Tsachor, & Welch, 2016).

Fortunately, studies have also demonstrated that we can access positive emotional states by changing our postures. Peper et al. (2017) showed if people sat upright or tried skipping instead of slouching, they elevated their mood and subjective energy levels within a few minutes. Communication between the mind and body is a two-way feedback loop, one influences the other. The following sections describe simple movement activities you can use to regulate emotional states.

Movement to regulate fear and anxiety

When clients are stuck in the emotion of fear, they tend to lean or move backwards and enclose or constrict their bodies. Energy tends to be directed toward the legs to help the client run away from a perceived threat. To counter the posture of fear, invite your client to lift the chin, open and expand the chest area, and walk forward. Walking will also discharge the excess adrenaline circulating through the lower body. If your client is unable to walk, invite him to sit upright or lean slightly forward and move his legs or feet up and down in a rhythmic marching movement. Experiment with how it feels to speed the movement up or slow it down with a more deliberate stomping motion.

Movement to regulate anger and resentment

When a client is stuck in the emotion of anger, energy is directed toward the upper body. The jaw clenches. The face flushes. The shoulders and arms tighten to prepare them to fight. There is an impulse to move forward with a sudden, direct motion to make something stop or get out of our way. Expressing compassionate curiosity toward your client's angry feelings will help calm the arousal down a bit. But if they're still outside their window of tolerance, suggest doing a movement activity together.

To discharge the anger, the body needs to feel the sensation of pushing something away. Invite your client to *slowly* push his arms out against an imaginary resistant force or against a wall. Pushing away from the body in this slow, deliberate way is more satisfying than punching a pillow because the body feels like it is actually moving a threat out of its space. Additionally, assertively commanding "No," or "Stop," or "Get away from me!" while pushing against resistance can help the client give voice to his anger and release the tight energy in the jaw.

Movement to regulate depression, shame, and helplessness

Movement is also extremely helpful in lifting depression. As discussed earlier, research has shown that sitting upright, instead of slouched, enables us to access more positive memories and thoughts. In 2016, Shafir et al. found that positive emotional states could be elicited with movement that was light, rhythmic, and free-flowing. Spreading the arms wide and lifting the arms or head also correlated with more positive feelings. Jumping, skipping, and dancing elevated both energy and mood. You may not be able to invite a client to skip around your office, but I've found inviting depressed clients to lift their arms into a V-shaped "victory pose" above their heads or move their arms in a rhythmic flowing motion like an orchestra conductor has been energizing and uplifting.

TOOLS FOR CALMING AND SELF-SOOTHING

Clients who have been impacted by trauma, particularly attachment trauma, may have no idea how to comfort and soothe themselves. They may have *attempted* to soothe themselves in unhealthy ways with drugs, self-harm behaviors, avoidance, or bad relationships. To replace these unhealthy habits, they need to learn alternative, natural ways to help themselves feel better. The tools in this section not only calm and soothe the nervous system, but help clients develop the skills of self-compassion needed to heal attachment trauma.

Paced diaphragmatic breathing

As cliché as it sounds to tell your clients to "take a deep breath," diaphragmatic breathing at the rate of about six breaths per minute reduces negative affect, balances the nervous system, decreases anxiety, and lowers blood pressure and heart rate (Steffen, Austin, DeBarros, & Brown, 2017; Xiao et al., 2017). Moreover, our breathing and emotional states are closely connected. A study led by French psychologists Philippot, Chapelle, & Blairy (2002) discovered distinct breathing patterns evoked by specific emotions and found people could change their emotional state by altering their breathing.

Feelings of fear and anger are characterized by irregular, short, shallow breaths. Sadness can be evoked by moderate breathing marked by sighs on exhalations. Feelings of joy can be elicited with paced diaphragmatic breathing through the nose while keeping the ribcage relaxed.

In sum, paced diaphragmatic breathing not only calmed the nervous system, but reduced negative affective states in these studies. To guide your client into paced diaphragmatic breathing, invite him to:

1. Take a slow breath through the nose and breathe into the lower belly for 4 to 6 seconds.
2. Pause for 1 to 4 seconds.
3. Exhale slowly through the mouth for 4 to 6 seconds.
4. Repeat for 4 breath cycles or approximately 1 minute. Work up to 2 to 5 minutes.

Self-soothing techniques

Merely focusing on the breath can cause some clients to feel more anxious or experience intrusive images and thoughts. Traumatized clients do better when they have something else they can focus on while doing paced breathing. Self-soothing statements, gestures, and imagery help the client comfort herself and feel understood, accepted, and held.

Giving clients a simple phrase they can focus on while breathing can be helpful. For example, a person could acknowledge his emotion on an inhalation with the mantra, *"Breathing in, I feel my (anger, fear, sadness, etc.),"* and imagine releasing his emotion on an exhalation with the phrase, *"Breathing out, I calm my (anger, fear, sadness, etc.).* Not only does this give the client a mantra on which to focus, but it also teaches him to acknowledge and care for his emotions. In his book *Living Buddha, Living Christ* (1995), Buddhist monk Thich Nhat Hanh suggests thinking of an emotion like a baby who is crying and imagining sending loving kindness to the emotion as you are breathing to comfort and calm it.

Similarly, if your client likes imagery, she could imagine breathing in a healing light that soothes, comforts, and protects her body. Invite your client to imagine the light having a special color or quality that feels soothing. Other clients may enjoy imagining a peaceful place or visualizing a compassionate guide who is with them, sending love and healing. Often clients can identify an ancestor, pet, or spiritual figure they can visualize comforting and supporting them. You can find imagery scripts for these ideas at my website: www.courtneyarmstrong.net.

Last, you could invite clients to imagine breathing through the heart and visualizing a person, child, pet, place, personal talent, or thing for which they feel *appreciation*. At the Institute of HeartMath, McCraty and Childre (2002) discovered that focusing on the feeling of appreciation while engaging in paced breathing produced a more calming effect on the nervous system than focusing on other emotions. Participants in the study focused on feelings of gratitude, love, joy, and peace, but feeling appreciation seemed to generate the best results.

ADAPTING TECHNIQUES FOR EACH ATTACHMENT STYLE

Avoidant-dismissive: Because avoidant-dismissive clients cope by shutting off and avoiding feelings, they may not be able to identify or verbalize their emotions. Start with grounding and movement techniques first. This helps them begin to reconnect to the sensation of emotion in their body. Because they are logical, they can be resistant to any techniques that seem too "touchy-feely." Paced breathing combined with a mantra or simply counting their breaths mindfully can work better than imagery techniques.

Anxious-preoccupied: Anxious-preoccupied clients tend to be responsive to all the techniques in this chapter. Because they tend to look to others for self-soothing, they especially benefit from learning how to comfort and soothe themselves with compassionate attunement.

Disorganized-unresolved: Because these clients are the most prone to dissociation, they benefit from learning tools for grounding and orienting so they can stay present in times of stress. They tend to be very skilled at using imagery. Inviting them to create a compassionate guide, healing place imagery, or seeing different emotional states as various "parts" of themselves can be very effective. I'll talk more about working with parts in Chapter 6, How to Work with Dissociation.

6

How to Work with Dissociation

issociation is a complex phenomenon that involves a disruption in memory, awareness, identity, or perception. Dissociation typically occurs when a person encounters an experience that is so overwhelming to the nervous system that his brain can't fully integrate it. Therapists and clients alike can be frightened by dissociative responses. It's unnerving when a client says they feel "unreal," has gaps in memory, stares blankly into space, or "switches" to another personality. But dissociation is a natural survival mechanism designed to manage sensory overload and buffer the pain and terror of an overwhelming situation. If dissociation helped the client survive a traumatic event, she may dissociate when she encounters reminders of a trauma, or other forms of extreme stress.

In this chapter, you'll learn about the different types of dissociation, acquire tools to manage it, and learn how to work with personality states or "parts." Because the topic of dissociation is so immense, one chapter can't address every aspect of it. But my hope is that the information and tools shared in this chapter will increase your clinical understanding, comfort level, and confidence.

UNDERSTANDING TRAUMA-RELATED DISSOCIATION

In the DSM-5, the American Psychiatric Association (2013) classifies dissociation disorders into three major categories: 1) depersonalization-derealization disorder; 2) dissociative amnesia; and 3) dissociative identity disorder. Depersonalization and derealization involve a sense of feeling detached from yourself or your surroundings. Clients may describe it as feeling "unreal," or like they are watching themselves interact with the world but aren't really in it. They might feel like their arms and legs don't belong to their body, or that their external surroundings seem fuzzy or cartoon-like. Depersonalization episodes can be transient and aren't necessarily preceded by a traumatic event. Even healthy, non-traumatized individuals can experience depersonalization or derealization when in unfamiliar surroundings or under extreme stress (Simeon and Abugel, 2006).

Dissociative amnesia occurs when a person can't recall specific events or periods of time, and the memory impairment isn't related to drug use or another medical condition. While it is rare for people to have a complete loss of memory about themselves, people with dissociative amnesia report having no memory about a traumatic event or having no memory of their lives preceding the event. For example, my client Cindy was a 15-year-old girl who was traumatized by a violent melee that occurred during a basketball game in her school's gym. Although nobody was killed during the event, the terror of being pushed and shoved in a crowd while people were threating to shoot each other caused her to dissociate. The next day Cindy had no conscious recollection of the event, nor did she remember anything about her life before the event occurred. She knew her name and recognized her brother, but not anyone else. When her parents tried to jog her memory by telling her family stories or showing her photographs, Cindy felt like she was looking at another person's life. She had absolutely no recollection of historical events and said the girl in the photos seemed like a stranger. I'll address how I worked with Cindy to recover her memory in Chapter 12, Traumatic Grief and Loss.

Dissociative fugue is another phenomenon that the DSM-5 now classifies as a form of dissociative amnesia. This occurs when a person travels or wanders far away from their home with no conscious memory of it. My client Holly experienced this when she suddenly fled her home in Tennessee and spent three days in Chicago. She had no conscious awareness of driving to Illinois or how she spent those three days. She only recalled waking up in a hotel room in Chicago wondering how she got there. It wasn't until Holly called her husband that she learned she had been "missing" for three days and he had been frantically looking for her. Holly couldn't identify a particular event that triggered the fugue, but said her life had become overwhelmingly stressful. She and her husband were both working full time while trying to raise their autistic son and care for her elderly mother-in-law in their home. Holly joked, "I guess my brain had enough and decided to run away!" Even though Holly used humor as she reflected on the event, she was deeply frightened by her fugue experience and worried it might happen again. I'll discuss tools we used to help Holly manage dissociative triggers later in this chapter.

Dissociative identity disorder (DID), formerly known as multiple personality disorder, occurs when a person has two or more personality states that feel separate and distinct from one another. The person may or may not have conscious awareness of their alternate personality states, but they definitely feel as if they have no control over the thoughts and actions of each state. People who develop DID usually experienced profound trauma or neglect before age eight. Before age eight, a young child's prefrontal cortex hasn't reached a maturity level that allows it to integrate extreme emotional experiences.

In their book, *Neurobiology and Treatment of Traumatic Dissociation,* authors Lanius, Paulsen, & Corrigan (2014) explain that traumatic dissociation is "associated with the release of endogenous opioids and anesthetic neurochemicals that alter the communication between lower and higher brain structures" (p. 6). In particular, the flooding of endogenous opioids inhibits the thalamus—the brain's sensory relay station. As a result, sensory experiences, affective states, and survival behaviors related to a traumatic event get locked away in implicit neural networks that can feel like separate self-states.

TOOLS FOR MANAGING DISSOCIATION

Clients may not tell you they are dissociating because they are either not aware of it, haven't built enough trust with you, or simply don't know how to describe what they're experiencing. Signs that your client may be dissociating include a vacant look in her eyes or far-off stares in the session, having difficulty keeping track of the conversation, reports of feeling unreal, losing time, or hearing voices in her head. In more extreme cases, you may notice your client "switching" to another part that seems to have a significantly different affect, voice tone, or behavior than the she usually has.

Carlson and Putnam (1993) developed a 28-item screening tool called the Dissociative Experiences Scale-II (DES-II) that can be helpful in determining if your client experiences dissociation and the type, frequency, and intensity. The questions ask about common experiences like driving somewhere and not recalling parts of your trip, as well as more disturbing experiences like finding strange clothes in your closet that you don't remember buying. The DES-II is meant to be used as a screening tool only. It does not constitute the full psychological evaluation needed to confirm whether someone has a dissociative disorder or not. But it's a good way to start the conversation about dissociative symptoms and is fairly easy for clients to use. You can download the DES-II at http://traumadissociation.com/des.

Educate your clients

Educating your client about dissociation is essential for helping them manage it. Here is a way I explain it to my clients:

When we encounter something that overwhelms our nervous system, our brains release a flood of neurochemicals to help us survive and cope with the situation. Some stress hormones, like adrenaline, mobilize us to action. Additionally, our brains can release opiate-like neurochemicals to help us tolerate extreme pain and fear. But these painkilling neurochemicals can also cause us to feel disconnected from ourselves and our surroundings. Or they can cause us to lose conscious awareness of the present moment, have gaps in memory, or even to feel like there are different parts living inside of us who have their own thoughts and voices. Sometimes people worry they are going crazy because it feels strange and scary. But it's actually just an extreme stress response where different parts of an experience get split off to help you cope and survive.

This explanation puts clients at ease because you are reassuring them that they are not crazy and that you will not be disquieted by their dissociative symptoms. Next, you'll want to assist your client in developing tools she can use to manage her dissociative symptoms.

Orient to safety in the present moment

You can use the tools for grounding and orienting that I discussed in Chapter 5, such as having clients name five things they can see, hear, touch, smell, or taste in the room. For clients who dissociate, I like to start every session with this exercise, not only to help them get oriented but to help them practice getting present. I encourage clients to practice this exercise at home, at work, or anywhere else they need to anchor themselves to the present moment.

Encourage your client to focus on objects that signal safety, such as a pleasant image, soothing sound, or comforting smell. Because our olfactory bulb transmits information directly to the amygdala, smell is the fastest way to trigger a flashback, but it can also be the fastest way to stop a flashback. My client Holly, who experienced dissociative fugue, associated the smell of fresh coffee with her grandmother's house. Her grandmother's house was a safe place for her, and she noticed that inhaling the aroma of coffee grounds had a calming effect on her. She began to carry a Ziploc bag of coffee grounds in her purse to sniff anytime she needed to settle her nervous system and reorient herself.

If your client is dissociating during the session, call her name gently or ask her if she can tell you how old she is, what time it says on the clock, what your name is, or what color your hair or shirt is. If she's still not responding, I have a Tibetan chime that has a soft, pleasant tone that I ring, or I ask my client if there is something else I can do to help her feel safer in the moment. Whatever you do, refrain from touching your client to reorient them. They could be in the middle of a flashback, not realize who you are, and become combative. I know this seems obvious, but it's our natural instinct to touch someone when they are not responding. You'll need to restrain this urge.

Create an internal sense of safety

In addition to helping clients anchor themselves to external objects of safety, it's useful to help them find an internal sense of safety. Dissociative clients are usually very good at immersing themselves in imagery. Invite them to imagine a place that evokes a sense of safety, healing, or peace for them. Their healing scene may be a beautiful place in nature, a safe room, a nurturing or protective figure, a pet, or even the image of an energy force shield with which they could surround themselves. Once they have identified an image, invite them to get more absorbed in the experience by spending several minutes noticing and enjoying the pleasant visuals, sounds, smells, and sensations they associate with it. The point of this exercise is to help them develop an internal resource they can retreat to in times of stress. Guide your client to practice this on a daily basis so that it is easier to access this resource when she needs it. I've also created a 4-Point Daily Stress Shield activity my clients like to use for calming, grounding, and empowerment. You can find this activity in Box 6.1.

Physical gestures that evoke safety

Nurturing gestures and containment postures can help clients feel safe and protected. Inviting clients to place a hand over their heart area in the center of their chest as they slow their breathing and imagine sending loving kindness toward themselves is easy and effective. Similarly, placing one hand on the forehead or abdomen while placing one hand on the heart while doing paced breathing can be grounding and soothing. As clients are doing this, I invite them to imagine feeling supported and safely held. Peter Levine has shared another posture that evokes the feeling of being contained and safely held: Place your right hand under your left armpit, and the left hand on top of your right shoulder as you hug yourself and gently rock. The National Institute for the Clinical Application of Behavioral Medicine (2017) published a video of Levine demonstrating this containment posture at: https://www.youtube.com/watch?v=G7zAsealyFA.

Gently approach inner experience

In their excellent book, *Coping with Trauma-Related Dissociation* (2011), authors Boon, Steele, and van der Hart suggest clients with dissociative disorder struggle with a "phobia of inner experience." These clients feel frightened and ashamed of their inner feelings, thoughts, and sensations and seek to escape them, avoid them, split off from them, or shut down. Helping dissociative clients develop the ability to notice and nonjudgmentally describe what they are sensing inside is a vital skill.

Expressing acceptance and compassionate curiosity about all aspects of your client's feelings makes it safer for her to talk about them, but you have to move slowly. For example, if your client says she feels too scared to talk about something, you could say, "Let's honor your fear and let it know it is welcome here. Perhaps we can ask your fear what it wants us to know? What is it protecting you from? I want to respect its concerns." Guiding clients to have these compassionate conversations with themselves also sets the stage for working with parts.

WORKING WITH PARTS

Neurologically speaking, a "part" is an organized neural network that contains a pattern of thoughts, perceptions, feelings, or behaviors tied to a particular situation or developmental age. In a sense we all have "parts." For example, the part of you that feels anger may seem very different from the part of you that is loving, nurturing, or playful. Most people have awareness of these different states of self, and yet conceive of themselves as a unitary, whole person. When someone has dissociative identity disorder (DID), there is no integration among their self-states, and they seem like completely separate identities.

Each part or self-state represents an organized, coherent response to a particular experience at a certain point in time. For instance, a client who suffered childhood abuse may have one neural network that formed as a small child that holds feelings of helplessness, fear, and the urge to hide and withdraw. When this part gets triggered, the client may withdraw, think, speak, and react like a small child. Later, when this child became a teenager, perhaps becoming angry and combative protected her from abuse. Personality "parts" may have their own name, gender, style of dress, voice, and views of the world. In times of stress, the brain will activate the self-state that seems best suited to handle the current challenge.

Working with parts is a lot like doing family therapy. This is why Richard Schwartz's (2013) internal family systems model makes sense to many people. All parts of us are like members of a family who are trying to maintain the system and keep it alive. Some families are functional and some are dysfunctional. But all the members have to live together and figure out how to get along with each other. Therefore, when you're working with parts, it's imperative that you not give the impression that you want to eliminate a part or remove it from the system.

Modern approaches emphasize accepting all the client's parts, understanding their meaning and function, and exploring how they can function together in a more amicable, coordinated way (Boon et al.,

2011). This approach to working with DID differs from 20th century approaches that made the goal of therapy integration of parts into one central identity. If a part believes you are attempting to eliminate it or "kill it off," then it will wildly protest and sabotage therapy.

Types of Parts

Although every DID client's system is organized in a unique way, alters tend to fall into four categories: 1) functional adult parts; 2) child parts; 3) angry/protector parts; and 4) helper parts. In the following paragraphs I'll summarize how these parts appear.

Functional adult parts

Functional adult parts carry out the everyday activities of the system. These parts may go to work, raise children, and can interact socially. In their book *The Haunted Self*, van der Hart, Nijenhuis, and Steele (2006) refer to these as "Apparently Normal Parts" (ANP) because they seem to function normally on the surface. The ANPs may overwork and do their best to stay busy because they want to avoid traumatic memories and the traumatized parts as much as possible. Yet, if a traumatic memory gets triggered, the parts of the system that hold the painful memory will emerge and take control of the client's identity.

Child parts

Child parts tend to hold traumatic memories that occurred at different developmental stages of the client's life. A client could have multiple child parts ranging from infancy to adolescence. Child parts can manifest as helpless, frightened, and lonely, but there can also be child parts who are playful and hold positive memories. Child parts often feel abandoned by the client's adult self and long for comfort, help, and safety. Child parts can be receptive to interacting with a therapist they view as accepting, compassionate, and safe. But they can also distrust the therapist and be reluctant to get close due to of fear being abandoned. Many times angry or fight parts will prevent the child part(s) from speaking or showing themselves to the therapist in an effort to protect these younger alters.

Angry/protective parts

Angry parts can be frightening when they appear, but their ultimate job is to protect the system. Angry parts may see themselves as strong, tough advocates for the child parts. They may hold the anger the younger child was not allowed to express and can erupt if they believe the client is being threatened or disrespected. Alternatively, the client could have an angry part that mimics his abuser. This abusive part may be critical, mean, and even violent toward the vulnerable parts of the client's system. Usually, this alter develops if the client was punished by his caregivers for speaking up, crying, having needs, exposing family secrets, or even having joy or confidence. Although it doesn't look like directing hostility toward younger parts is adaptive, these angry parts believe silencing the child parts protects them from being hurt again by the outside world. The best way to communicate with an angry part is to appeal to its interest in protecting the system. Once the angry part feels like you understand and respect its role, it may be open to negotiating with you and the other parts. If not, then see if the client has a "helper" part that can mediate conflicts within the system.

Helper parts

Often clients have helper parts that take care of other parts. Sometimes this helper part is fashioned after someone the client may have perceived as nurturing and supportive when they were a child, like a teacher or grandmother, or even a character from a book or movie. At other times, the helper represents how the client sought to comfort and soothe herself as a child. Sarah Krakauer (2001), author and DID specialist, states: ". . . every individual, no matter how damaged and fragmented, has an inner core that, once potentiated, can guide the individual to a state of harmonious functioning" (p. 44). Similarly, Ralph Allison, author of *Minds in Many Pieces* (1999) believed that all

DID clients have an "Inner Self Helper" (ISH) that represents the client's pure spiritual essence and knows and loves all parts of the client.

Richard Schwartz (2013), developer of the internal family systems model, promotes a similar concept, proposing that every person has a Self (spelled with a capital "S"). He describes the Self as possessing qualities he calls the 8 Cs: compassion, curiosity, courage, confidence, calmness, clarity, creativity, and connectedness. Clients and therapists can call on this higher Self or other inner helper parts to comfort, encourage, and mediate other parts.

Communicating with parts

All the client's parts have to feel comfortable with you before they will let you venture into their inner world. It's important to go at the client's pace, create safety and trust, and work on skills for coping with dissociation first. You do not want to tackle traumatic memories until the client has built better coping skills and has the capacity to stay present. Usually a part will let you know if you're moving too fast.

For example, after working together for a year, a DID client of mine I'll call Dee Ann told me she was ready to review a traumatic memory that occurred when she was five years old. The memory involved Satanic ritual abuse. She would have flashes of terrifying images involving blood, sexual abuse, and animal sacrifices by day, and terrifying dreams at night. Dee Ann wasn't sure if the abuse really happened to her or if it was a dream. She hoped we could figure it out by revisiting the memory and find a way to stop these frightening images. Just as Dee Ann began to piece a past memory together, an angry part that I'd never met leapt to the surface. He let me know "he" was responsible for protecting Dee Ann's five-year-old part and was not going to put her through the horror of revisiting that memory. Furthermore, he warned that Dee Ann's abusers would kill me if I knew their secret, so he was protecting me too. I thanked him for his protection and asked him if there was anything else he wanted me to know so I could support him in guarding the system. We had a productive conversation, but he was reluctant for Dee Ann to revisit her five-year-old's memories. When I asked if the five-year-old part might be asking for help containing the nightmares, he said he'd look into it and get back with me. I thanked him and asked if he could let Dee Ann come forward again so she could drive home. He obliged and receded.

Dee Ann took a couple of minutes to reorient herself and asked, "What happened? Did you hypnotize me?" I reassured her that I did not, and got the sense another part of her wanted to protect her from revisiting disturbing memories. She smiled sheepishly and said, "Oh, you must have met Rocco." I smiled back at her and said, "Yeah, I think I did. He seems to really care about you."

Dee Ann nodded and murmured, "Yeah. He can be a little overbearing, but I think he means well." We agreed to have more conversations with Rocco before we attempted to review the memory again. Dee Ann opted to do most of her conversing with Rocco at home through writing and internal dialogues. Rocco didn't like coming out in the therapy room too much. He was a tough guy who didn't like all that "sissy" stuff. He just tolerated Dee Ann coming to see me because it made her feel better to talk to a "kind, older woman." We spent nearly another year getting to know all her parts before we revisited any memories again.

Talking with Parts

Guiding the client to have an inner dialogue with one part at a time is a good place to start. Sometimes a client feels reluctant to engage a part because she is scared or ashamed of what it might say or do. She might feel more comfortable if you start the conversation and model how to talk to the part. Or you and your client may ask if there is a helper part who can be with the client and guide her through the conversation.

Questions to ask Parts

Invite the client to notice when it feels like a part comes up and get curious about the role and function it serves for the system. You or she can ask the following questions:

1. Hello, welcome. Tell me what you want me to know about you. If the part can't talk, ask it to communicate to the client in images or feelings.
2. What is your role? What do you hold or do for everybody?
3. Do you like what you are doing and how you are doing it?
4. Is there something you would rather do or wish you could do more?
5. What are you afraid would happen if you did not do this job?
6. How would it be if you were able to get to know another part?
7. What if we could find a way to take some of the burden off you? What else would you like to do?
8. How do you feel about me? Is there something I could do to help you feel heard, acknowledged, or reassured?

Inner Meeting Room

Inner meetings are another way to facilitate conversations among parts. You can suggest that clients create a safe meeting room in their mind where parts can come together to get to know each other, work things out, and make decisions. In her book *Easy Ego State Interventions*, Robin Shapiro (2016) advises that the meeting be structured with one part that can serve as a "chairperson," mediate between the parts, and keep the meeting on task. Younger parts who can't talk can draw pictures or assign a "spokesperson" to represent their views in the meeting. Krakauer (2001) also suggests creating a "hall of safety" where each part has a safe room they can retreat to if the meeting gets too intense. DID clients have wonderful imaginations and are good at creating meeting places. I usually guide clients to create the meeting room first, then invite one part at a time to attend the meeting.

In sum, clients who struggle with dissociation need additional time to build trust with you and develop skills for managing dissociative phenomena. It is essential that you spend time helping them learn how to ground themselves, orient to the present, and get to know their parts before diving into traumatic memories. Otherwise they are prone to reliving a memory and believe the trauma is happening again in real time. While the work is challenging, it is also immensely rewarding as you witness clients who suffered profound abuse heal and reclaim their lives. Next, in Chapter 7, I'll address how to instill hope and empowerment and help your clients access positive emotional states.

Four-Point Daily Stress Shield Activity

1. **Ground:** *Connect at least four points on your body with a supportive surface. This could be as easy as noticing your left and right foot making contact with the ground, your back resting against the chair, and your bottom making contact with the seat beneath you.*

2. **Breathe:** *While remaining in your grounded position, inhale to a count of four, hold for a count of four, and exhale for a count of four and pause for four. Repeat four times.*

3. **Protect:** *Imagine breathing in a color that represents your healing life-force energy on an inhalation. Breathe it into any area that feels tense, tired, sore, tight, angry, or scared. As you exhale, imagine releasing what you no longer need while the light surrounds your mind and body with protection. Repeat four times.*

4. **Affirm:** *Repeat the phrase "I am surrounding myself with love, light, and protection," or any other phrase that feels supportive to you, four times.*

7

Instill Hope and Empowerment

When clients who've survived trauma come to us for therapy, they need hope, encouragement, and empowerment. But how do you uplift clients who feel devastated? If you move too quickly to suggest silver linings or solutions, they could feel like you're minimizing their pain. But if you focus solely on their misery, you and your client can *both* end up feeling stuck. In this chapter, I'll show you how to strike a balance between compassionate listening and uplifting support to help clients feel hopeful, empowered, and motivated.

TURN SYMPTOMS INTO STRENGTHS

Turning a symptom into a client's ally, rather than a nemesis, can empower clients. Clients often misinterpret symptoms of anxiety, depression, numbing, and avoidance as indications they are "broken." Reassure clients that their symptoms are normal responses to trauma and actually indicate their brains are working properly. Explore how your client's emotional responses helped him survive and cope with tragedy. Not only does this help clients feel more competent, but it fosters self-compassion.

According to research by Martin Seligman (2011), clients who were taught that post-traumatic stress was not a debilitating disorder, but a normal reaction of grief and mourning, had better outcomes in treatment. Likewise, a Harvard University study led by Jamieson, Nock, & Mendes (2012) found that when people reinterpreted their stress response as a positive reaction that could help them overcome a challenge, their blood vessels dilated, instead of constricting. Their hearts were still beating fast, but with the blood vessels open instead of constricted, their electrocardiogram (ECG) measurements reflected cardiac activity associated with the emotions of courage and joy, rather than fear. In short, when people learned to view the physiological response of fear as a helpful ally, their emotions shifted from negative to positive.

For example, Monique, an 18-year-old client who survived a brutal rape, arrived at our first session in the midst of an intense panic attack. She was pacing in my waiting room fanning her flushed face with one hand as she wrapped her dark braided hair on top of her head with the other. At first she wanted to cancel our session and go home, stating, "I can't sit still and talk while I'm like this. I feel like a total freak. I'm sorry."

I reassured her, "No need to apologize, Monique. Your body is doing exactly what it needs to do. I know it feels scary, but your body is giving you extra adrenaline and strength right now to deal with a challenge. It's called the fight-or-flight response. When our bodies are in this state, they want to run or get away from something that seems threatening— like coming to a therapy session to talk to a total stranger about what was probably the worst day of your life."

Monique laughed and nodded in agreement. I suggested that since her body obviously wanted to move, walking might help her feel better. I offered to walk with her on a private walking trail behind my office. Monique was both surprised and relieved to find walking helped settle her nervous system. She continued to use walking and light jogging between sessions to manage her anxiety and reclaim her strength. She also responded well to guided imagery and did amazing inner work when we reprocessed her traumatic memories.

After several months of working together, she felt ready to go back to school. When I asked her what helped her most in our work together, she said, "You were the first person that saw me as a strong person, not a helpless victim. Getting me out on the trail to walk that first day was a huge turning point for me. It made me see I wasn't broken and helped me believe I could get better." I was heartened to hear this, but surprised. I felt certain the imagery tools and memory reconsolidation work we did had been the most helpful aspects of our therapy. But she emphatically stated that focusing on her strengths and reassuring her that her body was working normally was the best thing I did for her.

REFRAME SELF-DESTRUCTIVE BEHAVIORS

If a client is engaging in self-destructive activities like cutting, substance abuse, or eating disorders, get curious about how these behaviors have helped him manage emotional pain before you attempt to replace them. Lisa Ferentz (2015), author of *Treating Self-Destructive Behaviors in Trauma Survivors*, views self-harm behaviors as "creative coping-strategies" in disguise. As frightening as these behaviors appear, they've likely helped your client self-soothe, distract from pain, counteract numbing, or elicit care from other people. Gaining this awareness empowers clients and helps them feel less "crazy." More important, it paves the way for identifying healthier methods your client can use to replace self-harm behaviors and meet her needs.

My client Max thought the reason he cut on his arms and legs with sharp objects was because he hated himself. He viewed cutting as a form of self-punishment.

With compassionate curiosity, I asked him, "Does cutting give you any relief at all? Does it help drown out those tortuous thoughts or feelings, even for a moment?"

Max looked down at the scars on his arms and rubbed them, coaxing his wounds to give him an answer. After a few minutes he nodded, "Yes, I guess it does get my mind off my negative feelings and thoughts for a little while. The stinging sensation from the blade digging into my skin drowns out everything else at first. Then, I fixate on the blood and feel this weird sense of calm for several minutes. After that, I go through this ritual of carefully cleaning my wounds and bandaging them. So yeah, the whole process does take me out of my head for an hour or two. I never thought of it that way."

We got even more insight when I asked Max to tell me about the first time he cut on himself. He realized it was after an argument he had with his mother when he was 10 years old. She berated him for making a C in math on a report card and threw a glass at him for "not loading the dishwasher properly."

He recalled, "She had this crazed look in her eye and told me I was a selfish, lazy person who wouldn't amount to anything. I tried to tell her that I made a C in math because I didn't understand it and needed help. But she thought I was making excuses. Enraged, I ran out to a wooded area near our house. I had a pocket knife with me and started carving "Fuck You" into a piece of wood I found. Carving into the wood relieved a little tension, but I was still feeling pissed. So I carved the letters "FU" into my arm. I don't know who I wanted to hurt more—me or my mom."

I nodded compassionately and replied, "Well it sounds like you were trying to communicate your frustration. Did you show your mom the "FU" cuts on your arm or did you hide them from her?"

Max answered, "I hid them. But she eventually caught me cutting on myself. At first she yelled at me. Then, after she got over her initial shock, she tried to help me. She started listening to me a little more and wasn't as harsh with me. I stopped cutting for a while after that. Hmmm . . . now I'm realizing I cut on myself whenever I feel like nobody is listening to me or treating me like I don't matter. Maybe I'm not punishing myself as much as I'm frustrated nobody seems to care about me."

ATTUNE, LIFT, AND LEAD

Understanding and validating how trauma symptoms served your client is essential for building trust and rapport. But you also want to help them clarify a goal that is more compelling than their pain. As psychologist Clifton Mitchell (2007) explains in his book *Effective Techniques for Dealing with Highly Resistant Clients*, being unhappy with the status quo is what pushes a person toward change, but identifying something they desire more pulls them toward action. Instead of running away from what they don't want, we want clients running toward what they do want. To help clients make this shift, I recommend a communication pattern I call "Attune, Lift, and Lead." With this approach, you attune with the feelings and beliefs your clients are experiencing in the present moment while gently leading them toward what are more desired feelings and beliefs. I'll give examples in the following paragraphs.

Attune with clients by validating their feelings, but as you're reflecting back your understanding, change the tense of the verb to "has been." This implies that although something has been occurring, it doesn't necessarily mean it will continue to happen. For example, I said to to Max, "So cutting on your body *has been* a way that you've managed the pain of not feeling understood, accepted, or supported." Max nodded his head and said, "Yeah, I guess it has."

If I had said, "So cutting *is* a way to manage the pain . . .," then I would have subconsciously implied that cutting is still the solution. Saying "cutting *has been* a way to . . ." implies that it was a way to manage pain, but it's not the only way to manage it.

Second, it is helpful to "lift" and "lead" your clients by stating what they want instead of what they don't want. While looking compassionately and deeply into Max's eyes, I relayed, "What you'd really like is for your feelings to be recognized and know that they matter. And more important—to know that *you* matter, Max." When I reflected this back to him, his eyes welled with tears. Feeling like he mattered was the desire that was more compelling than his pain. We had to address this deeper wound first. The cutting was a superficial wound.

Treating Max like a valuable person for whom I had respect and helping him feel safe communicating his feelings became the focus our sessions. If I'd begun treatment by focusing on how to get him to stop cutting with a cognitive-behavioral treatment plan, he probably would have dropped out of therapy. Healing his heart was the first goal. Healing the cuts on his arms was secondary.

More than the words you say, remember that your client's attachment system is paying close attention to your eye contact, tone of voice, and body language. As Dan Siegel (2010) writes, our clients have to "feel felt." In addition to understanding what has been troubling your client, ask yourself, "What does this client seem to long for and desire deep down in her heart? What is she telling me she wants? What would she need to feel or believe in order to not feel depressed, anxious, and so on?" Clarifying what your client wants uplifts clients, too. This is why I call them lift and lead statements. For example, compare the following two statements a therapist might reflect back to a depressed client, and tell me which one causes you to feel better:

Response 1: "So, you've been feeling really down and it's been hard to get motivated."

Response 2: "So, you've been feeling really discouraged and you'd like to feel more hopeful and believe it's possible to enjoy life again."

After reflecting back your understanding of what your client wants, invite him to tell you how he wants to be feeling, thinking, or responding in his words. Of course, you could ask your client directly what he wants before suggesting your own ideas. But I've found clients will tend to reply in terms of what they don't want with answers like, "I don't want to be depressed anymore. I want these panic attacks to stop. I don't want to feel anxious."

Unfortunately, our emotional brain doesn't hear the word "don't" and focuses on the dominant thought in a sentence. For instance, if I ask you not to think about a pink elephant roller skating down Fifth Avenue in Manhattan, that roller skater just popped into your mind, didn't it? The same thing happens when we tell our minds not to be worried or sad. For the emotional brain to evoke the desired responses, you have to describe the attitudes and qualities your client wants to feel.

Once you and your client have clarified what she wants verbally, then it's helpful to lead your client into an experiential activity that *physically* evokes her desired responses and feelings. Remember, the emotional brain learns through experiences. It has to *feel it to believe it*. In the following sections, I'll share three experiential activities you can use to help your clients embody desired traits and feelings. My clients consistently enjoy these activities and have been surprised at how helpful they are in accessing positive feelings about themselves.

DESIRED FUTURE SELF

Envisioning one's desired future self is not a new therapeutic technique, but it's an incredibly powerful one. In fact, studies have shown that visualizing one's "best possible self" for anywhere between four days to four weeks elicited immediate positive affect and spurred motivation for study participants (King, 2001; Sheldon & Lyubomirsky, 2006).

Psychiatrist Viktor Frankl's story provides a dramatic example the power of envisioning one's future self to survive trauma. In his book *Man's Search for Meaning* (2006), Frankl describes a moment when he was forced to march through a field by Nazi soldiers even though he was feeling terribly cold, weak, and ill. He collapsed to the ground during the march, stating he could not go on. One of the guards beat him mercilessly with a club, threatening to leave Frankl to die if he didn't get up. Frankl thought he would die in that moment, but all of a sudden he had the vision of giving a passionate lecture to hundreds of people on "the psychology of death camps" and receiving a standing ovation.

From that day forward, he focused on his vision daily, working out what he would say, and imagining how many people he could help and inspire if he survived. His desire to fulfill this dream strengthened his resolve and buffered his spirit from being broken. Not only did he survive the concentration camps, he went on to become one of the most admired leaders in the psychology field. Indeed, his vision did come true when he received a standing ovation for his talk to an audience of 7,000 people at a conference in Anaheim, California (O'Hanlon, 2011).

Following is a guided imagery script you can use to help clients envision their desired future self. Invite your client to close her eyes so she can really get in touch with a clear sense of how it would feel to be responding to life in her desired way. If she's not comfortable closing her eyes, invite her to cast her gaze wherever it feels comfortable and kind of daydream about this idea for a moment with you. I tell clients that they are in charge of this experience and that they can talk to me while they're doing it, or stop if it becomes uncomfortable. You can download a copy of this script at www.courtneyarmstrong.net.

Imagine future you having moved forward in a positive way in your life in spite of this negative event. Acknowledging that you've been through something really painful and difficult, but imagining what it would be like to be on the other side of that now . . . . You might imagine yourself standing on one side of a bridge and looking over to the other side where you see your future self having moved forward successfully . . . (pause 10 seconds) . . . what would she look like? What would she be doing? (pause 10 to 30 seconds, or for 1 to 4 full breath cycles). *You may or may not get a clear mental image, just let yourself get the sense of what it would be like . . . How would you like your future self to be feeling? How would she be taking care of herself?* (pause 10 to 30 seconds). *How would she be interacting with the world?* (pause again) *Who is she with? How has she adjusted things so that she can now feel more alive, secure, satisfied, and happy with herself and her life?* (pause 20 to 30 seconds).

Perhaps you could see your future self taking anything that was useful from her past experiences like increased wisdom, depth, compassion . . . or increased clarity about what is important to her . . . and leaving behind what was not useful . . . knowing she did what made sense with the resources she had then . . . and using new knowledge and resources she has now. See the world through her eyes for a moment—checking out what it would be like to be on the other side . . . feeling clear, secure, focused, and even joyful . . . doing things that are in both your short-term and long-term best interest . . . (pause 20 to 30 seconds).

And you can talk to your future self if you'd like . . . What advice would she give you?. . . Let her show you what she did to get where she is now . . . (pause 30 to 60 seconds) . . . See her looking at you and thanking you because right now you are making her life possible . . . (pause) . . . feel her gratitude as you let her know you are setting an intention to heal and begin moving your life in this direction . . . and whenever you're ready, take a deep breath and find your way back here.

Suggesting clients think of their preferred future as an intention, rather than a goal, eases the pressure and allows for flexibility as they pursue their desires. If your client is having trouble imagining an positive outcome for her future self, ask her to imagine someone who has been through a similar trauma and consider what they would want for that person. Clients may not be able to imagine themselves feeling differently, but they often have compassion for someone else. I suggest clients not use a celebrity or anyone they know, but make up a fictional person. Not only can clients project onto a fictional person more easily, but they are less likely to compare themselves negatively to an imagined character. Jon Connelly (2014) introduces the concept to clients this way: "Let's imagine someone who has been through something very similar to you. Not anybody you know, just a person we make up who would be similar in age, background and has gone through a similar experience. She would understand exactly how you feel. What would you want for her future? What would you say to her? What would you want her to be feeling, thinking, and doing so she can be functioning in the most optimal way?" (p. 9)

Even though it's easier for a client to project onto a fictional person, some clients choose to imagine what they would want for a close friend or family member. For example, a combat veteran had trouble forgiving himself for killing an innocent civilian he thought was carrying explosives. But when he imagined how he'd want his son to feel if his son encountered the same situation, he realized he would want his son to understand it was an unfortunate casualty of war and not berate himself for it. Getting in touch with the compassion he would have for his son helped him get in touch with the compassion he could finally give himself.

BREATH-SYMBOL IMAGERY

Another technique that clients enjoy is to let their imagination show them a symbolic image or metaphor that would represent their mind working in the desired way. I also learned this concept from Jon Connelly (2014), the developer of Rapid Resolution Therapy, and have found it to be a powerful way to move clients forward and help them believe change is possible.

To begin, collaborate with your client to identify how she would like to be feeling and responding to things in her life now. I've included a list of positive qualities you can share with clients at the end of this chapter. Clients only need to select four or five desired qualities from this list—any more than that can feel overwhelming. Next, suggest clients let their imagination show them a symbol that would represent those qualities. Following is an example:

> Imagine what it would be like to be feeling strong, at ease, compassionate, and secure (or whichever four or five qualities your client chooses). Then ask your mind to show you a symbolic image that would represent your mind working this way. It could be something in nature, an animal in the wild, or another type of symbol or metaphor. Usually the first thing that comes to mind is best, even if it doesn't make logical sense to you at first.

Connelly suggests the symbol be something in nature or an animal in the wild. While these organic symbols work well, clients may select archetypal images, mythological or spiritual figures, or other objects that have meaning for them. I've seen clients select Cleopatra, Moses, Harry Potter characters, and even an image of a spreadsheet as their personal symbols. As long as the symbol has meaning and evokes the client's desired qualities, it will work. Once your client has identified his or her symbol, use the following script to invite them to deepen their connection to the symbol and their desired qualities. Again, you can download this script from my website at www.courtneyarmstrong.net to use in your sessions.

Imagine your [name client's symbol] *as you take a deep breath in and hold it for a moment. Good. Then, slowly exhale, letting go of what you no longer need right now. Let's do it again. See your* [symbol] *and breathe it in all the way to your belly this time. Yes, that's it. Now hold it for a moment as your mind takes it in . . . and then slowly exhale. Good. One more time, imagine your* [symbol], *breathe in . . . perhaps this time imagining the qualities of that* [symbol] *filling your lungs and moving into your bloodstream where it can circulate throughout your body. That's it. And if you like, you can gaze down or rest your eyes closed as you slowly exhale, releasing any excess tension or anything else you no longer want or need.*

That's right . . . and every time you inhale, imagine breathing in [name the four or five qualities of your client's symbol one word at a time every time they inhale for the next several breaths] . . . *letting the essence of what's represented by* [symbol] *infuse every cell, every tissue, every fiber of your being . . . as it supports healing, clarity, and inner wisdom.*

And you might even imagine what it would be like to be that [symbol] *as if you could inhabit it or ride behind the eyes of* [symbol]. [Pause for at least 30 seconds to 1 minute to let the client imagine and integrate this experience]. *What is your symbol showing you? How does it carry itself in the world? How does it respond to things? What can you learn from it?*

Yes . . . that's it . . . and you can continue breathing in the energy of [symbol] *as it clears, heals, organizes, and supports all of those things that are in your best interest . . . revealing peace, light . . . wisdom. And any time you want to access and enhance these qual-*

ities within yourself, all you have to do is imagine your symbol and take a deep breath . . . knowing it will activate and strengthen those qualities of [name each quality of the client's symbol one word at a time] . . . and all of that will continue working for you whether [symbol] comes to mind or not. That's it . . . and when you're ready, ever so gently, find your way back here, and take a big breath in . . . and slowly open your eyes.

INNER LIFE-FORCE ENERGY

I believe that beneath a person's pain and trauma lies a pure life-force energy that has sustained them and is continuing to help them heal. The concept of a life force is found in most ancient cultures of the world. In Asian cultures, it's called *chi* or *qi*; In India, it is called *prana*; in the Bible, it's called the *Holy Spirit*. No matter what you call it, I describe this life-force energy to clients as being loving, wise, strong, resilient, and creative.

Every living thing contains this internal energy that compels it to grow and thrive, no matter the circumstances. I compare it to a flowering plant that may have grown in dry soil, darkness, or even turbulent weather conditions. Inside that flower's seed is an unstoppable energy force that seeks light and growth. If it was planted under a dark deck, it finds cracks where light breaks through and grows through and around the deck. If it was planted in dry soil, it extends its roots deeper into the soil where it can find moisture. If it was raised in a stormy environment, it devotes energy toward strengthening its stems and roots to survive strong winds. Maybe it hasn't flowered yet, because most of its energy had to be devoted to strengthening its roots and its stem first. The plant may look withered or different from the other flowers because of how it had to grow. But it is still alive. It is still has worth. It is still beautiful.

Even if a plant's physical body doesn't make it through harsh circumstances, the energy and molecules that were part of that plant return to the Earth to support new life or be a part of another life. I affirm that I know my client has this life-sustaining energy because they are alive and sitting in my office. Even if they feel weary, ill and exhausted, that life-force energy continues to seek healing and resilience and is likely what led them to therapy. To help them access a sense of their own life force, I use the following imagery script. Again, some of the language in this script was inspired by Connelly (2014), who uses a similar imagery exercise he calls Changing Perceived Identity (p. 12). I've created a variation on this concept with a script that resonated more with my clients. Feel free to use it for your clients, too.

> *Recall a moment when you've seen something in nature that filled you with a sense of awe, peace, comfort, or joy. Perhaps you can remember the beautiful scenery, soothing sounds, feel of the air, or any pleasant smells you enjoyed there. And as you breathe in the essence of this place, perhaps you can realize that moment was a reflection of the peace, wisdom, and beauty you have inside of you. In fact we know those qualities are inside you because you are accessing them right now.*
>
> *When bad things happen, they can cast a shadow over our awareness of our brighter qualities . . . But just as we know the sun is shining even at night, the light of your essence is still alive and was never destroyed. Your body may have been hurt, but you are more than your body. Your feelings may have been hurt, but you are not your feelings because your feelings change. Someone may have messed with your thoughts, but you are not your thoughts, thoughts can change. And you're not other people's thoughts either.*
>
> *So, who are you? You are part of that light that you got in touch with in that beautiful place and that light can never be destroyed. Someone may try to block the light, but the light always finds a way. Even the tiniest pinpoint of light can penetrate the darkness. So knowing this light still exists within you and will continue to lift, soothe, and support you—you can find your way back here to this time and space. And every time you notice a light in the sky, in a room, or in your mind's eye, it can be a reminder that your light is alive and still shining.*

FOR CLIENTS WHO DON'T LIKE
IMAGERY

For people who have trouble with imagery, you can use pictures or picture cards to help them identify a metaphorical image of what they want. Because the emotional brain is more responsive to images than words, I still like to invite them to consider an image that would represent their desired qualities. Clients can select images from magazines, or you can purchase card decks with archetypal imagery like Caroline Myss's (2003) *Archetype Cards* or Kate Cohen-Posey's (2016) *Brain Change Cards*. Likewise, I've used Sams's and Carson's (1999) *Medicine Cards: The Discovery of Power Through the Way of Animals* to help clients select a symbolic animal image for the Breath-Symbol exercise. Invite your clients to pick the cards that move them emotionally instead of analyzing which image or card is "right." After they choose their pictures, ask them to describe the feelings the image evokes in them or notice which aspect of the image speaks to them most to help them more deeply connect with it.

Finding a song or creating a music playlist that evokes desired feelings is also a wonderful way for clients to get in touch with their desired feelings. A client of mine who survived childhood abuse chose the song "Rearview Mirror" by Eddie Vedder (1993) and Pearl Jam because it connected him to the sense of freedom from abuse and the belief he could move forward. Another client chose the song "Good Woman Down" by Mary J. Blige et al. (2005) because it reflected her desire to be resilient and set a good example for her daughter. For more ideas that help clients emotionally connect to desired goals, see my book *The Therapeutic Aha!:10 Strategies for Getting Your Clients Unstuck* (Armstrong, 2015).

In sum, helping clients get in touch with their strengths, envision their preferred future, and embody the qualities they desire is just as necessary as validating their pain and problems. Without a desired destination, therapy can ramble aimlessly. Before I introduce uplifting material, I make sure clients feel that I have a good understanding of their feelings and frustrations. I don't want them to think I'm dismissing their distress or sugarcoating their sorrow. Clients are usually open to exploring their strengths, positive emotions, and preferred futures by the third or fourth session.

Additionally, I strongly recommend the activities in this chapter before you attempt to reconsolidate traumatic memories with clients. First, they positively resource clients before they explore painful material in detail. Second, you can easily integrate these tools into the memory reconsolidation process to give their traumatic experience a new meaning. Next, in Chapter 8, I'll outline a simple five-step memory reconsolidation protocol you can use to help clients update traumatic memories, so they don't haunt them anymore.

Active	Firm	Perceptive
At ease	Flexible	Purposeful
Assertive	Focused	Positive
Authentic	Fair	Prepared
Balanced	Forthright	Present
Bold	Free	Playful
Brave	Grateful	Resilient
Calm	Grounded	Resourceful
Capable	Honest	Satisfied
Clear	Healthy	Secure
Comfortable	Humorous	Self-assured
Compassionate	Insightful	Sincere
Confident	Intentional	Skillful
Connected	Joyful	Spiritual
Content	Liberated	Strategic
Courageous	Loving	Strong
Creative	Motivated	Sturdy
Curious	Open-minded	Supported
Determined	Optimistic	Trustworthy
Energized	Passionate	Whole
Empowered	Peaceful	Wise

PHASE II

Transform
Traumatic Memories

8

Memory
Reconsolidation

Recalling and revising traumatic memories is an essential part of trauma therapy. As discussed in Chapter 1, post-traumatic stress disorder (PTSD) symptoms are caused by implicit memories that cause the amygdala to overact any time it encounters reminders of the traumatic event. Initially researchers thought the best way to tame the amygdala was through behavioral therapies such as prolonged exposure (PE). Foa and Kozak (1986), the developers of PE for PTSD, hypothesized the avoidance of reminders of traumatic events was similar to a phobia. They reasoned that you could train the brain to inhibit fear responses by repeatedly exposing it to reminders of the event without anything bad happening. Foa produced multiple studies evidencing the effectiveness of PE (Foa, Hembree, & Rothbaum, 2007). Yet, PE has several clinical limitations.

First, dropout rates are high because PE calls for clients to repeatedly reexperience painful memories as early as the third session (Najavits, 2015). Marylene Cloitre (2004, 2010) and her colleagues found that clients need skills for regulating strong emotional responses before launching into vivid recollection of traumatic memories, especially if they've experienced multiple traumas. Second, neuroscientists observed that even after a course of prolonged exposure, the same fears can resurface when the client is under extreme stress—a phenomenon known as *spontaneous recovery*. Neuroscientists like Joe LeDoux (2015) at New York University realized exposure doesn't update the original fear memory network, it only creates a new neural pathway that competes with the old fear learning. Fortunately, in the year 2000, LeDoux's lab discovered the brain does have an innate mechanism for updating fear memories: a process called memory reconsolidation (Nader, Schafe, & LeDoux, 2000).

MEMORY RECONSOLIDATION: A BREAKTHROUGH IN TRAUMA TREATMENT

When information is converted from short-term to long-term memory, it's called memory consolidation. Memory *reconsolidation* refers to retrieving a long-term memory, updating it with new information, and restoring it in its new form. Reconsolidation is triggered when the brain encounters a reminder of the traumatic event and simultaneously encounters a "mismatch experience"—a new experience that contradicts what the brain expects to happen and changes the context and meaning of the memory (Ecker, Ticic, & Hulley, 2012).

You might ask: "Isn't exposing yourself to a feared stimulus repeatedly without anything bad happening a mismatch experience?" Not entirely. Exposure attempts to teach the brain that something associated with danger in the past is not necessarily dangerous anymore. In contrast, memory reconsolidation focuses on changing the person's *relationship* to the feared stimulus. For example, if you had a fear of snakes, exposing yourself to hundreds of snakes without getting bitten wouldn't convince the amygdala that snakes are safe. An effective mismatch would be an experience that helps you believe you have the resources to protect yourself from getting bitten by a snake, or that you could survive if a snake bit you. In other words, a mismatch experience changes the meaning of the event and what you *believe about yourself* in relation to the event. Rather than call it a mismatch experience, I call it a *new meaning experience*.

Reconsolidating my dog phobia

To illustrate the difference between exposure and memory reconsolidation, I'll share how I overcame a dog phobia after our family dog Rocky attacked me when I was a teenager. Rocky was a large Chow Chow who was quite temperamental and had already bitten two of our friends in the nine months since we'd rescued him. We should have removed him from our home, but my mom was determined to rehabilitate him.

One day when I was preparing to take Rocky for a walk, our elderly next-door neighbor stepped into our yard to say "Hi." Rocky snarled and attempted to charge toward the man aggressively. Terrified, I yelled, "No!" and yanked Rocky's choke collar forcefully, pulling him toward me as hard as I could. Rocky didn't like that one bit! He turned, dug his teeth into my abdomen, then lunged toward my throat, knocking me down. Feeling helpless to stop him, I curled into the fetal position, wrapped my arms around my neck, and covered my head with both hands. Rocky continued to bite and pull at my arms until my brother lured him away with slices of Oscar Mayer Bologna, his favorite treat. Meanwhile, our neighbor called animal control.

When animal control arrived, they demanded we put Rocky down. My mother was completely distraught by the thought of ending Rocky's life and became hysterical. She begged animal control not to take him, insisting that Rocky was a "good dog" and that *I must have done something to trigger him.* I was shocked. Did my mom think I caused the attack? Did she want animal control to take me away instead of him? I looked away, trying to hide my angry tears, but caught a glimpse of my bloody shirt and mangled arms instead. Nausea welled up from my stomach, the ground started spinning, and my legs gave way. I fainted next to an Azalea bush in our front yard.

Upon my collapse, my mom immediately rushed me to the hospital for treatment. My physical wounds healed, but the emotional wounds from her insensitive comments continued to weep. Within weeks, she wanted to get another dog. When I angrily protested and told her I still felt scared of dogs, she chided, "You've got to get back on the horse that threw you, girl!"

Then my mom proceeded to do her own brand of exposure therapy, cajoling me to be around canines as frequently as possible. She insisted I read books about dogs. She dragged me to the Humane Society to look at dogs. She asked her friends to let us pet-sit their dogs. None of it worked. No matter how many friendly dogs I encountered, my brain still held the belief that a formerly friendly dog could turn aggressive on me suddenly. Worse, my mom's eagerness to get a new dog and her belief that Rocky was not to blame sent my brain these implicit messages: 1) I caused the attack; 2) my feelings don't matter, 3) my mom loves dogs more than me; and 4) I do not feel safe in her house. On a rational level I knew this wasn't true, but it *felt* true, and feelings are all that matters to the emotional brain.

My dog phobia didn't abate until my cousin came to visit us a year later. A dog lover like my mom, she asked us where Rocky was. My mom looked down and wrung her hands as I proceeded to tell the horrific story. When I tearfully confessed that I believed my mom blamed me for the incident, my mom's eyes widened and her jaw dropped open. She shook her head as she reached over to hug me and said, "No, Courtney. I don't blame you. Rocky was a rescue that was probably abused. Somewhere in his life, he learned to fiercely defend himself if someone suddenly moved toward him. I'm so grateful you had the courage to stop him from attacking our neighbor and found the strength to protect yourself. You handled the situation correctly. I blame myself for the incident. I should have never brought home a dog with those tendencies. We don't need to get another dog. You need to feel safe in this house."

And just like that, my mom reconsolidated the traumatic memory. Within a few weeks, my fears remitted and I felt ready to get a new dog—albeit a smaller breed that we could train. To unlearn the fear, my emotional brain didn't need to be exposed to more dogs. I needed an experience that confirmed my mom still loved me, valued my feelings, and would prioritize my safety. Additionally, I didn't need to believe all dogs were safe. The target learning was for me to: 1) learn how to tell the difference between a family-friendly dog and a potentially aggressive dog; 2) how to properly train and communicate with dogs; and 3) how to protect myself if a dog became aggressive. Exposing myself to friendly dogs didn't accomplish this. Reading dog-training books and learning skills from Humane Society staff during those forced visits with my mother taught me those skills. Yet, without the experience of my mom reassuring me of her love and commitment to protect me, the trauma would not have resolved.

RECON: A Five-Step Protocol for Reconsolidating a Traumatic Memory

Upon studying and being trained in several types of trauma therapies, I realized there are five steps common to every trauma treatment when memory reconsolidation occurs. I use the acronym RECON to describe these five steps:

1. **R**ecall one moment of the traumatic memory, briefly.
2. **E**xplore negative beliefs attached to the traumatic event and the client's desired beliefs.
3. **C**reate a new meaning experience that evokes the client's desired beliefs.
4. **O**bjectively describe the event while integrating the client's new meaning experience.
5. **N**ew narrative integration—retell the story until the new meaning of the event feels true.

In the following section, I'll go through these steps in more detail.

Step 1: Recall one moment of the memory, briefly.

Ask your client to recall one moment of the memory. This need not last longer than a minute, just enough to activate the implicit memory network. Recalling one moment rather than the whole event helps clients stay within their window of tolerance. To capture the implicit components of the memory, ask your client:

1. What is the main image that comes to mind when you recall it?
2. What sensations do you feel in your body?
3. What emotions do you feel as you recall it?
4. What did you want to do physically in that moment, but felt like you couldn't? (*I ask this question because the helplessness a client feels is often connected to a truncated physical survival response. If that is the case, I may invite the client to complete the physical action they wanted to take in Step 3 of the RECON process.*)

Step 2: Explore negative beliefs attached to the event and the client's desired beliefs.

Traumatic events can dramatically change a person's beliefs about themselves, other people, and the world. Because cortisol inhibits the prefrontal cortex and verbal centers during a traumatic event, these beliefs aren't stored as conscious, intellectual thoughts. They feel like essential truths about our identities and our lives that we can't reason away. I call these "embodied beliefs" because they feel true, even if we realize intellectually they aren't true. Negative implicit beliefs related to trauma usually center around these five issues: safety, trust, power/control, responsibility, and self-defectiveness. (Resick, Monson, & Chard, 2017; Shapiro, 2017). Following are examples of negative beliefs in each of these five categories:

Safety: I can't protect myself. If I leave my house, I will be hurt.
Trust: I can't trust other people. I can't trust myself. I won't let people close to me.
Power/Control: I have no control over my life. Bad stuff always happens to me. I need to be in full control or something bad will happen.

Responsibility: It's my fault. I should have done something. I
caused this.

Self-defectiveness: I'm a bad person. I'm unlovable. I'm not good
enough.

To explore your client's negative embodied beliefs attached to an
event, use Worksheet 8.1, Exploring Embodied Beliefs, at the end of
this chapter, which asks the following questions:

1. How did this event change how you feel about yourself?
2. How did this event change how you feel about other people?
3. How did this event change how you feel about your life, the
   world, or your future?

Once your client has identified negative beliefs associated with the
memory, ask her what she'd like to believe about herself, others, and
the world instead. Identifying desired beliefs creates the blueprint for
new meaning experiences that will help your client heal. You can use
Worksheet 8.2, Discovering Desired Beliefs, at the end of this chapter,
which asks:

1. What would you like to believe about yourself? What strengths
   or insights have you been able to develop in spite of this event?
2. What do you want to believe about the people involved in the
   event? How do you want to feel around them? What do you want
   to believe about people, in general?
3. What would you like to believe about life, the world, or your
   future? What is the best possible outcome you can imagine for
   yourself?

If your client has trouble identifying desired beliefs, invite her to
imagine what she would want for someone else who had been through
a similar experience. Clients may find it easier to feel compassion for

another person than for themselves. Additionally, you could share your vision of what you think is possible for your client. In the next step, I'll share ideas for creating new meaning experiences that help your client *feel* that her new beliefs are true and possible.

Step 3: Create a new meaning experience that evokes the client's desired beliefs.

The emotional brain needs a *felt experience* to harness new learning, realizations, and meanings. It's not enough for us to intellectually identify preferred beliefs and expect them to stick. Creating a new meaning experience initiates the mismatch required for memory reconsolidation. For this new meaning experience to be effective, it has to be: 1) felt, 2) believable, and 3) disconfirm negative beliefs the client had attached to the event.

In the following paragraphs, I'll share three new meaning experiences my clients and I have found to be most helpful. These are all future-oriented imagery techniques that put the traumatic event into a new context and encourage clients to get in touch with the strength, wisdom, power, and general goodness they still possess. These exercises are also effective in calming the nervous system before reviewing traumatic memories in more detail.

1. *Finish the story in a new place:* When something traumatic happens, the memory of the event tends to end at the point where the client felt devastated, helpless, or hopeless—but that's not where the story ends. I ask clients to "finish the story" by telling me when the event stopped and how they survived. Or, they can finish the story at later time in their life when they had an experience of feeling competent, empowered, grateful, or loved.

   Similarly, you can invite your client to complete the physical response they wanted to take during the event, but felt like they couldn't. For more guidance on how to use somatic movement interventions, I recommend Ogden and Fisher's (2015) *Senso-rimotor Psychotherapy: Interventions for Trauma and Attachment* or Peter Levine's (2015) *Trauma and Memory: Brain and Body in Search of a Living Past.*

2. *Desired Future Self:* If the client doesn't have a positive new ending to the story, invite her to imagine what she wants for her future self. I shared this exercise in Chapter 7, Instill Hope and Empowerment. If you and your client have already done this activity in a previous session, you can simply revisit it and add any additional beliefs they want their future self to have regarding the traumatic event.

3. *Breath-Symbol Imagery:* Another exercise I shared in Chapter 7 (Instill Hope and Empowerment), the Breath-Symbol Imagery exercise invites clients to identify a symbolic image that would represent their mind working in the desired way. For example, my client Tracy was raped by an acquaintance at a party. Her desired beliefs were: 1) it wasn't my fault; 2) I will heal from this; and 3) I can protect herself from being attacked in the future. She wanted to feel secure, strong, and resilient. I invited her to imagine what it would feel like to embody those beliefs and let her mind show her a symbol that would represent her desired qualities. She got the image of an oak tree. I invited her to take three deep breaths as she imagined being like the oak tree. After a few minutes of enjoying this imagery, she reported feeling more calm, secure, and hopeful.

Imagery is not the only way to elicit new meaning experiences—any experiential intervention that evokes the client's desired beliefs will work. I've used movement, music, metaphors, stories, and role-playing activities too. In Box 8.1 (page 107), I've summarized methods other trauma therapy approaches use to create new meaning experiences.

Step 4: Objectively describe the event while integrating the new meaning experience.

Next, invite your client to tell you the entire story of the traumatic event and integrate the new meaning experience into the story. I coach clients to describe the memory objectively, as if they were watching it on a small television screen. Describing the facts from an objective perspective helps your client stay in the present moment and avoid reliving the event. Integrating the new meaning experience triggers memory reconsolidation and updates implicit learning in the emotional brain. Telling the story out loud helps the prefrontal cortex and left hemisphere integrate the memory into a coherent narrative that can now be stored into explicit memory.

During this step, your job as the therapist is to: 1) assist your client in staying within her window of emotional tolerance; 2) guide her to integrate the new meaning experience into her narrative; and 3) reframe any additional negative beliefs that are revealed as she tells the story.

If your client experiences excessive hyperarousal or hypoarousal that takes her out of her window of tolerance, ask her to stop the story for a moment. Use one of the tools for grounding, calming, and soothing discussed in Chapter 5 to regulate her nervous system. Once she is back in her window of tolerance, ask if she would like to continue the story or stop. If she wants to stop, invite her to imagine putting the memory into a sturdy, locked container that only she can unlock. Advise that if any intrusive thoughts or images of the memory arise between sessions, she can tell them that she'll deal with them at another time and put them back into the container.

To help your client integrate new meaning experiences into her new narrative, invite her to pause at the moments where she notices feelings of shame, fear, anger, or helplessness. These are usually the moments of the memory where a negative belief was formed. Integrating the new meaning experience at these moments creates the mismatch experience that updates the memory network. For example,

Tracy felt intense shame when she remembered kissing and dancing with her attacker at a party before the rape occurred. This was one of the moments that had caused her to harbor the belief, "This was my fault. I caused this."

At this point, I suggested she recall the image of her oak tree, seeing it as pure, strong, and resilient and then imagine a boy walks by and pees on the tree. I asked Tracy, "Is it the tree's fault the boy peed on it? She laughed and said, "Of course not!" Then I asked, "Is this tree any less pure, resilient, or strong because a boy peed on it?" She blurted, "Absolutely not!" Looking at it from this perspective helped her separate her beliefs about herself from the behavior of another person.

Step 5: New narrative integration—repeat and revise the story with new experiences until the new meaning of the event feels true.

Once you and your client have gone through the full story, integrating new meaning experiences, have her repeat the story back to you again. Repeating the new story helps solidify new meanings and gives you an opportunity to see if there are still places in the story where the client feels stuck. Sometimes as clients review the story they realize they have an inner conflict about moving past the trauma, forgiving themselves, or believing they can be okay. Following are three effective new meaning experiences that can help clients resolve these inner conflicts. I'll share examples of how to apply these interventions for specific types of traumas and inner conflicts in Chapters 9 through 13.

1. *Internal reparenting:* Invite your client to imagine reassuring his younger self that he did the best he could to handle the situation with the resources he had then. Or, imagine having his older self step into the traumatic scene to nurture, protect, and guide his younger self. The adult self could explain to the younger self that the actions (or inaction) that other people took during the traumatic event didn't mean anything about the client's worth. The actions of other people only reveal how their

minds were working at the time and show us flaws in their thinking and functioning. Let the older self show the younger self positive things that will happen later in the client's life, and what he'll be able to do in spite of the tragic experiences.

2. *Imagine perpetrators as childlike, immature, and irrational:* One of the issues that causes fear and confusion for trauma survivors is the implicit belief that someone who hurt them has power over them. Or, the survivor can feel like they caused the perpetrator to harm them. Reduce feelings of weakness, guilt, and shame by validating that something was obviously wrong with the way the perpetrator's mind was functioning. When someone's brain is malfunctioning, they are not reading situations accurately. Their minds distort things and cause them to say and do childish, hurtful things that are completely irrational. Invite your client to imagine the perpetrator as being smaller in size, operating at the maturity level of a child, or with a brain that is not firing on all cylinders. Suggest the client view himself as a more competent person who did what he needed to do to survive and has more resources, insight, and intelligence now.

3. *Imaginal conversations:* If a client is struggling with guilt or resentment around a deceased person, invite him to have an imaginal conversation with the deceased. I suggest the client imagine the deceased speaking from a place of enlightened awareness where they have more insight, compassion, and understanding. Not only have my clients found this exercise reassuring, Columbia University researchers demonstrated imaginal conversations help resolve complicated grief (Shear, Houck, & Reynolds, 2005).

How do you know when the memory is reconsolidated?

On average, clients only have to retell the story one or two more times after they complete Step 4 of RECON. You'll know the memory is reconsolidated when the client can tell the story from start to finish without abreacting and naturally integrates his desired new meaning into the story. Clients are often surprised by how differently they feel about the memory at this point. They'll remark that the event seems more factual, less disturbing, and doesn't feel as heavy as it once did. They'll notice that they feel lighter in their bodies and will look more relaxed and peaceful in their affect. When they say their old negative beliefs out loud, they won't feel true anymore. Their new beliefs will feel true, or at least resonate more strongly.

What if my client doesn't have a clear memory of the event or can't verbalize it?

Invite your client to make up what she thinks might have happened and work with that narrative. Memory is fallible, so we rarely remember the details of an event accurately anyway. The story we tell ourselves about the event is far more important. Whether the client's story is factually accurate or not, the goal is still to put the imagined experience of the event into a new context that liberates the client from suffering. Of course, if there is a legal case involved, I make it clear to clients that we are making up a narrative of the trauma for therapeutic purposes. We are not attempting to reconstruct a narrative for legal or investigative purposes.

I also take this stance if a client believes a family member may have molested them and wants to recover a "repressed" memory. False-memory research by Loftus and Pickrell (1995) demonstrated that even mentally healthy people can create a pseudomemory they believe is real based on a mere suggestion. Therefore, I caution clients not to take the story they make up literally, but to work with it metaphorically, as if it were a bad dream.

Do all five steps of RECON have to be done in one session?

You can space the steps of the RECON process across three or more sessions, depending on your client's needs. For instance, you might use a full session for Steps 1 and 2: Recall a traumatic memory briefly and explore the client's negative beliefs and desired beliefs about the event. Likewise, you may use a full session for Step 3: Create a new meaning experience that evokes the client's desired beliefs. Then, in the next session, you can do Step 4: Objectively describe the memory while integrating the new meaning experience. However, if you are doing step 4 in a separate session, you'll need to ask your client to briefly recall the memory (Step 1) and connect to the new meaning experience (Step 3) before describing the memory in detail. For memory reconsolidation to occur, the client has to juxtapose the memory of the trauma directly with the new meaning experience (Ecker, Ticic, & Hulley, 2012). It's this simultaneous recollection of the two experiences side by side that causes the synapses holding the memory to unlock. Otherwise the old memory and the desired meaning experience stay in two separate neural networks that aren't linked to one another.

Takeaways

Understanding the brain's natural process for updating emotional memories has led to significant breakthroughs in trauma therapy. We now know we can permanently change a traumatic memory network so that it doesn't haunt a client anymore. The RECON protocol gives you the steps and tools to successfully facilitate memory reconsolidation. It provides the structure needed to effectively address each aspect of the memory reconsolidation process. Yet, it's flexible enough to integrate into any therapy method you already use and adapt to your client's needs. To make the process easier, I've included three worksheets at the end of this chapter that walk you through the RECON protocol. The first is Exploring Embodied Beliefs (Worksheet 8.1). The second is Discovering Desired Beliefs (Worksheet 8.2). The third is a RECON Cheat Sheet (Worksheet 8.3), which guides you through the full process. You can also download copies of these worksheets at my website: www.courtneyarmstrong.net.

In the next five chapters, I'll address how to use the RECON process for specific types of trauma, including sexual trauma, childhood physical abuse, attachment trauma, traumatic grief, and combat trauma. While each client's experience of a trauma is unique, I'll discuss the recurring themes found in each type of trauma and demonstrate how to create new meaning experiences to resolve them.

How other trauma therapies create "mismatch" experiences

Most modern trauma therapy methods appear to be inducing memory reconsolidation. Yet each therapy method has its own approach to creating new meaning experiences that change the context of the event at the emotional level. Watkins & Watkins (1997) ego state therapy and Richard Schwartz's (2013) internal family systems invite clients to engage in imaginal conversations with different "parts" of themselves to resolve inner conflicts. Francine Shapiro's (2017) eye movement desensitization and reprocessing uses dual awareness and bilateral sensory stimulation to prompt the client's brain to scan for and integrate positive personal experiences into the traumatic memory network.

Pat Ogden's (Ogden & Fisher, 2015) sensorimotor therapy and Peter Levine's (2015) somatic experiencing invite the client to reclaim his power by completing a physical survival action that got truncated during the traumatic event. Ecker, Ticic, & Hulley's (2012) coherence therapy helps clients recognize how their symptoms helped them survive and adapt to traumatic circumstances. Then, clients are invited to create new experiences that update prior emotional learning. Diana Fosha's (2008) accelerated experiential dynamic psycho-

therapy and Dan Siegel's (2011) interpersonal neurobiology use the therapeutic relationship to create corrective emotional experiences to heal attachment wounds and put traumatic memories into context.

Hypnosis and neurolinguistic programming (NLP) use imagery, metaphor, and multisensory communication to create new meaning experiences (Bandler & Grinder, 1982; O'Hanlon, 2011; Smucker & Dancu, 1999). There is not one "superior" approach. The effectiveness of an approach depends on whether your client finds it helpful and thinks it makes sense. Although I follow the structure of RECON to reprocess traumatic memories, I select experiential interventions according to my client's interests and preferences.

(Download a copy at www.courtneyarmstrong.net.)

Traumatic events can dramatically change a person's beliefs about themselves, other people, and the world. Because of the way the mind processes trauma, these negative beliefs can feel like essential truths about our identities and our lives that we can't reason away. This worksheet will help you identify the beliefs associated with a negative event.

I. **If this event were a book or a movie, what title would you give it?**

    _____

II. **Negative Beliefs Associated with the Event**

    A. How did this event change how you feel about yourself and your identity? _____

    _____

    _____

    _____

    _____

    B. How did this event change how you feel about other people? What does it *feel* like it meant about the people involved? Or people in general? _____

    _____

    _____

    _____

    _____

    C. How did this event change how you feel about life, the world, or your future?_____

    _____

    _____

    _____

    _____

WORKSHEET 8.2: **Discovering Desired Beliefs**

(Download a copy at www.courtneyarmstrong.net.)

A. How would you like to feel about yourself now? What strengths, talents, or insights have you been able to develop in spite of this event? _____

_____

_____

_____

_____

B. What do you want to believe about the people involved in the event now? How do you want to feel around them? How do you want to feel about people, in general? _____

_____

_____

_____

_____

C. What would you like to believe about life, the world, or your future? Is there a way you can imagine using this experience to live your life with a greater sense of strength, purpose, or meaning? What is the best possible outcome you can imagine for yourself? _____

_____

_____

_____

_____

D. If this event were a chapter in book or a movie, how do you want the story to end? How could the main character in the book or movie reclaim his or her life and move forward in spite of this negative experience? _____

_____

_____

_____

_____

(Download a copy at www.courtneyarmstrong.net)

1. **Recall one moment of the memory, briefly.**

   A. What images, sensations, and emotions come to mind?

   B. What did you want to do physically in that moment, but felt like you couldn't?

2. **Explore negative beliefs attached to the event and the client's desired beliefs.**

   A. How did this event change how you think or feel about:

      1. Yourself?

      2. Other people?

      3. Life, the world, your future?

   B. What do you want to believe now? What is the best possible outcome you can imagine for yourself? What have you been able to do in spite of this event?

3. **Create a new meaning experience that evokes the client's desired beliefs.**

   Choose from any of the following or create a new meaning intervention:

   A. Finish the story at a new place.

   B. Desired future-self imagery.

   C. Breath-Symbol imagery of the desired beliefs and responses.

   D. Physical movement to complete a survival response.

   E. Internal reparenting: rescuing, comforting or guiding younger self through scene.

   F. Imagining perpetrators as weaker, smaller, and incompetent.

   G. Imaginal conversations with other people or inner parts of oneself.

   H. Song or music playlist representing desired perspectives and beliefs.

continued

4. **Objectively describe the memory while integrating the new meaning experience.**

Retell the story out loud, or in writing, with the awareness that you survived, handled it in ways that made sense, and can respond to reminders of this event in your new desired way.

5. **New narrative integration**

Repeat and revise the story with new experiences until the new desired personal meaning about the memory feels true.

9

Sexual Trauma

Restoring a person's sense of safety, trust, and personal power after sexual trauma is challenging. Even if clients intellectually realize they didn't cause the sexual trauma, it's hard for them to reason away disturbing images, physical sensations, and feelings of shame. Moreover, when a friend or family member was the abuser, it creates a profound rupture in the client's attachment system and her ability to trust you. Before they divulge the details of a sexual trauma, clients need to feel that you are nonjudgmental, respectful of their boundaries, and won't be vexed by disturbing stories about sex.

In this chapter, I'll share three case examples that highlight the most common issues with which sexual trauma survivors struggle. In each case, I'll demonstrate how I applied the RECON protocol to update negative beliefs with new meaning experiences. You'll see examples of how to use metaphor, storytelling, imagery, and the therapeutic relationship to disconfirm negative beliefs and elicit the client's desired beliefs.

WHEN SEXUAL TRAUMA DISRUPTS SECURE ATTACHMENT

Tracy was a 21-year-old female who had no prior trauma and a secure attachment style before she was raped by three men at a fraternity party. After the rape, Tracy was experiencing classic PTSD symptoms of intrusive memories of the event; avoidance of men; alternating between feelings of numbness and anxiety; and persistent negative thoughts about herself.

In our first session, I educated Tracy about the way trauma impacts the brain and nervous system so she could understand her emotional responses. In our next session, we worked with tools that could help Tracy feel grounded, calm, hopeful, and empowered. She particularly enjoyed the Breath-Symbol Imagery exercise I shared in Chapter 7. She chose the image of an oak tree as her symbol because "it is rooted and secure but also able to stand tall and beautiful—even after a turbulent storm." By our third session, Tracy felt ready to reprocess the traumatic memory. In the following paragraphs, I'll illustrate how Tracy and I worked through each step of the RECON protocol.

Step 1: Recall one moment of the memory, briefly.

To open the implicit memory network, I asked Tracy to recall one moment of the memory and give me a short summary of what happened:

Tracy: A guy I liked invited me to a fraternity party. We were drinking, dancing, and having a good time. I guess I took it too far when I started booty dancing to a Beyoncé song. He grabbed me around the waist while two other guys grabbed my arms and legs. They carried me to a back bedroom and all three of them raped me. (*Her eyes welled with tears and she hung her head in shame and sorrow.*)

Therapist: Tracy, I am so sorry this happened and I'm glad you're here so you can heal. What emotions and sensations are you noticing in your body as you recall this memory?

Tracy: I feel sad, ashamed, and kind of sick to my stomach. My legs feel weak.

Step 2: Explore negative beliefs attached to the event and the client's desired beliefs.

Therapist: You're doing great describing the feelings attached to this event. Now I want to understand any negative beliefs your mind may have attached to it. How has this event changed how you feel about yourself? What has it felt like it meant about you?

Tracy: It's my fault. I took it too far by booty dancing. I feel dirty and broken.

Therapist: That's a good example of how our minds can attach unhelpful meanings. I don't think you took it too far—it sounds like those boys took it too far. Let me illustrate it by using a metaphor. Imagine if a guy invited a lady to his birthday party. He asks if she would like to try a bite of chocolate cake. She liked the cake, so he asked if she'd like to have a whole piece. She says, "Sure!" Then, instead of giving her one piece, he smashes the entire cake into her face and tries to shove it down her throat. Do you think something is wrong with this lady, or that something is very wrong with that guy?

Tracy [Laughing]: Well, the guy of course!

Therapist: Right. So we know something was wrong with this guy. Has this event changed how you feel about men?

Tracy: Yes. I feel like all guys are pigs. You can't trust them. They only want sex.

Therapist: Ok we'll look at that in a moment. What has it felt like it meant about the world, your life, or your future?

Tracy: The world isn't safe. Sex will never be enjoyable for me again. I'm not sure if I'll be able to have a normal relationship now.

I used the chocolate cake metaphor to begin reframing Tracy's negative beliefs and demonstrate that I was not going to blame or judge her. The emotional brain understands metaphors better than it understands intellectual reasoning. I reassured Tracy that her emotional brain wasn't broken. It just needed information in a context it could understand to put the event into perspective. Then, I asked Tracy how she'd like to feel about herself, others, and the world.

Tracy: I'd like to believe that I'm still a good person. And, like you said—I want to recognize *they* took it too far, not me. I'd like to believe there are still men out there who respect women and will respect me. Yet, I realize there are men who abuse women, too. I want to discern whom I can trust and whom I can't trust. I want to believe I can recover and have a normal relationship with somebody.

Therapist: Yes, that's what I want for you too, Tracy. What words or feelings come to mind when you imagine your mind working in your desired way?

Tracy: Strong, resilient, secure, and . . . maybe innocent? Innocent doesn't really seem like the right word, but I don't want to feel dirty or ashamed anymore.

Therapist: How does the word "pure" feel? I'm remembering you described the oak tree as pure and secure, even after a strong storm. The storm doesn't change the tree's pure essence. If some guy peed on the tree, we wouldn't think the tree is disgusting. We'd think what that guy did was disgusting. The tree is still pure.

Tracy: Yes, I like that. Let's go with the word "pure."

Step 3: Create a new meaning experience that evokes the client's desired beliefs.

The next step is to collaborate with your client to create an *experience* that evokes her desired beliefs and meanings about the event.

Since Tracy identified the symbol of an oak tree and enjoyed doing the Breath-Symbol Exercise, we used this to deepen her sense of feeling pure, strong, secure, and resilient. I guided her through the activity, suggesting she imagine admiring the oak tree, observing its branches and leaves, smelling its scent, feeling its bark, recognizing that it had been through hundreds of storms and survived. I offered that she could also imagine feeling what it's like to be the oak tree, securely rooted, with a stable core, yet able to stretch and grow. Tracy engaged in this imagery experience for several minutes. When she opened her eyes, her facial features softened, her shoulders relaxed, and she was actually sitting taller. She commented, "That felt good. I feel relaxed, but strong inside."

4. Objectively describe the memory while integrating new meaning experiences.

Next, I invited Tracy to describe the memory of the rape. I coached her to describe the memory like she was watching it on a tiny television screen so she wouldn't relive it. My job was to: 1) help her stay emotionally present; 2) listen for opportunities to reframe her negative beliefs; and 3) bring her awareness to actions of strength and resilience she used to survive the event.

Tracy: A guy I met through a friend invited me to a fraternity party. He picked me up at my dorm and we walked over to his frat house. There was a great DJ at the party who was playing my favorite songs. We were drinking beer, dancing, and having a good time. Then we did a shot of tequila. He gave me this starry-eyed look and started kissing me. I felt flattered and thought maybe this was the start of a new relationship. Then we started dancing again. A Beyoncé song was playing, and I did a booty dance like she does in her videos. I was joking around, but he took it the wrong way and started pulling me against his crotch as he gyrated up and down. I tried to pry his hands off me, but he locked his arms around my body. Then, two of his friends came over, lifted up my legs and arms, and carried me to a back bedroom. *(At this point, Tracy's face started to flush and her breathing became more shallow, indicating she was experiencing hyperarousal.)*

Therapist: Tracy, you're doing great, but let's pause for a moment and tell me what you are noticing in your body right now.

Tracy: My heart is beating faster. I feel a little hot and nervous.

Therapist: That's understandable. Let's give your nervous system a moment to get back in this time and space. You can look around and tell me a few objects you can see, hear, or touch in this room. Or take a few deep breaths as you focus on your tree imagery, perhaps planting your feet on the floor so you can feel firmly rooted here in the present.

Tracy took a few breaths as she imagined her tree, grounded her feet on the floor, broadened her shoulders, and extended her spine, stating, "Okay, that's better. I'm back." I asked her if she wanted to continue the story or stop for now. Tracy wanted to continue and began to describe the moment when the rape occurred.

Tracy: They took me to a back bedroom that was dark with wood paneling. There were two twin beds in it. They pulled my dress up over my head and pulled off my panties. Then they took turns—two of them holding down my arms and legs while another one had sex with me. It was happening so fast that I was kind of in disbelief. I tried pull away, but I felt like I had lost all strength in my limbs. I cried and begged them to stop, but they just laughed and said, "You asked for it, booty dancer!" After that, I gave up and think I blacked out for a little while. I'm disappointed I didn't fight back harder.

Therapist [seeing an opportunity to reframe this negative belief]: You did fight back, Tracy. You fought them when they picked you up on the dance floor, you fought them when they took you to the bedroom, and you repeatedly asked them to stop. What I'm hearing is that the more you fought them, the more aggressive they became. In this situation, it's not unusual for our bodies to activate the freeze survival response. You could literally feel like you can't move or black out. It feels scary, but it's your brain's way of deterring further aggression from predators and buffering the pain of the moment. All your responses make sense. Tell me how you escaped after it was over.

Tracy: Hmm. I haven't thought about how I got out of there.

Therapist: Yes, our minds can stop the movie in the worst place. But, the movie doesn't end there. Tracy survives and goes on.

Tracy: I guess they finished their business and left me in that room. I remember waking up and feeling sick. I saw my dress and underwear, grabbed them, and found a bathroom. I vomited a couple of times and cleaned myself up. I wanted to get out, but was scared they might be waiting for me. Looking for something I could use as a weapon, I saw a razor and a can of Raid bug killer on the counter. Armed with my bug spray and razor, I peeked out the door and tiptoed quietly toward the front entrance. Luckily nobody saw me. I dashed through the front door and ran to my dorm as fast as I could.

Therapist: Yes, good! If you like, you could explore what it feels like to pump your legs up and down right now like you did when you were running. Feel what it's like to move that energy through your body, realizing your legs are not weak or immobilized anymore.

Tracy (pumping her legs and arms up and down like she is running): Yes, it feels good to remember I can move. I remember more of . what happened after I got to my dorm now.

Therapist: Yes, continue. Tell the story until it feels like it has the ending you want it to have.

Tracy: Well, I didn't have my key and had to bang on the dorm's steel doors. The resident assistant let me in. She wrapped a warm blanket around me and told me the same things you're telling me—that it wasn't my fault and those guys had no right to do this to me. She offered to take me to the hospital and call the police, but I was too scared. I wanted to get some sleep first. The next day she went with me to campus health services. The nurse practitioner checked my body for injuries, gave me an antibiotic, and recommended I do a rape kit. She said that even if I didn't press charges, it was good to take bodily samples in case I changed my mind later. I'm not sure I want to press charges and go through the ordeal of court. But it makes me feel better knowing the DNA evidence is there, should I decide to pursue charges later.

Therapist: Yes, I know those exams can feel invasive and uncomfortable, but I'm glad you did it too. It's a way of taking care of yourself. How are you feeling now as you think back on that story?

Tracy: I feel calmer and lighter. It helped to remember how I got out of there. I can see now that I didn't do anything that justified them raping me. But now I feel angry. How could those guys do this to me? What is wrong with them?"

Therapist: Yes, their thinking is obviously twisted. There are plenty of men who would never dream of doing that to a woman. But there's a small subset of the population that confuses sex with power. We can talk about ways to protect yourself from that kind of person in the future. For now I just want you to realize you did a good job surviving it.

Will I ever be able to enjoy sex again?

Next, we addressed Tracy's fear that she wouldn't be able to enjoy sex or have normal relationships again. I asked her to imagine how caring, consensual sex felt with someone who respected her. She replied, "Soft, sweet, free. It doesn't feel pressured or forced."

"Yes," I affirmed. "What you experienced with those guys wasn't sex, that was assault. Imagine someone slapping a girl on the cheek, versus someone she trusts lovingly caressing her cheek. Same body part, different sensations. The intention is different. Get your mind to notice these differences, not the similarities. Close your eyes and send your body loving kindness. Show your body that it's still pure. Show your body it's okay to enjoy loving touch from someone who respects you and it's okay to set boundaries with those who don't. Someone who respects you will honor your body and respect your boundaries."

Tracy closed her eyes and tearfully nodded, "I see what you mean. I think I had cut off from my body. Sending my body loving kindness feels good. It feels healing."

Tracy and I went back through her story one more time. I wanted to be sure the memory was reconsolidating with her desired meanings. She was able to go through the full story with no feelings of anxiety or shame. She still felt sad that the rape happened, but the memory felt like it was in a context that would allow her to move forward. When someone has a secure attachment history, it's easier for them to reconsolidate a memory because they have a frame of reference for normal relationships. For clients with insecure attachment styles, reframing negative beliefs is more challenging.

ANXIOUS ATTACHMENT AND SEXUAL TRAUMA

Clients with anxious-preoccupied attachment styles can be more vulnerable to sexual trauma. First, these clients have been taught they must acquiesce to another person's needs while denying their own. Second, they only feel lovable or worthwhile when they're getting attention and approval from other people. Third, if they experienced sexual abuse as children, they may believe the only way to get love is to be sexual.

My client Mallory, whom I referred to in Chapter 4, How to Engage Insecure Attachment Styles, is a good example of a woman with an anxious attachment style that was exacerbated by sexual abuse from her stepfather. A charming young lady with dark wavy hair, emerald green eyes, and an infectious smile, she'd learned to use her sexuality to get attention from men. Mallory was married and loved her husband, but their romance had taken a backseat to the demands of rearing children and paying bills. He wasn't giving her as much of his attention, and she felt undesirable, empty, and depressed.

Her spirits lifted when she reconnected with an old boyfriend from high school on Facebook. Initially, they only chatted online, reminiscing about old times. Then, they progressed to sexting and meeting secretly. This affair sustained her for a while until the man called it off. Mallory was devastated until she began having another affair with a man with whom she worked. When that affair ended, she looked for another man on Facebook. The cycle continued until Mallory collapsed into a deeper depression and called me for therapy.

Our initial sessions focused on exploring her relationship patterns, helping her realize she wanted emotional intimacy more than sex, and how to nurture herself emotionally. When we began exploring where she learned to equate sexuality with love, she revealed that her stepfather starting molesting her when she was 12 years old. The abuse stopped when her mother caught them having sex when Mallory was 14. She promptly kicked Mallory's stepfather out of the house and filed for divorce. Mallory hadn't had any contact with him since then.

Something is wrong with me because I enjoyed it

When we explored her negative beliefs attached to the sexual abuse, Mallory confessed, "I feel ashamed because I enjoyed it sometimes. It made me feel special. Sometimes I even initiated sexual contact with him."

When we explored her desired beliefs, Mallory wanted to believe that she didn't want sex from her stepfather, she wanted his love. She also wanted to believe that having pleasurable responses to sexual touch was normal, and didn't make her a bad person. To update this belief, I validated that being held, kissed, or caressed feels soothing, exciting, or pleasurable because of how the nerve endings in our skin and body register this activity. I used the metaphor of being tickled. I asked, "If someone tickled you and you laughed, does that mean you wanted to be tickled? You may have experienced a sensation that felt pleasurable, but it may have also felt weird, painful, or uncomfortable."

Mallory agreed, "That's true. There were lots of times I didn't like it."

It's my fault/I caused it/I led them on

To help Mallory clear the guilt around initiating sexual contact with her stepfather, I reassured her, "You liked getting attention and love from your stepfather. You learned that he responded to you if you let him touch you in a sexual way. You didn't know another way to get his love, attention, and approval."

She agreed somewhat with this assessment, but her tentative nodding and inability to meet my eyes told me her emotional brain didn't quite buy my interpretation. So, I followed it with a metaphorical story.

"Let's say this little boy grew up with a mom who was depressed. She loved him, but she was so tired and preoccupied with her problems that she couldn't give him consistent love and attention. One day he dressed up in women's clothing as a joke to cheer his mom up. It worked. She laughed and laughed. Because his mother was so amused by this, he started dressing up like a girl anytime he wanted his mom's love, attention, or approval. Then it got out of hand. She insisted he dress up in drag whenever she wanted to be cheered up. No matter what he was doing or what kind of mood he was in, she'd interrupt him and insist he perform for her. He got tired of having to perform all the time, but he continued to do it because his mom liked it. Does that mean this boy really wanted to be a woman or a drag queen?"

"No," Mallory replied. "He's just doing it because it's something his mom encouraged, and he knows it makes her happy. It's the only way he can get her attention."

"Right," I affirmed. "Sometimes he enjoyed it. Sometimes he hated it. But he hadn't found a better way to get his mom's attention, so he learned to connect with her this way. Now that he's an adult, we want him to real-ize there are a variety of ways to connect with people, and most people won't expect him to dress up like a woman to feel loved. Likewise, we want your mind to get that there are a variety of ways to feel loved, and most people won't expect you to be sexual in order to get their attention."

Internal reparenting imagery

As we moved to Step 3 of RECON: Create a new meaning experi-ence that elicits desired beliefs and meanings about the event. We used internal reparenting imagery. Internal reparenting imagery helps clients release shame by reassuring their younger self they did the best they could. It also helps clients with anxious attachment learn how to give themselves love and support instead of believing they can only get it from other people.

I invited Mallory to imagine her adult self reassuring her younger self that she didn't do anything wrong and that her stepfather's mind was malfunctioning. I encouraged her to show her younger self other quali-ties that made her lovable, like her compassion, creativity, and sense of humor. Mallory teared up during this experience and said it felt good to console and nurture herself in this way.

Next, I invited Mallory to create a symbolic image of the adult woman she wanted to be: strong, intelligent, caring, able to respectfully express her feelings, and keep healthy boundaries. She imagined a lioness, a powerful animal that could be playful, caring, and even sexual—but could also maintain her boundaries and protect her children.

Now that Mallory felt more resourced, I suggested she could briefly recall a memory of a time her stepfather abused her and imagine step-ping into that scene as an adult to comfort and protect her younger self in any way that made sense to her. Mallory imagined stopping the abuse and taking her younger self away from her stepfather. She comforted her younger self and reassured her that she didn't do anything wrong. She explained that even though her stepfather could be kind, he had really mixed-up ideas about sex and shouldn't be doing those things to her.

She held her younger self and said, "You don't have to do this anymore. I'm stepping in now to protect you. You never need to feel like the only way to get a man's love is to be sexual with him. You are lovable just the way you are." She then imagined herself growing up to be the lioness, connecting to qualities of strength, resilience, and self-compassion.

Because we had connected her to positive experiences before reviewing her memories in more detail, Mallory found recounting the story wasn't as difficult as she'd imagined. She noted that her beliefs about being a bad person began to feel absurd as she repeated the story out loud. In subsequent sessions we continued to work on expanding her capacity for self-care, setting boundaries, and respectfully expressing her feelings to her husband. Employing these new skills took practice, but they were easier for her to implement after the memory reconsolidation was done because it helped her get a new perspective of herself.

AVOIDANT ATTACHMENT AND SEXUAL TRAUMA

When people with avoidant-dismissive attachment encounter sexual trauma as adults their primary issues center around control and power. They feel extremely frustrated when they can't control PTSD symptoms and ashamed they weren't able to prevent the trauma. If avoidant attachment *resulted* from childhood sexual abuse, the client may avoid sex, emotionally detach during sex, or view sex as simply a way to relieve stress or feel excitement. They may prefer to engage in sex at a distance through porn, one-night stands, prostitutes, or other situations where they don't have to be emotionally close to a partner.

Because it's difficult for these clients to show vulnerability, they may not reveal incidents of sexual trauma right away. If they do reveal sexual trauma, they tend to be focused on how to get rid of their memories rather than work through them. Education about how trauma impacts the brain and the body is essential to help them make sense of their symptoms. I also provide these clients with education about memory reconsolidation. Once they understand that the goal of reviewing trauma memories is not to relive them, but to rewire them, they're receptive.

Jack was 45-year-old man referred to me by a couples therapist to address sexual abuse he'd experienced as a preteen from a baseball coach. He'd never told his wife about the abuse until they entered marital therapy. He confessed, "I definitely detach during sex. My wife was worried I wasn't attracted to her, but that's not the case. I learned to detach as a way to cope with what happened to me as a kid."

Jack explained that his father died when he was two years old. He didn't have many male role models in his life until one of his baseball coaches took an interest in him. He thought Jack had a lot of talent as a pitcher and wanted to spend extra time with him to work on his skills. They got close as his coach took on other fatherly roles, like helping him with his homework, paying for him to go to baseball camps, and taking him and his mom to dinner. Jack said his relationship with his coach didn't become sexual until a year later, when his coach offered to buy him a porn magazine.

Jack's face flushed as he nervously confessed, "We looked at the magazine together and laughed at first. Then, my coach asked me if I'd ever masturbated and offered to show me how to do it. It sounds dumb to say it out loud. But I trusted this guy and I didn't have a dad. I thought maybe all fathers did this with their sons. I convinced myself it was normal."

"Of course you thought it was normal," I replied compassionately. "He started out by acting like a father toward you. You didn't have another frame of reference."

Jack shrugged his shoulders and said, "Yeah. Well, it started with us masturbating together and then it progressed to other stuff. When I told him I didn't want to do it anymore, he got mad and threatened to kick me off the baseball team. Furthermore, he told me that if I ever told anyone, he'd say I was the one who initiated sex and that's why he kicked me off the team!"

I can't trust myself/I won't let myself be vulnerable again

In Step 2 of RECON, Jack identified these negative beliefs: "I'm gullible. I'm weak. I don't trust people. I won't let myself be vulnerable again." When we explored his desired beliefs, Jack said, "I'd like to believe I have good judgment now. I'm not sure I'll ever trust people, but I want to feel comfortable making love to my wife. I trust her. I know she loves me."

To create a new meaning experience for Jack when we moved to Step 3 of the RECON process, I asked him to tell me when the abuse ended. I hoped this would reveal a moment when he realized he took his power back. Jack said, "I quit the baseball team and avoided him. I never told anybody, not even my mom."

"I understand. Sounds like you did what you needed to do to protect yourself. Even though you still wanted to play baseball, you made your safety a priority."

Jack nodded and sighed, "Yeah, I guess so."

Seeing he didn't feel quite proud of that decision, I asked, "What else is your mind telling you that you could have done?"

Jack rubbed his forehead and bemoaned, "I should've told somebody so they could fire the guy and make sure he didn't do it to anyone else."

I should've told someone

Many sexual abuse survivors struggle with whether it was their responsibility to tell someone so the perpetrator wouldn't harm someone else. I commend them for having compassion for others, while also bringing to their awareness that it wasn't their responsibility. The survivor's responsibility is to do what they have to do to continue surviving, like a prisoner of war. I invited Jack to imagine telling someone about his coach back then, and examining if it was a realistic option. He looked out the window as he thought about it. "No. Nobody would've believed me. He would've denied it, and I would've been completely humiliated if my mom or the whole school knew what happened."

"Right," I replied. So there's been a lot of news lately about athletes who experienced sexual abuse from coaches and doctors associated with their teams. They couldn't speak out until they felt like they had the support of other survivors and people in power who could take action. Do you think they would understand why you didn't tell anybody?"

Jack exclaimed, "Are you talking about the USA Gymnastics Team doctor and the Jerry Sandusky scandal at Penn State? Yeah, I know how they feel."

To help Jack consider how he might offer that same kind of compassion toward himself, I asked, "So, if a young baseball player told you he had this experience, how would you build his morale and help him refocus on his strengths so he could enjoy the game again?"

Jack rubbed his hands together and said, "I'd tell him that I know it screws with your head, but that it's the pervert's fault, not his. I'd want him to feel like he could talk to me about it when it was bothering him. Then, I'd want to help him build his talents and confidence again."

"Yes," I agreed. "See what happens if you visualize that more fully. Imagine how you might help this kid reclaim his confidence and dignity and go on to win the Little League World Series or something."

Jack laughed, "You mean like the Chicago Cubs? Just kidding. I know what you're saying. Yeah, I can kind of picture that. I see your point."

As is typical with avoidant clients, they feel reluctant to do any activity that might make them feel emotional, vulnerable, or silly. While Jack was showing a positive response to this metaphor, he wasn't willing to close his eyes and take it into a deeper imagery experience. He tried to deflect with humor and tell me he got the point. I didn't want him to be uncomfortable. But I knew we needed to create a more deeply felt experience to help his emotional brain release the shame and embrace the concept of self-compassion and resilience.

Leaning in, I tried again, supplicating, "Jack, I know it feels silly to do guided imagery. But remember how I was telling you the emotional part of your brain doesn't understand logic or words? How else could we show that part of your mind that felt ashamed that it doesn't need to feel that way anymore? How can we show your 11-year-old self that this weirdo guy—who probably did care for you and wanted to help you, also had a side of him that was totally wacked? Once you saw the wacked side of him, you got away from him. Even though you didn't win the World Series, you handled that season's challenges successfully. Now you're in a new season where you're free to make a fresh start."

Jack covered his face with his hands and tried to hold back tears. I encouraged him to let them flow. His 11-year-old self was finally letting go of all the grief, shame, and anger associated with this experience. As he cried, I offered words of reassurance, saying what that 11-year-old boy needed to hear: "I'm so sorry he turned out to be crazy. You did what you needed to do to manage him until you could get away, Jack. You've turned out to be a fine man, and life is going to get so much better with this monkey off your back."

Jack drew in a deep breath and sighed. He wiped his eyes with his shirtsleeve and said, "Whoa! I didn't see that coming. I guess that's been buried inside me for about 34 years. I'm glad to finally let it out."

I nodded, "I'm glad you did too, buddy. You've held it long enough."

Once Jack's tears settled, I suggested we could move to Step 4 of the RECON process to fully integrate this new meaning into the traumatic memory network. I suggested he pull up one memory of the abuse and retell the story as we coached his 11-year-old self through the experience, knowing he handled it the best way possible. I suggested Jack end the story at a new place—such as when he got away from the man, graduated high school, or married his wife, to show his 11-year-old self that he would prevail in the end.

Jack told the story of his most disturbing memory—a time when his coach forced Jack to give him oral sex in the backseat of a car. As Jack described details of the event, I guided him to pause at the most disturbing moments, imagine stepping into that scene, and tell his younger self what he needed to hear. Initially Jack imagined telling his younger self, "I'm sorry this guy is doing this. You'll get away from him, finish school, and marry a great gal named Sally." Jack clinched his jaw and narrowed his eyes, "I don't like that version. Can I do it a different way?"

"Sure," I offered.

Jack sat up tall. This time he stepped into the remembered scene and imagined dragging his coach out of the car by his collar. He declared, "Listen, you sick son of a bitch, don't you ever touch this kid again or I'll kick your ass! Stay away from him, stay out of my head, and don't come near me again. My life is good now. Don't fuck with me anymore. It's over!" Jack crossed his arms, puffed out his chest, and gave me an affirmative nod. "How's that?" He smirked.

Seeing his pleased expression, I cheered, "Bravo! How does that ending feel to you?"

Jack gave me a playful grin and said, "I like it. I don't know why, but I feel better. All of a sudden I realized he's an idiot who is probably dead by now. I'm not going to let him have power over me anymore. I survived that crazy experience. I don't have to dwell on it. It's done."

In subsequent sessions, we worked on a couple more of Jack's abuse memories. After reconsolidating the first one, he found the other memories not nearly as disturbing. He also continued to work on skills for emotional intimacy in marital therapy with his wife.

Working with Jack, I learned the "mismatch" experience doesn't have to be a contrived technique you've learned in a workshop. Using the therapeutic relationship to convey your sincere belief in your client as you provide the attuned attachment experience they didn't get can spark the memory reconsolidation process, too.

For these corrective emotional experiences to be successful, you have to have a trusting therapeutic alliance with the client first. Otherwise the client will not trust your words, no matter how sincere you are. This is especially true for clients who've suffered chronic childhood abuse and have disorganized attachment styles. I'll address how to earn trust and revise traumatic memories with these clients next, in Chapter 10.

10

Childhood Physical Abuse

Forming a secure therapeutic alliance with clients who've suffered childhood abuse and neglect can be challenging. If the abuse was severe, repetitive, and began at a young age, it is likely the client developed a disorganized attachment style. With disorganized or unresolved attachment, the client has intense conflicts about getting close to people. As children, the very people with whom they needed to attach for survival were also the people who posed the greatest threat to their existence. They long for loving, caring relationships, but expect to be betrayed, abandoned, or hurt by people.

As a result, people with disorganized attachment have a blend of both avoidant and anxious attachment traits. They can be preoccupied with having close relationships one moment, then suddenly distance or cut off from a relationship the next. They can feel fragmented as they vacillate between different "parts" of themselves. Not all people with disorganized attachment styles develop dissociative identity disorder. But they can quickly regress to traumatized states when stressed and appear to have different personas.

When these clients come to therapy, they are usually in crisis—either struggling with suicidal ideation, a destructive relationship, or chronic health problems. Before you can reconsolidate their traumatic memories, you have to stabilize the crisis, and patiently work to build trust and rapport. Once the crisis is sufficiently stabilized, it is helpful to reconsolidate traumatic memories so clients can begin to build new perceptions of themselves, the world and others. These clients can struggle with inner conflicts through the memory reconsolidation process, as they attempt to reconcile their longing for love with their fierce instincts to protect themselves. Through a case example with my client Pamela, you'll see why it can feel like you're moving one step forward, then two steps back, when working with these clients. Yet the effort to patiently walk through the difficult journey with these clients is worthwhile, as they have the greatest need and capacity to heal.

SUICIDAL IDEATION AND INNER CONFLICTS

My client Pamela, whom I introduced in Chapter 4, How to Engage Insecure Attachment Styles, was an impressive woman who managed to build a remarkable career and survive a lifetime of violent relationships. Although she desperately wanted to put her traumatic memories behind her, the more urgent issue was resolving her persistent suicidal ideation. She cried, "Even if you can help me make peace with my past, I'm not sure I have the will to go on living. I'm tired. I have trouble believing life will ever be good. It's been one disappointment after another."

I replied, "You've certainly had more than your fair share of trauma, Pamela. But you're still here. I understand the suicidal part of you wants to end the pain. Yet, there is another part of you that seems determined to survive and not let the world break you. Tell me about that part. What gives her the will to keep living? What does she want that suicidal part to understand?"

Pamela declared, "I live for my nieces and nephews. Our family is so screwed up. I want to help them live normal lives and break the family cycle of abuse."

I was relieved to hear Pamela had an inspiring reason to continue her life. To reinforce her fortitude, I replied, "Yes, breaking the cycle of family dysfunction so the next generation can have a better life is an extraordinary mission. Tell me about your nieces and nephews. They seem like a special part of your life."

Guiding Pamela to tap into the positive feelings she had for her nieces and nephews did shift her affect. She showed me pictures and shared warm and humorous stories about them. She said whenever she felt suicidal, looking at their photos or speaking to them over the phone would temporarily lift her spirits.

Thinking we'd found a way to instill hope and reinforce her motivation to live, I asked, "What would be the best outcome you can imagine that feels possible for you, your nieces, and nephews? Can you see yourself enjoying spending time with your nieces and nephews as adults, being grateful you all survived, and creating new, happier family memories?"

Pamela sighed, "Sure, I'd like to see them grow up and be happy. But when do I get to be happy? I'm tired of being the rescuer in this family. When will someone come rescue me?"

My attempt to create a compelling future vision backfired, but her response revealed her deeper desire: a healthy, loving adult relationship. The problem was that she was confusing a healthy, loving relationship with someone rescuing her. Worse, it felt like she was inviting me to step into the rescuer role. While my compassionate side wanted to rescue her, I knew it would thrust our relationship into a lopsided dynamic, with her in the role of helpless victim and me charged with the endless responsibility of saving her life. Inevitably, there would be a moment when I wouldn't be available to rescue her from a crisis or would need to set a boundary with her. Then, she'd perceive me to be like all the other abandoning, persecutory people in her life.

Conveying compassion while choosing my words carefully, I offered, "Yes, I wish you'd had a strong protector who could have rescued you from the unfathomable violence you endured. Yet, looking for a rescuer sets us up in a trap. We end up giving all our power to that person and inevitably they will let us down. Do you think that has happened in some of your relationships? You've been drawn to someone because they seem like a strong nurturer or protector and then they end up smothering you, or becoming violent and controlling?"

Pamela's eyes narrowed as she leaned away from me and furrowed her brow. I feared I had offended her and braced myself for her combative comeback. Instead, she said, "That's an interesting observation. I am drawn to big, confident men because they feel safe. Like a big bear who can protect me. But, then they also wind up being controlling, needy, and abusive. So how do we break the pattern?"

Preparing for the RECON process

I explained to Pamela that the emotional brain sets up relationship templates based on our past experiences. Since she was an engineer, I compared it to a virus or software program with a bug that gets downloaded to a computer. To update the program, I told her, we can do a process called memory reconsolidation. It requires us to review the memory and recode it with new information.

Pamela frowned, "But I've talked about the abuse before and it didn't change anything. It just made me feel worse."

I agreed that talking about the event over and over doesn't change the way we feel about the memory. Instead, the memory reconsolidation process is intended give the event a new meaning that would help her feel more worthwhile and empowered. Additionally, I reassured her that she wouldn't have to relive the memories, and we would prepare her with tools to calm and resource herself first.

Pamela expressed a little skepticism, but was open to the process, "Sure, we can try it. At this point I don't have much else to lose."

In the next session Pamela and I worked on tools for grounding, orienting to the present moment, and calming her nervous system. She liked focusing on a painting of a sailboat that I had in my office, noting, "That painting makes me feel peaceful, calm, and strong. You know, I built a sailboat once."

"No kidding! Tell me about that," I encouraged.

"Yep, a 38-foot cutter. A project my first husband and I did together.

That was one of the first moments I felt really proud of myself. It helped me realize I was smart, good at mechanical things, and enjoyed working with my hands."

"That's impressive, Pamela. That could be a new ending for a childhood abuse memory. Our minds tend to stop abuse memories at the point where we felt helpless. Showing your mind that you survive and go on to do something positive helps change the context of the memory."

"Yes," Pamela agreed. "That might work. But, since my first husband killed himself, it also brings up sad feelings for me. A better ending would be the moment my dad apologized for the abuse and told me he was proud of me. That didn't happen until right before he died. But it meant a lot to me. That would be a better place to end those memories."

RECON for memories of physical abuse

When we started the RECON process, the first memory Pamela chose to reconsolidate was a time when she actually stood up to her father. He beat her so badly that he dislocated her jaw, then kicked her out of the house. At this point she left home and joined the military. I asked her to bring up one moment of the memory, briefly. Then, I asked her to quickly describe the images, emotions, and physical sensations that came to mind.

Pamela said, "I see his flushed face as he's hitting me and pushing me out of the house. I feel angry and scared. I don't know where I'm going to go. My jaw is hurting as I think about it."

"Okay. Good job. Take a deep breath and maybe cradle your jaw in your hand to give it some love. Remind your body where it is now and that your dad is not here in this room. Show your mind that not only do you survive, your dad is going to apologize for this one day. I know that it doesn't make the event any less horrific, but I want your mind to see that you prevail." Pamela looked at the painting of the sailboat on my wall and took a deep breath. A few tears came to her eyes, then she quickly wiped them away, looked at me, and said, "Okay, I got it. What's next?"

I could have explored her tears, but at this point it's more useful to keep the client present so she doesn't relive the event. I told her she'd successfully completed Step 1 of the RECON process. The next step was to tell me what it felt like that event meant about her, other people, and the world.

Pamela cried, "It felt like I was worthless and unwanted. My parents didn't care about me, and the world wouldn't care about me either. I thought I would die homeless and alone."

"Okay," I replied, "Knowing what you know now, what do you want to believe about that event instead? What would you tell your younger self if you could step back in time?"

Pamela drew a deep breath and said, "I would want her to know that she survives, that her dad would apologize eventually, and that she's smarter and stronger than she thinks she is."

"Yes," I affirmed. "What other assets do you want her to realize she has, or will develop later? What kind of relationships do you want her to have?"

Pamela gave me a confused look and said, "I don't know. What does a healthy relationship look like? What should I want for her?"

I offered, "Perhaps you could see her feeling secure, with intelligence, compassion, and resourcefulness. Because of what she's been through, she has strong survival skills and street smarts. She's interested in being with people who respect that and care about her. She protects herself from people who don't respect her. Now she's ready for a mutually respectful relationship with someone who is mature, stable, understanding, and appreciates her good qualities. If he's upset, he can talk about it rationally and be considerate of her feelings and boundaries. If she's upset, he's interested in understanding the problem and finding a way to work it out amicably."

Pamela gave me her full attention as I was describing this potential new relationship template. Nodding, she replied, "That seems reasonable. Do you think we can get my mind to believe that, though?"

Seeing this as an opportunity to move to Step 3 of the RECON sequence (Create a new meaning experience that elicits desired beliefs), I explained, "Yes. But the part of your mind where we need to install this new template only speaks in images, metaphors, and symbols. It doesn't understand words. So, let's create an image that would represent your mind working in the desired way. It could be something in nature, an animal, or other image. Imagine how you want to be feeling, and see what symbol your mind shows you that would represent that."

Pamela closed her eyes for a moment, then chuckled, "I see dolphins. They are powerful, strong, and intelligent—but also compassionate and playful. They work together as a team. They protect each other, but they don't hurt each other."

"Beautiful," I echoed. Then I guided Pamela to immerse herself more deeply in the dolphin imagery to fully connect to her desired beliefs and feelings. Her face looked calm and peaceful as she vividly imagined swimming with the dolphins for several minutes. When she opened her eyes, I asked if she felt ready to review the memory of the abuse in more detail so we could integrate her new beliefs into it. She nodded, "Yes. Let's do it."

As we moved to Step 4, I coached Pamela to review the memory as if she was watching it on a small computer monitor so she wouldn't relive it. I suggested that she could imagine having a remote control that would allow her to "freeze" her father in the scene or make him smaller so he was less intimidating. Likewise, she could step into the scene to act as a competent protector for her younger self or nurture and guide her younger self through the experience.

Pamela proceeded, "I had just graduated high school and was hanging out with some kids from the neighborhood. I got home late for dinner and my dad told me since I was late, I would not be eating and he ordered me to go to my room. I ignored him and went to the kitchen to get an apple. He followed me into the kitchen, grabbed the apple from my hand, and threw it against the wall. Then he noticed I smelled like cigarettes and asked me when the hell I picked up smoking! I said 'None of your business, old man! I'm 18 now and it's legal.' Out of nowhere, he hurled an explosive uppercut punch to my chin. That's when my jaw dislocated. But he wasn't finished. He dragged me by my hair upstairs to my room. He grabbed handfuls of clothes and shoes out of my closet and threw them at me, yelling, 'Get out, you worthless bitch! Don't ever come back here again. You think you're better than me? Well, try living on your own! Nobody is going to help you. Nobody is going to want you. And you'll probably die alone on the street.'

"After that I pulled myself up, threw my things in a bag, and left. I stayed a couple of days with my friend, Nancy. Then, I got the idea to join the Navy and met with a recruiter later that week. I didn't go home again until 15 years later, when I found out my dad was dying. My sister said he wanted to see me and apologize for being so cruel to us growing up. He cried and told me he was proud of me the night before he died. He looked so frail and weak. Maybe that weak man was who he really was inside."

"Yes, what else are you noticing?" I asked.

Pamela shook her head and said, "Gosh, right now I almost feel sorry for him. He looks so pitiful, even when I think about the abuse. I can see that mean, puffed-up persona was just a mask to cover up how insecure he felt inside. I think he wanted me to leave because I was smarter than him and he felt threatened. My siblings looked up to me. A lot of times I protected them from the abuse. They were beginning to see me as the leader of the family, not him. He felt threatened when I talked back to him. That's why he needed me to leave."

"Makes sense," I replied. "Make sure your younger self sees that. What else do you want her to realize, so she knows she doesn't have to find some burly dude to take care of her? How can she take care of herself?"

Pamela closed her eyes and said to her younger self, "You're going to be okay. You're smart enough and strong enough to take care of yourself. You don't need a protector. You need a compassionate companion. Like the dolphins—they work together as a team."

For Step 5 of the RECON process, I asked Pamela to tell the story one more time to be sure the memory was fully integrated as a coherent narrative. She was surprised by how differently she felt as she retold it, commenting, "That's strange. I feel sad for my dad, but proud of myself. He doesn't seem as frightening. He just seems crazy. I can see myself as competent, smart, sane—just doing what I had to do to survive in that house. He was the one with a problem, not me." Pamela reflected on a few other memories of her dad, applying the same perspectives by contrasting the abuse memories with the image of her dad as frail and weak. Rather than view herself as an unlovable failure, she began to see herself as a smart, obedient child who was trying her best to hold things together. We ended the session with her imagining holding, protecting, and comforting her younger self. She left the session feeling tired, but hopeful. She asked if we could work on memories related to her mom in the next session.

Working with flashbacks

After Pamela had such a positive response to the RECON process, I was shocked when her 16-year-old niece brought her to our next session in a completely dissociated state. Her niece explained, "Pam does this sometimes. She thinks she's a little girl and her mother is chasing her with a shotgun. When my mom and Pam were little, they tried to run away from home because of all the abuse. My grandmother went hunting for them in the woods with a shotgun, and threatened to kill them once she found them. Pam thinks that's happening again right now. I'm glad she has this session with you. My mom would've come, but she had to work. I look like my mom when she was younger, so right now Pam thinks she's nine years old and I'm her sister."

I admit I felt panicked, unsure of what to do in this situation. When a client dissociated or had flashbacks during a session, I usually recognized the signs early enough to reorient them before they fully relived a memory. Initially I tried to see if I could reorient Pamela by asking her if she knew who I was or remembered my office. I even showed her the sailboat painting she liked, hoping that would prompt her memory. Pamela merely looked at me with big doe eyes and said, "No, ma'am. I don't remember this place. My sister said you're a counselor."

Going with the moment, I decided to interact with her as I would if a nine-year-old showed up to my office in crisis. I sat down on the floor to appear less threatening and said, "That's right. This is a safe place. Nobody can hurt you here. I know your mom and dad get really mad and do scary things sometimes. You and your sister can stay here until they cool off."

Pamela looked at her niece and asked, "Do you think it's okay? She's not going to tell mom or call the police, is she?"

Her niece said, "No, she's okay. She's not going to hurt us."

Pamela's niece explained that the during the incident, Pam and her sister ran away from their mom and hiked through the woods for two days to the next town. When they got there, they went to the sheriff's office to tell them their mom was trying to kill them. The sheriff treated them like runaways and turned them in to a juvenile detention center. When they were finally released home, their mom beat them with switches from a peach tree until their legs bled.

Hearing the story was heartbreaking, and I realized in her nine-year-old state, Pam may be worried I was going to send them to the juvenile detention center. My first goal was to help her feel safe with me. I offered her a box of crayons and asked if she wanted to draw or color with me. She took out a blue and green crayon and began to draw. At first I quietly drew with her and commented on how pretty her pictures were. She gave me a shy smile. Then, she asked, "Do you work for the police?" I told her I did not, that I worked with people who felt scared, and my job was to help them feel safe and figure out how they can make their home lives better.

Pamela asked, "You're not going to send us to that children's jail are you? I don't like that place."

I reassured her, "No, I am not. I don't like that place either. The sheriff made a terrible mistake. You and your sister don't need to be in detention. That's not going to happen again. You did good getting away from your mom until she can calm down. She doesn't think clearly when she's mad, does she?"

Pamela shrieked, "No, she's crazy! She tried to shoot us with a shotgun! I don't want you to tell nobody, though. I don't want her to go to jail. I just want her to quit hurting us."

"Me too," I said. "I know your mom and dad hurt you when they're mad. But I don't think they're going to kill you. They know if they do that they will go to jail. They're too scared to do that. What happens after they calm down when they are mad? What do they do then?"

"They just act like nothing ever happened, and then it's kind of quiet for a couple of days. They tell us we're bad kids and they have to hit us to keep us in line," Pamela mumbled.

She told me some of the "bad" things that would warrant a beating from her parents included playing and laughing too loudly, not eating all their vegetables, and not doing their chores perfectly. For instance, Pamela could get a whipping if she missed one crumb on the floor after she attempted to sweep it with a broom twice her size. I reassured her that she did not sound like bad kid, but that her parents seemed to have really unrealistic expectations of children. I commented, "Sometimes adults are really confused and think kids should act like grown-ups or robots. But you're not a robot. You're a person with feelings. But you're having to work around parents who don't get it. Sounds like you are doing the best you can. That's all any of us can do. One day you'll be a grown woman with your own house, and can make your own rules."

Pam looked up at me and said, "Yeah, I'd like to have my own house."

In an attempt to orient her again, I looked at her shoes and said, "Wow, you have really big feet for a little girl! I'll bet you can run fast with those. What size shoes are you wearing?"

Pam glanced down at her feet and looked surprised. She pulled off one of her shoes and looked inside to see what size they were. She wrinkled her nose, "These are ladies' shoes."

I mirrored her confused expression and said, "Wow, and it looks like you have ladies' feet. Look, they are the same size as mine!"

Pamela looked at my feet and then back to her own feet. Then she looked at her hands and down at her clothes and mused, "These are ladies' clothes!"

"Yeah," I said. "Let's see how tall you are."

Pamela and I both stood up and realized she was taller than I. At that point she looked at her niece, then looked around the room. Then she looked back at me and said in her adult voice, "How did I get here? I don't remember driving to your office, Courtney."

I breathed a sigh of relief. She was back. Her niece and I explained what happened. I told her how I attempted to help her work through the memory and asked her how she felt. She replied, "Um, okay, really. I feel a little tired and just want to go home now if that's okay."

Inner conflicts about resolving abuse memories

Though her father was pretty violent, Pam had the most conflicting feelings about her mother. Her mother was still alive. She lived 800 miles away from Pam, but she continued to guilt Pam into taking care of her, and often left hateful messages on Pam's voicemail.

As we explored her relationship with her mother, she said, "You know what? I don't want to change the memories of her abuse. If I make peace with those, then it feels like I let her off the hook. I could forgive my dad because he acknowledged what he did and apologized. She never will."

Rather than push her, I honored Pam's request to let those memories lie for a while. We continued to focus on skills for managing dissociation, depression, and social anxiety. A few months later, Pam came to a session after having a horrible argument with her mother. She huffed, "What do I need her for? I raised myself and can be my own damn mother. She's fired! I'm releasing all responsibility for her. I can't fix her."

After Pamela reached this empowered emotional place, we were able to reconsolidate several memories of her mom's abuse, finishing the story at the point where she "fired" her mother. Fortunately, she was able to revisit the memory of her mother chasing her with a shotgun without dissociating, finishing the story by affirming that the sheriff made a mistake by sending her and her sister to the juvenile detention center. In subsequent sessions, we'd look at one memory at a time, finishing the story with Pam realizing that her mother was mentally ill and imagining ways she could nurture, guide, and protect her younger self. Yet, there were many sessions when she didn't want to work on memories and preferred to focus on ways to deal with her current life stressors.

When working with clients who have such a violent and chronic abuse history, it's important to work at their pace. I tell them, "You didn't have control over the event when it happened, but you have control over the story. It's your story, and you get to decide when you want to tell it, to whom you want to tell it, and where you want it to fit into the narrative of your life. You own it now, it doesn't own you."

Even though I've witnessed amazing emotional changes in abused clients after they've reconsolidated traumatic memories, they still tell me that the most helpful element of our therapy was my willingness to work at their pace and not push them. In effect, the ultimate "mismatch" experience that helps rewire insecure attachment patterns is being in a relationship with someone who can accept them as they are and patiently dance with their defenses. It's the day-to-day stability of you showing up, being honest, and expressing compassion that restores these clients' faith in humanity again. Remember that on the days you think you're not being effective enough with these clients. Being on the journey with them through all their ups and downs is the way to build trust, hope, and healing.

11

Relational and
Attachment Trauma

A t the core of attachment issues is the experience of relational
trauma at a young age. It may not involve physical or sexual
abuse, but repeated experiences of rejection, criticism, neglect,
or chaos that left an indelible mark on the client's self-esteem. Relational
trauma isn't always caused by negative experiences with caregivers. Bul-
lying, racism, or experiences of betrayal, rejection, and criticism by other
authority figures, peers, and siblings can cause clients to have negative
perceptions of themselves and relationships.

Clients may not describe painful relationships as a form of "trauma."
They are more likely to complain about recurring depression, anxiety,
or low self-esteem and deny a history of trauma. I explain to clients
that the emotional brain may keep overriding their best intentions to
change because it keeps activating coping strategies that worked in the
past. To reveal past experiences contributing to their current problems,
I ask, "Where do you think you learned that pattern?" Or, "Tell me the
first time you can remember having that thought, feeling, or impulse."

In this chapter, I'll share two examples of the way early relational
trauma creates avoidant and anxious attachment patterns and how to
use memory reconsolidation to begin installing more secure attachment

patterns. While every type of relational trauma can't be addressed in this chapter, I am hopeful these examples will demonstrate how to identify early attachment breaches and ways to use memory reconsolidation to begin healing them.

"IF I ALTER ME, THEN I CAN CHANGE HIM"

Madeline came to therapy due to recurring struggles with anxiety, depression, and codependent relationship patterns. Witty and intelligent, she had a great deal of insight into her issues and we seemed to build rapport quickly. She'd been in therapy previously, was an active member of Al-Anon, and often read self-help books. Yet, with all her knowledge and insight, she couldn't seem to stop putting others' needs ahead of her own, and blamed herself when relationships didn't work out.

When I asked about her childhood, Madeline readily acknowledged that her upbringing was likely the source of her problems. Her father was bipolar, alcoholic, and abused her mother emotionally and physically. Although her father didn't physically abuse Madeline and her brothers, they were still terrified of him. Madeline said her dad had a soft spot for her and seemed to favor her over her brothers. While this favored position helped her feel a little more loved and supported amid the family chaos, it also left her with a distorted sense of guilt and responsibility. She felt like she was the only person in the family who could manage her father or keep the household running when her mom couldn't function.

Madeline's mother eventually left her father, got a good job, and raised her three children as a single parent, but relied on Madeline for emotional support. Madeline's father died from cancer a few years before I met her. Fortunately, he did make peace with her before he passed away. Although she no longer held resentment for him, she still struggled with flashbacks and nightmares of his violent tirades. We agreed to do memory reconsolidation on these past experiences, in hopes it would stop these intrusive images and release her from the belief she had to care for others in order to be loved.

For our first memory reconsolidation session, Madeline chose a memory of her father putting a fishing knife to her mother's throat after she and Madeline went to pick wildflowers in a nearby park. Madeline was eight years old at the time. Her mother was depressed, so she suggested they go to the park, thinking that would cheer her mom up. When Madeline's father learned they'd gone to the park, he became enraged. He didn't like for Madeline's mother to go anywhere without him out of fear she would leave him. After they returned from the park, a violent argument ensued between her parents that ended with her dad threatening to kill her mother if she left the house without his permission again.

Moving to Step 2 of the RECON process, I asked Madeline what it felt like that event meant about her, her parents, and her world. She looked down at the floor and said, "I blamed myself. I was the one who talked mom into going to the park and thought dad was going to kill her. I feared I would be responsible for her death."

In an effort to console her and reframe this belief, I replied, "Oh my goodness. You were trying to help your mom, but didn't realize your dad would be threatened by such an innocent gesture."

Madeline added, "Yeah, after that I thought the only way to keep it from happening again was to not want to pick wildflowers. Basically, I learned how to not have wants."

"Wow," I replied. "What do you want to believe now?"

Tilting her head to the side, she pondered, "I guess that it wasn't my fault that things got so bad and that the family violence doesn't define me. But, the main message I want to unlearn is that *if I alter me in some way, then I can change him.*"

Both our mouths fell open after she made this statement. It was such a clear articulation of the core implicit belief that had been ruling her life. I commended her insight and suggested we rework her statements into positive declarations. She'd described her desired beliefs in terms of what she didn't want, but the emotional brain is more responsive when we define clearly what we do want.

Madeline redefined her desired beliefs as follows: 1) That was a dark chapter in my life, but my family and I overcame it; 2) Picking wildflowers was not the cause of the violence; my dad's mental illness was the cause; 3) My feelings and my safety are important; and 4) It's okay for me to have wants. Reasonable people are willing to find a compromise between my needs and their needs.

For Step 3 of the RECON process, *create a new meaning experience that elicits desired beliefs,* I asked "How would you feel inside if you really embodied these beliefs? What personal qualities would you possess?"

To assist Madeline, I invited her to look at Worksheet 7.1, Positive Qualities for Desired Future Self and Breath Symbol Imagery that I shared in Chapter 7. Madeline identified these four qualities: strong, confident, clear, and self-assured.

Next, I invited Madeline to create a symbol that would represent her mind working in her desired way. She sat up tall and laughed, saying, "I just got an image of a big bear. It's strong, and people are not going to screw with it. A bear's roar is bigger than an alcoholic dad's. One roar from the bear and he'd sit his butt down! I know I couldn't have been a bear then. But imagining what a bear would do helps me tap into what it's like to feel strong and secure enough that very few things would be able to hurt me."

Once she had accessed this feeling of power within herself, I invited Madeline to move to Step 4 of RECON, *Objectively describe the memory while integrating new meanings.* She decided to describe the memory from the bear's perspective, considering what a bear might think if it had walked up on this violent family scene.

"So this little bitty dad, who thought he was big, began beating his wife because she went to pick wildflowers with her eight-year-old daughter. The bear didn't see anything wrong with picking wildflowers. He likes wildflowers! But the dad thought the mom went to the park to meet another man. He was screaming and yelling at his wife, while their daughter kept getting out of bed to check on them. At one point, the dad held a fishing knife to the mom's throat and threatened to kill her . . . ugh, what do I say now?" Madeline asked me.

I suggested, "How do you want the story to end? Your emotional brain thinks your mom died at that moment. Show your eight-year-old self that she lives. In fact, your mom outlives your dad."

Madeline gasped, "Oh my gosh—you're right. I mean it's obvious she outlived him, but something just clicked when you said that. She was actually stronger than him."

"Yes, take that in for a moment so you can feel the truth of that emotionally," I guided.

Madeline drew a breath and said, "Yeah, okay. So the bear knocks the knife out of the little dad's hand so he accidentally cuts himself instead of his wife. After that, the mom realizes she's had enough and decides she's going to leave him. She saved up money and made a plan for her and her kids to go live with her sister. The dad tries to follow them at first, but he gives up. Then the mom raises the kids and realizes how strong she really is. Sadly, the dad gets cancer later. But before he dies, he tells Madeline he is sorry. Madeline realizes that he had a mental illness that caused him to do those things. She realizes it wasn't her fault. He had problems she couldn't fix, and it wasn't her job to fix them."

"That's right," I commended. "How did it feel to tell the story from that perspective?"

Madeline reflected, "I feel calmer and lighter. As I look back on it now, it doesn't have the same sting it did. That's weird. Could it really be this easy?"

I laughed. "Sometimes it is. But let's go through it again to make sure the new meaning fully resonates with you. Not only do we want that event to be less disturbing, but we want your prior negative beliefs to feel inaccurate and for your desired beliefs to feel true."

Madeline went through her story again. This time she told it as her adult self observing the scene, without the bear. At the point where she remembered her dad holding the knife to her mother's throat, I invited her to step into the scene to protect and comfort her younger self. I wanted her to have the experience of what it felt like to advocate for herself and soothe herself emotionally.

Madeline closed her eyes and said to her younger self, "I know you're scared right now, but he's not going to kill your mom. He's just trying to scare her so she'll do what he wants. This is not your fault. Dad's got mental problems and your mom has problems, but eventually she is going to get away. Things are going to get so much better after that."

Then she imagined looking at her dad in the scene and roared, "Sit down, drunk dad guy! Leave Madeline and her mom alone."

Madeline opened her eyes and chuckled, "He sat his ass down that time! It helped to feel like I was protecting my younger self. I think that's why the bear came up as my symbol—it's about protecting myself. I got love from both my parents, but not much in the way of guidance or protection. I guess that's why I doubt myself or don't realize when I need to protect myself."

"Yes, that makes sense," I agreed. "It wasn't modeled for you, so how could you know how to do it? You're learning these skill as an adult, though. We can keep refining and developing these skills in future sessions. But first we needed to update the message you got as an eight-year-old girl. Adapting to what other people wanted was the best strategy for you as an eight-year-old—especially when dealing with a dad who had a mental illness. A part of your mind kept running that program because it worked for you earlier in life. We're helping your mind update to a new strategy that works better for you as an adult."

Madeline nodded, "Yeah—I see that now. So do we need to do more memories, or will my mind generalize this to other memories?"

"That's a great question," I responded. "My experience is that your mind will generalize this learning to similar memories. But there may be memories that happened at a different age, or the issues were different, so they have different meanings we may need to update. Let's check in next week and see what you want to do. In the meantime, you can use your bear imagery meditation as a way to calm, encourage, or empower yourself."

Madeline laughed, "That's so cool. This bear is going on parade, baby—all through my childhood!"

FEELINGS DON'T MATTER, ONLY ACHIEVEMENTS MATTER

While Madeline was very motivated to update past memories, my client Craig was reluctant to revisit his childhood. He was the client with an avoidant-dismissive attachment style that I referred to in Chapter 4, How to Engage Insecure Attachment Styles. He was referred to me by his physician because he was having unusual bouts of nausea and abdominal pain. Even though Craig didn't think his nausea was stress-related, he admitted it could be related to a series of painful losses. Within the last five years, his oldest son died at the age of 25, his 23-year-old daughter had estranged herself from him, and his 20-year-old son was missing.

Reluctant to discuss his grief, Craig asked if we could focus on pain management skills in the beginning of our work together. Surprisingly, mindfulness meditation proved to be an effective tool for him. I introduced mindfulness to Craig through the book *Full Catastrophe Living*, in which author Jon Kabat-Zinn (2013) provides an eight-week, mindfulness-based stress reduction plan to help chronic pain patients. In the book, Kabat-Zinn reassures clients that their physical pain is real. But he also makes a good argument for the way one's mental and emotional responses can ease pain or exacerbate it. Kabat-Zinn's straightforward and scientifically supported approach appealed to Craig's intellect. Clients with an avoidant-dismissive style are more open to try a technique if they understand the logic behind it first.

Craig struggled with the mindfulness practices at first. Kabat-Zinn's program encourages people to practice a 45-minute body scan meditation, which was too long and intense for Craig. I suggested he start with mini-mindfulness practices for only 5 to 10 minutes at a time, and suggested a few mindfulness apps he could download on his phone to guide him. Sitting still was difficult for him, so we did mindful walking on a trail behind my office during our sessions. As he got comfortable walk-ing with me, he began talking more about his internal experiences. This is not unusual for clients with avoidant-dismissive attachment. Sitting in an intimate space looking at you as they're exploring painful issues can make them feel vulnerable and uncomfortable. Having another task on which they can focus while talking with you makes the experience of sharing personal feelings less threatening.

On one of our mindful walks, Craig exclaimed, "I'm realizing how cynical and critical all my thoughts are! I was trying to focus on these pine trees as we walk, and my mind tells me this is stupid. I try to enjoy the fresh air, and my mind tells me I better enjoy it now because climate change is destroying the atmosphere. Then I tried to focus on my footsteps, and I noticed the arthritis in my knee. It's so frustrating."

"That's awesome!" I cheered. "You are doing it exactly right. The point of mindfulness is not to quiet your mind, but to notice the unhelpful chatter in your head. As Michael Singer (2007) writes in his book *The Untethered Soul*, it's like an obnoxious roommate living with you who has to make running commentary on everything. The skill is to notice what this voice is saying without judgment. You can seek to understand why the voice thinks it has to tell you these things. Or you can sim-ply acknowledge this voice with compassionate awareness and gently refocus your attention with the part of your mind that wants to take in beauty, stillness, or peace."

Craig continued to walk quietly as he considered my response. Then, he suddenly stopped in his tracks and said, "Shit! I just realized the obnoxious roommate in my head sounds a lot like my father. I haven't talked to him in years, but apparently, he's still living with me."

Excited for the opportunity to help Craig explore the root of his critical thoughts, I asked him to tell me more about his father. Craig grumbled, "Well let's just say, I didn't feel like his son, I felt like his racehorse. He treated me like an animal."

Craig's tall stature, muscular build, and eye for strategy made him a good athlete, especially in football. His father was certain he could be a pro football star and began grooming him for the NFL after Craig made quarterback on his middle school's team. Instead of offering Craig positive support, his dad attempted to motivate him by relentlessly criticizing him and pushing him beyond his physical limits. For instance, he'd force Craig to get up at 4 a.m. to work out before school, restricted his diet, and humiliated Craig by heckling him during team practices and games.

Craig bellowed, "I told him all his pushing, prodding, and nagging was making me perform worse, not better. He ignored it and insisted he had to toughen me up for the big leagues. We had college recruiters lined up to look at me by the end my junior year in high school. But two weeks into my senior year, I tore my ACL, the anterior cruciate ligament in my knee. That ended my career right there. I had to have surgery to reconstruct my ACL, and eight months of physical therapy. To make matters worse, my mom got sick and died a year later. That was more than I could take, so I started drinking and doing drugs. I stopped the drugs after my kids were born, though."

"My God," I said. "No wonder all these losses with your kids have been so hard on you. You've been dealing with loss since you were a teenager."

I suggested to Craig that it might be useful if we addressed memories of his childhood. I explained that we can internalize negative messages from our parents and early experiences of loss that continue to haunt us as adults. I suggested memory reconsolidation could be another way to update those messages. Craig said he'd think about it.

At our next meeting, Craig stormed into our session announcing, "We found my 20-year-old son! He's home, but he's struggling with an opiate addiction. He's in rehab right now. I've been through addiction and realize this isn't going to clear up overnight. We need to put all that other stuff on hold so you can help me deal with this." I agreed. While reconsolidating memories is useful, current crises take precedence. For the next month, our sessions focused on how to cope with this situation and support his son in getting sober.

Another opportunity to look at his past arose after a family meeting at the rehab center where his son was being treated. Craig lamented, "In the family session, my daughter told me she distanced from me because I'm cold and critical. Maybe I'm more like my dad than I thought. Can you help me be a better father?" I suggested we start by revisiting memories of *his* father. I added, "It starts with learning how to be a better father to yourself. As you learn to have patience and compassion for yourself, I think you'll be better able to give it to your kids."

Reconsolidating memories of a critical father

In our next session, Craig brought up a memory of his father dragging him out of bed at 4 a.m. to run six miles with nothing but a glass of orange juice in his stomach. Craig felt dizzy and vomited during the run, and told his dad he had to stop. His dad called him a "sissy" and insisted that he keep going. Craig finished the run, but collapsed from dehydration when they got home and had to be taken to the hospital for intravenous fluids. His mother seemed concerned about Craig overexerting himself, but his father dismissed it and said Craig just needed to drink more water every day.

Now that Craig had activated a memory, we moved to Step 2 of the RECON process. I asked Craig what it felt like this event meant about him, his father, and his life. He said, "That's when I realized he doesn't think I'm a human being, he thinks I'm a racehorse. My well-being doesn't matter. My achievements are all that matter. I felt like my father was a cruel, selfish jerk. I felt like my mom cared, but wasn't strong enough to do anything about it. In terms of my life, I thought I had two choices: give up or buck up. So, I bucked up. But, I didn't do it for him. I did it for me. I decided I wanted to be a pro football player so I could get away from him. I fantasized about being rich and famous and rubbing it in his face by cutting him out of my life."

"Okay, what do you want to believe now? What would you tell your younger self knowing what you know now?"

"I'd tell him your well-being is important. Because you push yourself so hard, you're going to tear your ACL and blow the whole thing!" Craig barked.

"Whoa!" I interrupted. "Why are you giving this kid a hard time? Is his life going to end because he doesn't become a pro football player?" I wanted to help Craig break out of these self-critical patterns and develop self-compassion.

Craig conceded, "No. You're right. I guess I want him to know that achievements are nice, but they're temporary. They won't make you happy. You can't let them define you because things are always changing. That's what I'm learning from the mindfulness practice. There are moments of victory. There are moments of loss. There are moments of joy. There are moments of sorrow. There are moments of pleasure. There are moments of suffering. You can only take each moment as it comes."

"Yes!" I cheered. "That's a very astute insight, and so true. How does it feel as you say those things to yourself?"

Craig pursed his lips and nodded, "Hmm. Strangely comforting."

"Yes, so as you think about that concept and look back on this scene with your dad, what else are you realizing? Are you seeing him any differently?" I asked.

Craig replied, "Yeah, he seems like an idiot."

I tilted my head to the side and paused. Craig's avoidant attachment style caused him to dismiss other people's intelligence if they were critical of him. Underneath the resentment he had for his dad, I suspected there was a deep longing to be accepted by him. I wasn't sure if I should push Craig to get in touch with this pain, or ask him to consider why his dad was so demanding. I wanted him to realize his dad acted the way he did because of his own issues, not because of anything Craig did.

Craig picked up on my hesitance. Before I could say anything, he blurted, "I guess thinking he's an idiot is not a skillful way of looking at it?"

"Well, writing him off as an idiot doesn't seem like a full explanation of his bizarre behavior. What made this man so obsessed with making his son a football star? What made him so out of control?"

"Pfft!" Craig sputtered, "He had to win at everything. In his mind, you're a winner or a loser. There's no in between. So, if I'm not the best, he's not the best. I don't know what made him like that. It's sad, really. Nobody likes being around him."

"Yeah," I replied, "Black and white thinking puts you in a trap. As you said earlier, life is full of ups and downs. You can't attach your identity to all of it. What do you wish you could've gotten from him? What do you wish your relationship had been like?"

Craig frowned. "I just wish we could've enjoyed things together. You know, play sports together just for fun, not competition. I wish he would have been more loving toward my mom. He misses her terribly. But he made her a nervous wreck, too. He was obsessed with being this rich, successful guy with a beautiful wife and perfect kids so people would admire him. We just needed him to love us. But he didn't care about us."

"He didn't care? Or do you think he didn't know how to love?" I asked. "Sounds like he equated love with being admired. But what creates love between people is when they can share their successes *and* their failures together without judgement."

Craig shook his head and stammered, "He was wound so tight, he couldn't let love in. I'm afraid I'm just like him. I don't let love in because I don't want to be hurt."

"Okay, I understand. So how do you want to feel and think instead? Imagine your future self just the way you want him to be."

Craig answered, "Patient, wise, compassionate, open. That's the kind of father I wish I had and the kind I want to be."

"Yes," I answered. "What does it feel like in your body as you imagine these qualities? Perhaps you could breathe in each quality one at a time and notice what it feels like."

Because Craig had been practicing mindfulness, I thought meditating on the way each of his desired qualities felt in his body would be more effective than imagery. Matching the rhythm of Craig's breath, I softly repeated each one of his preferred qualities. Craig closed his eyes and took a deep breath as he meditated on each quality. He sat back on the couch and dropped his hands to his lap with his palms up. His posture began to shift from rigid and tense to relaxed and open. I suggested that, when he was ready, he could imagine sending patience, wisdom, compassion, and openness to his younger self.

Craig stayed with the meditation for several minutes, then I noticed hidden tears peeking through his eyelashes. He swallowed hard and whispered "I love you, son. I love you."

I didn't want to interrupt him, but I wanted to make sure he was having a healing experience, not a painful experience. Softly, I asked, "What are you noticing right now, Craig?" He kept his eyes closed and said, "I just thought of my son who died and wanted to tell him I loved him. I'm okay. I want to tell each of my kids that I love them. I just need another minute."

"Okay, take your time. Do whatever feels right for you," I replied.

He stayed with the meditation another couple of minutes while I sat mindfully breathing with him as a supportive presence. When Craig opened his eyes, he released a long exhale. "Wow. That was intense. Good, but intense."

He explained that as he got in touch with the qualities of feeling patient, wise, compassionate, and open, he felt his heart soften. When I suggested he could send those feelings toward his younger self, he felt his heart welling up with emotion and didn't know what to do with it. Then he got the idea to send those qualities to his children. Craig explained, "When I sent the feelings toward my kids, that's when I felt this huge shift. It was like these tight bands around my heart began to release and break open. I tried to send love to my dad, but I couldn't quite get that. So, I simply thought of him and said, 'May you be free from suffering.' Those are words from a meditation script that I like. That felt right."

I was so grateful that Craig was able to open up to his emotions and this experience within himself. He was learning how to accept his tender feelings and feel comfortable expressing his love to others. He seemed to be recognizing that opening his heart to love wasn't weak, but took deep courage and strength.

To finish the RECON process, I asked Craig to describe the memory again from this enlightened perspective. He was able to tell the story of his father's abuse again, this time describing his dad as a misguided man caught up in his own suffering. He saw his younger self as a well-intentioned kid doing the best he could. He finished the story by saying, "I'm not a racehorse anymore. Life isn't a race. It's journey you take one step at a time."

Even though clients report significant breakthroughs after successful memory reconsolidation, they still need help reinforcing new patterns and learning new skills. They didn't just miss out on attachment experiences, they often weren't taught skills for managing stress, handling conflicts, setting boundaries, or problem solving. With both Madeline and Craig, we alternated between memory reconsolidation and skill-building sessions. I'll share several of these skill-building interventions in Phase III of this book. But next, in Chapter 12, I'll discuss tools you can use to help clients heal traumatic grief.

12

Traumatic Grief
and Loss

T he sudden or violent loss of loved one can certainly thwart a
person's sense of safety and the feeling of secure attachment in
relationships. As Panksepp and Biven (2012) describe in their
book, *The Archeology of Mind: Neuroevolutionary Origins of Human
Emotions*, we're hardwired to experience grief and panic when we feel
separated from a loved one. Panksepp asserts that the emotion of grief is
meant to be an adaptive response. Grief's sadness is meant to cause us
to withdraw, slow down, and reflect on the meaning of our relationship
with the deceased. Feelings of anxiety and panic are meant to compel
us to reestablish connections with our lost loved one, pack, or tribe.

When children experience early loss or separation from caregivers,
they may develop an anxious attachment style. As adults, they may still
may find themselves panicked if they think someone is distancing from
them. Or, they may cling to loved ones in an effort to avoid perceived
abandonment. Alternatively, children may cope with loss by developing
avoidant attachment patterns, denying their need for relationships and
becoming overly self-reliant.

Western cultures tend to promote a self-reliant approach to grief,
suggesting the bereaved accept the finality of the loss and move on

with their lives as soon as possible. But research has demonstrated that the best way for grievers to move forward is to give themselves time to reflect on the meaning of the loss, access social support, and internalize a healthy continuing bond with the deceased (Bonanno, 2009; Klass & Steffen, 2018).

Reconsolidating memories of the death or unresolved conflicts with the deceased is also helpful for integrating the loss. Complicated grief expert Katherine Shear (2010) explains, "not only does revisiting the story of the death help the griever feel less afraid of her emotions and her thoughts around the loss, but it provides the opportunity to identify problematic beliefs that are sticking points in processing the loss" (p. 5).

The most common issues that keep people stuck in complicated grief include: 1) feeling responsible for the death or ruminating over what could have done to prevent the loss; 2) intrusive images of the deceased suffering and in pain; 3) survivor's guilt, or beliefs they are being punished; 4) feeling like life isn't fair, or has lost all meaning or spiritual purpose; and 5) beliefs that they will not be able to function or experience joy without the deceased loved one. In this chapter, I'll share how you can you use memory reconsolidation to reverse these negative beliefs, clear intrusive images, and repair attachment wounds.

HEALING RAGE AFTER GRIEF

Dixon was the client I introduced in Chapter 1, who struggled with incessant road rage after he and his sister were in an accident that killed his sister and left him with third-degree burns. The car accident occurred while he and his sister were driving to a family gathering, and a teenage drunk driver swerved onto their side of the highway and hit them head-on.

After a few sessions with Dixon, I surmised that he'd developed an avoidant attachment style prior to the loss. His father abandoned the family when he was a toddler, and his mother was not emotionally available because she worked two jobs. Dixon's sister was the main attachment figure in his life. After she died, it seemed Dixon made an unconscious decision to shut down his attachment needs completely, emotionally distancing from family and friends.

Dixon ruminated over what he could have done to prevent the car accident, and expressed his rage at drivers he perceived to be reckless and dangerous. Anger is usually an easier emotion for clients with avoidant attachment to access. It allows them to express their pain without feeling so vulnerable. Dixon's wife Katie urged him to review the memory of the accident with me so he could stop ruminating and calm down.

Dixon snapped, "That's the problem, Katie. I don't *want* to calm down. Reckless drunk driving killed my sister! I can't let people get away with it, especially now that I have kids."

When Dixon said this, it hit me—perhaps his road rage wasn't just a post-traumatic response, it served a purpose. He was attempting to *raise awareness* of the dangers of drunk and reckless driving, albeit in a misguided way. He needed someone to validate the deeper purpose of his anger before he would be open to changing his behavior.

So I echoed, "I don't want you to calm down either, Dixon. I think you've got an important message and the scars to prove it. Obviously, you're attempting to get people to stop driving recklessly. The problem is the way you've been delivering your message. Driving up and down the freeway honking your horn and shouting from your car isn't an effective strategy. In fact, it may be making you one of those reckless drivers yourself. The anger's not your problem—it's your strategy that's not working."

Dixon smirked. He said: "Okay, shrink. What do you suggest?"

I ignored his sarcasm, and thought about how he might channel his anger into advocacy for his sister's life. "Well, you're a teacher, in a high school, no less. You've already got access to an audience of hundreds of potential drunk, reckless drivers who could benefit from hearing your message. Have you ever talked to your students about what happened to you?"

"Yeah, a few," he said, shrugging. "But I like to keep it a mystery and make them think I got these scars by being a badass so they don't mess with me." His eyes twinkled.

"You *are* a badass!" I cried. "You survived a burning car crash!"

The intensity of my response got Dixon's attention. He sat up tall and gazed at me curiously. Then, he looked down and rubbed the scars on his arms as he mulled, "I've never thought of it like that before. I'm no hero, but I tried to pull my sister out of that car for as long as I could."

"That took a lot of courage and shows how much you loved her," I said softly.

Dixon wiped a tear away and said, "Yep. I would've done anything for her."

"What was your sister like? What did you love about her?" I asked.

Access positive memories of the deceased

In my book *Transforming Traumatic Grief* (Armstrong, 2011), I discuss the importance of inviting grievers to share stories about the deceased. Other people in the griever's life have likely avoided talking about the deceased, fearing they could cause the griever pain. But sharing stories about the deceased helps grievers process the meaning of their relationship and internalize a healthy, continuing attachment bond with their loved one.

Dixon seemed grateful for the opportunity to tell me about his sister. He recounted how she loved animals and music. He told me about rock concerts they'd attended together. He licked his lips and gloated about the way he'd been trying to re-create her delicious fried chicken recipe. His affect broadened and his body seemed more relaxed as he spoke of her.

I nodded, "Wow—she sounds like a really enjoyable person to be around."

Dixon affirmed, "She was. Maybe I am trying to avenge her death by yelling at other drivers. It could be why I get so resentful when my wife tells me to calm down. It feels like everyone wants me to move on, like my sister's life didn't matter."

"Her life *does* matter," I said. "How would she want you to keep her legacy alive?"

Dixon gazed out the window for a moment. "She'd tell me the best way to honor her is to be good father to my kids," he said, his voice suddenly low and soft. "That would make her happy. You know, our dad left us and didn't come around much. She was my best friend. I miss talking to her."

"What would you want to tell her, if you could talk to her right now?" I asked.

Imaginal conversations

Imaginal conversations can be powerful interventions that help clients work out unresolved issues with the deceased and foster positive continuing bonds. My experience has been that clients almost always find this exercise meaningful. The only time clients haven't found it useful is when they feel like they can't imagine a response from their loved one. Yet, when I remind them that they can make up what their loved one might say, they succeed.

If the client's relationship with the deceased was difficult, I invite them to imagine that their deceased loved one is now free from a malfunctioning brain and body, no longer in pain, and able to speak to the client from a place of enlightened awareness. Enlightened awareness means improved insight, clarity, compassion, and understanding. Of course, you'll want to set up the intervention in a way that fits with the client's spiritual beliefs. I'm not suggesting they have to believe their loved one is actually talking to them, just to imagine it. Our emotional brains process imagined experiences similarly to real experiences. The imaginal conversation often feels real and meaningful, even when they believe they are making it up (Shear, 2010).

As Dixon considered what he'd like to say to his sister, he wiped his eyes and sniffed, "First, I'd want to tell her that I appreciate everything she did for me. If it wasn't for her, I don't know where I'd be. I'd tell her I'm sorry about the accident. I feel guilty because I was driving. I've replayed it over and over in my mind to see if there was something else I could have done."

"So, perhaps you could close your eyes and imagine telling her that right now," I offered. For the emotional brain to integrate an imaginal conversation, the client needs to fully imagine and experience it in some way. They don't have to do it in your office. They may prefer to do it outside the session, in a special place they shared with the deceased, or visiting the deceased's memorial site or gravesite. Clients could also do this by writing a letter to the deceased, and then write a letter back to themselves, imagining what the deceased might say to them now.

Dixon opted to continue the conversation in my office. He closed his eyes and whispered, "I'm sorry. I miss you, sister. I wish there was something else I could have done."

I guided, "Now imagine what she might say back to you. Perhaps you can envision her free of pain and speaking to you from a place of clarity, compassion, and understanding. What would she say?"

Dixon sat quietly with his eyes closed for several minutes. He wiped tears from his cheek, "She'd tell me the accident wasn't my fault and that I did everything I could. She'd want me to stop dwelling on it and focus on being a good husband and father. But I still wonder if there was something else I could have done."

"Hmm," I replied. "Perhaps the road rage has been your brain's way of completing an action you wanted to take during the accident, but couldn't. Would you be willing to run back through the memory of the accident with me, so I understand exactly what happened? I don't want you to relive it. Let's see if we can look at it together objectively."

Release self-blame with memory reconsolidation

Dixon said he'd be willing to review the memory with me if it served a purpose and he wasn't just rehashing it over and over. I coached him to describe the memory objectively, as if he was watching it on a small television screen. He was doing well, giving me details while staying within his window of tolerance. Then he suddenly stopped at the point before the drunk driver swerved into their lane. He looked down at his feet and winced. "I was looking down, changing the station on the car radio instead of watching the road. If I hadn't looked down, maybe I could've moved out of the way sooner."

I reassured him, "I don't know, Dixon. Our brains remember traumatic events in slow motion, making us think we had more time to respond than we really did have. How long do you think it takes to change a station on the radio? Pretend like you're doing that right now, and I'll count the seconds."

Dixon looked down and pointed his finger at an imaginary radio while I watched the second hand on my clock. He clocked in at two seconds.

Next, I invited him to replay this section of the memory again, but to imagine not looking down to change the radio while I counted out loud for two seconds. I asked, "Did that two seconds give you enough time to get out of the way of the other driver?"

He shook his head, and said: "Nope. He was coming too fast. Even if I'd had two seconds to swerve right, there was nowhere to go. He still would have hit us."

In an effort to learn from an experience, the emotional brain will imagine all kinds of alternative actions we might have taken to prevent an accident. Although the emotional brain is well intentioned, it often imagines scenarios that were not possible at that time. Inviting the client to imagine these alternative responses while you offer a realistic perspective helps him to disconfirm these erroneous beliefs. Because the emotional brain learns through experiences, you can't just verbally reassure the client he did all he could do. It's more helpful to walk through the details of the memory with him and assist him in seeing that he did all he could do with the information, skills, and resources he had at that time.

Although I didn't follow the RECON protocol in the five-step sequential pattern I've shared in previous chapters, we were still able to change the meaning of the memory for Dixon with the interventions I used in this session. You don't have to follow every step of the RECON protocol rigidly. As long as the client recalls the memory and simultaneously connects to a felt experience that changes the meaning of the event, the memory will change. Shortly after this session, Dixon did begin giving talks to high school students about the dangers of drunk driving. I'll discuss how he did this in Chapter 14, Post-Traumatic Growth.

NIGHTMARES AND DESPAIR AFTER SON'S SUICIDE

Lydia was a 49-year-old nurse referred to me by her physician because she was engaging in out-of-control eating binges that were wreaking havoc with her diabetes. Lydia said the binging began three years earlier, after her son Logan died from a drug overdose at the age of 25. She blamed herself for her son's death and explained that the eating binges simultaneously numbed her pain and served as a form of self-punishment.

She had recurring nightmares of Logan lying on a gurney and being rolled into a flaming furnace. In the dream, he'd reach out to her for help, but Lydia felt like she couldn't move. She believed the nightmares symbolized her feelings of helplessness and guilt, stating: "I had to cremate him because I couldn't afford a burial, but I'm not sure if he wanted that. But I'm more worried that the dream means my son is in hell, and I can't do anything to stop it."

Lydia was deeply religious, and her son was homosexual. She worried he wouldn't be allowed in heaven since he had committed the double "sins" of being gay *and* committing suicide. She wondered if God was punishing her, too. "Maybe I should have raised him differently," she sobbed as she buried her head in her hands.

I assured her: "No, you loved your son unconditionally. I think that is beautiful."

She wiped her face with a tissue and looked at me, "Thank you. He was a sweet boy. He was just prone to depression, like me. I don't know what made him gay."

"Well, I don't think anybody knows what makes a person straight or gay. Love is love. I don't think you should be punished or judged for who you love or how you love."

"Me either," Lydia sniffled.

Since she was capable of unconditional love for her son, I wondered if she believed God was capable of unconditional love, too. I asked, "Do you believe that God is more intelligent and compassionate than you or I?"

Lydia nodded, "Yes, absolutely."

"So, if you and I understand Logan and have compassion for him, I've got to think God understands him and has compassion for him."

Lydia touched her fingers to her lips, "Ahh. I hadn't thought about it that way before."

Because she'd struggled with depression herself, she agreed that suicide is really someone's attempt to end emotional pain. She was comforted by the thought that God probably understood that, too, and would have mercy on her son. Our conversation seemed to be easing her guilt and fears that God was punishing her and her son. She asked if we could do something to stop her nightmares in our next session.

Rescripting nightmares

Though analyzing the symbolic meaning of a nightmare can be useful, rescripting dreams is actually more helpful. In fact, imagery rescripting is the most empirically supported treatment for reducing nightmares (Kunze et al., 2017). With imagery rescripting (IR), you ask the client to recall the dream and vividly imagine changing the dream scene with an outcome that would be more satisfying.

Clients are usually most disturbed by feeling paralyzed or helpless in a dream. Inviting clients to imagine completing the action they want to take in the dream is often very helpful. Clients can even imagine that they have superpowers in their dreams. I invite them to consider that they could fly, make themselves larger or smaller, or make something that seems threatening become smaller or disappear. Sexual trauma survivors have reported that such imagery rehearsal therapy not only reduced their nightmares, but gave them a sense of mastery over their dreams. (Germain et al., 2004).

Similarly, sleep researcher Anna Kunze (2017) and her colleagues in the Netherlands have done studies comparing the effectiveness of imagery rescripting to other interventions for nightmares. It is best for clients to change the dream in their imaginations as they are simultaneously recalling it. In a 2017 article, Kunze and colleagues report that IR is *not* effective if clients *think* about how to change the nightmare without mentally rehearsing the new ending. Kunze and her colleagues hypothesize that IR may elicit memory reconsolidation because the person is recalling the nightmare memory and experientially integrating a new experience into it.

To rescript Lydia's nightmare, I invited her to close her eyes, recall the dream, and change it in any way that felt more satisfying to her. For example, I suggested she could imagine being able to move and respond to Logan. I told her I would stay silent while she worked this out in her imagination, but that she was welcome to describe what she was experiencing, or ask me for support through the process.

Lydia closed her eyes and stuttered, "Oh . . . Oh . . . okay, I see him on the gurney and it's moving toward the flames. He's reaching out to me. This time I walk over to him." She fell silent for a few minutes, but I could see her eyes moving back and forth beneath her eyelids, suggesting she was imagining a new scene. Lydia smiled softly, and a few tears streamed down her cheeks. She commented, "He is standing beside me now with his arm around my shoulder, assuring me that he will be all right. He's not upset with me. He said he was confused and upset with himself. But he is at peace now. I'm hugging him and telling him I love him. He kisses me on the cheek and tells me he loves me too. Now he's telling me goodbye. I don't want to let him go, but he says he'll be with me in spirit and we'll be reunited in Heaven."

Lydia put her hand over her heart, took in a deep breath, and opened her eyes. "How are you doing?" I asked.

She replied, "That helped. I think I've been wanting a chance for us to tell each other 'goodbye' and affirm our love for each other." Lydia replayed the dream this way several times before she went to bed that night, and the nightmares did not come back.

Although the client's ideas for new dream outcomes are often relevant and insightful, occasionally a client may suggest a dream outcome that does not provide a peaceful resolution. When this occurs, I explain to the client why the solution may not have been advantageous and explore ways we might improve it.

For example, a client of mine who dreamt of her deceased mother chasing her with a knife decided she wanted shoot her mother in the dream to stop her from chasing her. But the client's mother had died from a suicidal gunshot wound. We both realized that shooting her mother symbolized the anger she felt toward her mother regarding the suicide, but we agreed that metaphorically shooting her mother exacerbated her feelings of sadness and guilt. Therefore, I suggested she stand still peacefully, knowing that her dream body could not be hurt and she could let her mother come toward her with the knife. I told her, "Whatever is trying to scare you is scared. See what happens if you reassure your mom that you're not going to hurt her."

To her surprise, when she played the dream this way, her mother appeared confused, dropped the knife, and hugged the client instead. Not only did changing the dream this way stop the nightmares, but it also helped the client begin to release guilt and anger, and feel compassion for her mother.

Dissociative amnesia related to grief

Cindy was the 15-year-old client I mentioned in Chapter 6, How to Work with Dissociation. If you recall, Cindy was traumatized in a violent melee at her school and developed amnesia about the event, as well as her entire life before the event. I had never worked with a client who had this type of dissociative amnesia, and consulted Jon Connelly for assistance.

Connelly is the developer of Rapid Resolution Therapy, and I had seen him have success with cases like this. Luckily, he was doing a workshop in my area and offered to sit with me in a session with Cindy. Cindy and her parents were agreeable to letting Connelly join us.

Connelly began our session by explaining that when we are not able to retrieve a memory we know we have, such as recalling the name of someone we know, we often get stressed. The stress impairs our ability to think clearly, causing the information we are seeking to elude us. Later, when we are more relaxed and not looking for it, the information we were trying to remember suddenly comes to us.

He suggested he and Cindy could play a game in which he would guess some things that might have happened in her childhood. Her job was to tell him if she thought he was right, or correct him with what she guessed might be more accurate information. He encouraged her to have fun with the game and not worry about whether her guesses were correct. Connelly started by saying: "When you were a little girl you had a doll. It had long green hair."

Cindy laughed and said, "No, I don't think I had a doll with green hair."

Connelly teased, "Well, what color hair do you think it had, then?"

Cindy chuckled, "She had long brown hair, and I used to braid it."

"Great! You also had a toothbrush. It was pink and shaped like a pig," he joked.

Cindy giggled, "No. I had a white toothbrush."

"Really?" Jon replied. "Are you sure it wasn't pink and white striped?"

Cindy tilted her head to the side for a moment, then grinned, "Oh my gosh, I am really remembering that I had a white toothbrush!"

"Awesome," Connelly cheered. "You also had a teacher in the first grade. She wore glasses and smelled like onions."

Cindy smirked, "You are silly! No, my first-grade teacher was nice and smelled good. She had pretty red hair, and gave us stars when we did our homework."

"Her name was Mrs. Jenkins," Connelly mused.

Cindy shook her head slowly. "No. Her name was Miss Lynn. Yes! Her name was Miss Lynn. I remember her!"

Cindy's mother clapped her hands and exclaimed, "That's right, baby! Miss Lynn was her name. Can you remember your second-grade teacher's name?"

Connelly held up his hand, motioning for her to stop. He explained,

"You can't do it like that. You have to keep it light and fun. The information will come to her memory as it's ready. I know you mean well, but don't pressure her."

We continued the whole session like this, with Connelly humorously suggesting absurd things that may have happened in Cindy's childhood, and Cindy giggling as she countered him with different stories. She noticed that as she started making up answers, actual fragments of memories and information came to her mind. Connelly commended her and said her mind could show her anything else it felt like she was ready to know.

Cindy touched her fingers to her mouth as her eyes widened. She whispered, "I think I just remembered the fight at the game."

Connelly replied, "Okay, what do you remember?"

Cindy took a deep breath, "After the game, a fight broke out. I was pushed between two chairs where these two boys were punching each other."

Connelly teased, "Two boys were punching each other while sitting in chairs?

Cindy sneered, "No! They were standing up, but they were fighting where the chairs were on the side of the gym. Somehow I got pushed over there and was between them. One of them hit me in the back of my head."

Connelly replied compassionately, "Oh goodness. Then what happened?"

Cindy shuddered and said, "I was trying to get away from them. My friend Miranda helped me get up into the bleachers. I fell and hurt my knee. People were screaming and shoving. Then I heard a boy shout, 'I'm going to get my gun. This school's going down! I don't care. I'll kill you all!'"

Connelly humorously remarked, "Wow. These were pretty serious sports fans!" He didn't want to minimize her pain, but used the humor to help her stay present and avoid reliving the terror of that moment.

Cindy looked up at Connelly and laughed, "Yeah, I guess so. But, when I heard somebody was going to get their gun, I got worried about my Bubba. I couldn't find him. I was afraid he was going to get hurt or killed."

Connelly replied, "Your Bubba? You mean that doll with the green hair we were talking about earlier?"

Cindy furrowed her brow and scoffed, "No! My brother! I call him Bubba. I couldn't find him. I was scared so I just started screaming for him. I think that's when my parents found me and they got me into an ambulance."

Realizing the humor was beginning to annoy Cindy, Connelly shifted back to a more compassionate tone. He replied, "Good, I'm glad you remember that they found you. How about your brother? Is he okay?"

Cindy nodded, "Yes. He was the only person I recognized when I woke up in the hospital. But then I recognized my parents and a lot of kind people have helped me. Wow. I am so happy my memory is coming back. Now I'm remembering happier times too, like when I modeled for some pictures for Coca Cola."

Cindy's parents gasped and said, "Yes, yes you did! This is wonderful, honey!"

At that point, the session time was up and Connelly thought it would be good to end on this positive note. I was amazed to see how effective using play and humor could be in helping someone recover memories and avoid being retraumatized as they recalled a devastating experience.

But the work wasn't over. Cindy continued to struggle with anxiety and be sensitive to loud noises. She wanted to fully recover so she could return to school. We scheduled weekly sessions to help her work on these skills and further process the meaning of the traumatic event for her.

It wasn't until our fourth session that Cindy confessed, "I think I may know the boy who said he was going to get his gun at the fight. I think that's why my memory shut down."

"Oh, okay," I reassured her. "What do you know about him?"

Cindy winced, "Well, we were kind of talking to each other. He wanted me to go out with him. I knew he was in a gang but I never thought he'd do anything like that. I'm scared. I'm afraid he might come after me if I told somebody."

Worried she might dissociate upon the stress of this realization, I said "It's okay, Cindy. We don't have to do anything with that information right now. All you know is you saw the face of someone you think may have been involved. Fortunately, nobody was shot. The police and the school are handling the investigation and doing what needs to be done to secure the school. You don't have any concrete evidence, and nobody is blaming you for this. People only want for you to be okay and return to yourself again. Take that in and stay present here with me."

Cindy pleaded, "Okay. Don't tell nobody. You don't have to tell anybody, do you?"

"No. Not unless you tell me there is a current situation where someone's life is being threatened," I told her.

"No. I don't know about anything. And, you're right, I don't even know if that guy did it. He doesn't go to my school. I just knew he was with a gang and I heard a gang started this. So, I'm not sure. I'm not talking to him and he's heard I can't remember anything."

In the coming months, the police did arrest the offenders. Fortunately, the person Cindy thought was involved was not part of the shooting. Turns out, he came to watch the basketball game and see Cindy cheerlead. She still kept her distance from him and got more involved with her church. Her church community was very supportive and gave her and her family the sense of safety and stability they needed. Community is a very important part of recovery when violence affects an entire group of people. I discuss this next in Chapter 13, Combat Trauma, as well as in Chapter 14, Post-Traumatic Growth.

13

Combat Trauma

The devastating effects of combat trauma drove the psychiatric community to create a diagnosis for post-traumatic stress disorder (PTSD) in 1980. Prior to this, symptoms of flashbacks, hypervigilance, nightmares, and avoidance were described as "shell-shock" or "war neurosis" and viewed as a weakness in soldiers. One of the reasons the military was reluctant to embrace the diagnosis is because most combat soldiers don't develop PTSD. The United States Department of Veterans Affairs (2018) estimates that only 11 to 20 percent of combat veterans meet the full diagnostic criteria of PTSD symptoms. Yet the VA does acknowledge the stressors of war can contribute to other emotional issues such as depression, anxiety, insomnia, substance abuse, and readjustment difficulties.

Although the VA has come a long way in recognizing the legitimacy of PTSD, veterans and military personnel can still be reluctant to admit to it. In their article "The Darker Side of Military Healthcare," Russell, Schaubel, and Figley (2018) report that there is still a stigma associated with mental health issues in the military. Admitting that one has a problem can cost a soldier his or her job, thwart an honorable discharge, and impact future benefits. In addition, the military restricts which types of treatment can be offered for PTSD. Prolonged exposure (PE) and cognitive processing therapy (CPT) are still considered the "gold standards" of treatment by the VA. In recent years, the VA has also approved eye movement desensitization and reprocessing (EMDR), but veterans often have to go outside the VA to find an EMDR clinician.

Desensitizing soldiers to sensory reminders of war is an important component of PTSD treatment. But, veterans report they are far more disturbed by the moral injuries of war. The inability to save a comrade's life, remorse over killing people, feeling unappreciated by society, and the lack of support from the government are deeper demons that keep them awake at night. In this chapter, I'll share examples of how to use memory reconsolidation to treat combat trauma. But first, I'd like to share a cautionary tale about the dangers of rigidly following a manualized treatment protocol in lieu of attuning to your client's deeper emotional needs.

THE PROBLEM WITH MANUALIZED THERAPIES

In his book, *Evil Hours: A Biography of Post-Traumatic Stress Disorder,* David J. Morris (2016) reported how an overly manualized approach to treating PTSD worsened his symptoms and fed his sense of isolation and despair. Morris, a former US Marine infantry officer, developed PTSD after covering the Iraq war as a journalist between the years 2004 and 2007.

Upon returning from the war, Morris felt depressed, but didn't think he had PTSD. Yet when an explosion scene in a movie triggered a terrifying flashback, he reached out to the VA for help. After several weeks of completing paperwork and intake interviews, he was finally referred to an eight-week research study at the VA that was using prolonged exposure (PE) therapy to treat PTSD.

Morris said that, to avoid tainting the study, his VA counselor rigidly stuck to the PE manual and did very little to establish a personal relationship with him. The PE manual required Morris to begin recounting his traumatic memories in the third session, with little preparation other than a diaphragmatic breathing exercise. Morris left this session feeling very upset and anxious, but his counselor assured him the anxiety would remit if he stuck with the PE protocol. Unfortunately, things got worse. Morris professed:

"After a month of therapy and telling the story of my close call in Baghdad roughly 100 times, I began to have more trouble sleeping. Eventually I broke down altogether and was unable to read, write, or leave the house." He also became more angry and aggressive, describing an incident in which he stabbed his cell phone several times with a knife when it failed to dial out one day.

Morris talked to his VA counselor about the problems he was having with PE and asked if they could try another approach. Morris told him, *"Talking about a single incident with an improvised explosive device (IED) doesn't capture the reality of living under fear of constant threat and feeling like no one cared in the slightest when I got home."* He implored his counselor to take him out of the study, so he could use his therapy sessions to process his feelings of loneliness and isolation.

Instead of attuning to his client's feelings, his VA counselor insisted his painful emotions would resolve on their own if Morris stuck with the PE protocol. Morris opted to drop out of the PE study and joined a group utilizing cognitive processing therapy (CPT). Morris liked CPT better because it gave him tools for managing intrusive, negative thoughts. But he found the assigned homework worksheets impractical. At the end of his therapy, he realized it wasn't the CPT tools that helped him as much as being with a group of people who seemed to understand and genuinely care about him.

Morris's experience underscores that our attunement with our clients is still at the heart of trauma therapy. Even as I share examples of how to reconsolidate memories with RECON, the steps aren't meant to be followed like a rigid protocol. Work the steps into heartfelt conversations with your clients and adapt the interventions to their needs.

Reconsolidating survivor's guilt

Survivor's guilt can cripple a soldier as badly as missing limbs, disfiguring burns, and other injuries. In his book *On Killing*, Lieutenant Colonel Dave Grossman (2009) explains: *"A combat soldier seems to feel a deep sense of responsibility and accountability for what he sees around him . . . every enemy dead is a human being he has killed, and every friendly dead is a comrade for whom he is responsible."* It's difficult to release that responsibility once a soldier gets home.

Patrick was an Iraq war veteran who experienced debilitating flashbacks interfering with his ability to work, drive, and even play with his children. Patrick longed to enjoy his children, but when he played with them they would scream with laughter and excitement. Unfortunately, their screams triggered flashbacks from the war when he had heard people screaming in pain. The memory that haunted him most was an incident in which he witnessed his platoon leader's Humvee being blown up by an IED. Patrick was stuck in the gunner position in a Humvee traveling behind his leader's vehicle and could not get out. He attempted to get the driver of his Humvee to call the medevac helicopter, but the driver had gone into shock and wasn't responding.

Eventually Patrick was able to revive the driver and get medevac on the radio. But he felt guilty over not being able help his comrades and platoon leader sooner. Hearing screams, seeing fire, or smelling smoke brought him right back into the helplessness and horror he felt during the incident. The flashbacks were so bad that he traveled with a service dog named Brandy who was trained to sense when Patrick was on the verge of a flashback. She was trained to clear other people away from him, then lick his hand or face to orient him back to the present moment.

Prior to reconsolidating this memory, Patrick and I spent a few sessions getting to know one another and working on emotional regulation skills. Patrick's favorite tool was the Breath-Symbol Imagery I shared in Chapter 7, Instill Hope and Empowerment. He chose the symbolic image of a crane because it symbolized peace and resilience for him.

Along with this breathing exercise, Patrick and I also practiced grounding techniques to help him stay oriented to the present moment. By the fourth session, Patrick felt ready to reprocess the memory. I invited him to bring his service dog Brandy for added support and grounding.

Reconsolidating the memory of an IED explosion

At the beginning of our reconsolidation session, I invited Patrick to spend a few minutes grounding himself and using slow, paced breathing while he imagined his crane. When he signaled to me he was ready, I asked him to recall one moment of the memory and briefly describe any images, sensations, or feelings that came up as he recalled it.

Patrick recalled the image of his platoon leader's truck exploding and rolling over after hitting an IED. When I asked what sensations and feelings he was noticing in his body, he choked. "I realize I'm holding my breath right now and I feel like I can't move." Before we went further, I invited him to open his eyes, take a deep breath, and pet Brandy to remind himself where he was. Patrick took a deep breath and scratched Brandy's ears. She licked his hand gently, then he looked at me and said "Okay, I'm back now."

Next, we moved to Step 2 of the RECON process to explore Patrick's negative beliefs about the event. He frowned, "I felt useless and like I failed my platoon leader. He was like a brother to me. I wish I'd been in that vehicle, not him. The military suffered a great loss that day."

Before going any further, I wanted to get a sense of Patrick's spiritual beliefs about death. I asked, "What do you believe happens after people die?"

Patrick: "I'm a Christian. I believe they go to Heaven."

Therapist: "So, do you believe your platoon leader is in Heaven?"
I asked?

Patrick (looking confused and shaking his head): "What? He didn't die!"

Therapist: "He survived? The way you described it, I thought he'd died."

Patrick (chuckling): "No—he lost his legs and it took him months to recover from third-degree burns, but he is alive and living in Texas. I heard he is doing pretty well and has three different kinds of prosthetics: a set for running, a set for everyday activities, and a set for playing basketball! My buddy and I are going to go to visit him this summer. That's one reason I want to get over this PTSD. I don't want him to see me like this."

Therapist: "Wow! What would he say if you told him this event was still haunting you?"

Patrick: "He wouldn't want me to be troubled by it anymore. In fact, he'd probably give me crap if he thought I was still torn up over this. He'd tell me to move on so I could be a good father to my girls. He'd reassure me that I did what I could under the circumstances."

Even though Patrick intellectually understood that his platoon leader hadn't died, the implicit memory network that held the traumatic memory stopped at the point Patrick felt helpless and thought his leader had died. To help Patrick create a new meaning experience to elicit his desired beliefs, I suggested he finish the story in a new place, showing his mind that his platoon leader survived and wasn't blaming him for the incident.

Patrick closed his eyes and vividly imagined these scenes for several minutes. He visualized visiting his platoon leader in Texas and telling him that he was sorry he couldn't have done more to help. Upon imagining this, he realized his platoon leader would tell him he handled the situation well and that there was nothing more he needed to do. Patrick also imagined his leader playing basketball with his prosthetics, which lifted his spirits. He opened his eyes and wiped a soft tear from his cheek.

He added: "Another one of our brothers didn't make it out alive, so I feel bad about him, too. But I just remembered another thing our platoon leader told us. He said that if someone loses their life to save yours, don't waste it. Honor them by living the best life you can live. That's what my buddy would tell me, too."

Patrick and I talked a little more about his comrade who passed away. I wanted to be sure we gave this man's life meaning and helped Patrick integrate positive things he wanted to remember about his relationship with him.

Helping your client avoid flashbacks when describing a memory

To finish the memory reconsolidation process, I asked Patrick to objectively describe the memory and finish the story in a new place. Patrick tensed up, looked out the window, and paused for a moment before he continued. His dog Brandy stood up and nuzzled his arm. He patted her head, then winced, "It's still hard to talk about."

"I know—take your time," I coached. "Look at Brandy, let her presence ground and comfort you, and get here with us for a moment. Look around the room to remind yourself where you are right now. You're not in Iraq. There's no explosion. See your commanding officer in Texas telling you he's okay now and that you *did* help him by getting medevac on the radio."

Following my cues, Patrick regained his sense of presence and nodded. "Yes, okay. I was riding in a gunner position in a Humvee behind my platoon leader's Humvee on a mission we were doing in Iraq. Before we left, he warned us that there were likely to be IEDs along the road we had to travel. He wanted to be in the leading Humvee because he could recognize IEDs better than we could. I remember him now pointing out one to us and driving around it.

"But later his vehicle hit an IED that was better disguised. The sound of the explosion was so loud it was almost deafening. The ground shook, and I fell backwards as debris flew toward me. I managed to pull myself up and that's when I heard the ear-piercing screams for help. I saw somebody was trapped underneath the truck. I panicked and tried to get out of the vehicle, but I couldn't. The driver of my Humvee passed out and I kicked him in the head to wake him up. That sounds kind of mean, but he didn't respond to anything else. He finally came to consciousness and got medevac on the radio, and we waited for what seemed like forever.

Patrick grimaced and choked, "I still remember the stench of the smoke and burning . . . um . . . you know . . . skin."

Realizing he was starting to relive the moment, I gently nodded and said, "I know that must have been a horrifying experience, Patrick. So notice that and get back here with me and Brandy. Is there another smell you could tune into in this room right now that is very different from that smell?"

Patrick sniffed, looked around, and said, "Yes, I think I smell a peppermint candle in here or something like that?"

"Yes, that's right! I have a peppermint-scented candle on my desk. Would you like to hold it or sniff it up close? Smell is the quickest way to get present and stop a flashback."

Patrick shook his head. "Yeah. That would be good. I see a beach ball in the corner of your office over there. Holding onto that beach ball might help, too."

"Yes, that's a great idea. We can even toss it back and forth as you're telling the story, if that would help."

Patrick and I tossed the ball gently back and forth to each other for a few moments until he felt himself feeling more calm and present. Then he proceeded with the story: "So, it seemed like a long time before medevac arrived, but they did get there and loaded us all into their helicopters. They discharged me, and I heard one of our men died and my platoon leader was in the intensive care unit, fighting for his life. For months, I wasn't sure if he was going to make it. But he did. He lost his legs and had massive injuries. But he survived, is home with his family, and wants to see me and my buddy this summer. He knows I did what

I could and would not want me to have regrets. He'd want me to focus on living my life and not pity him—or myself."

Fortunately, Patrick responded very well to memory reconsolidation and did not have any more flashbacks after this session. However, we continued to work on desensitizing him to potential trauma triggers. To help him tolerate being around his daughters screaming as they played, we created a hierarchy of exposure events he could practice. He began by intentionally asking his girls to giggle and exert low-volume squeals, and worked his way up to being able to tolerate louder screams as he played with them in his yard. I also suggested he carry around a pack of mints he could sniff when he was around triggering smells like smoke or the scent of barbecued meat. Smells can activate a memory quickly, but countering the undesirable smell with a pleasant smell can quickly disrupt the memory, too.

Honestly, I was surprised how quickly Patrick reconsolidated his memories. Part of the reason may have been because he had secure attachment with no prior trauma. But reconsolidating traumatic memories was just one aspect of his treatment. Patrick had a traumatic brain injury (TBI) caused by the blast from the IED that left him with headaches, difficulty concentrating, and problems with short-term memory. Because I am not a TBI expert, I referred him back to his psychologist at the VA to address these issues. His VA psychologist also worked with Patrick on readjusting to civilian life, restoring social bonds, and finding a sense of meaning and purpose after military life.

Nightmares of the dead

While Patrick felt guilt over not being able to protect his comrades, my client Jeff felt remorse because he was such an efficient killer. He was part of a special operations unit in Afghanistan that carried out stealth missions to take out terrorist cells and high-value Taliban targets. As much as Jeff believed his missions were worthwhile, he had nightmares about the men he had killed. Jeff was particularly disturbed by intrusive images of a young Taliban fighter, no more than 14 or 15 years old, whom he had killed at close range. Jeff explained, "The boy was stationed as a sentry, guarding a passage to a compound we were targeting. I had to kill him with a knife, quickly and quietly, so we could carry out the mission. He died in my arms. Now I can't stop dreaming of his face."

Grossman (2009) asserts that humans, like most animals, are not wired to want to kill their own species. He describes studies during World War II by Army Brigadier General S. L. A. Marshall that revealed only 15 to 20 percent of American riflemen would actually fire at the enemy on the front lines. The other 80 percent opted to take intimidating postures and fire above the enemies' heads, hoping the enemy would retreat so they wouldn't have to shoot another human. This wasn't just an American phenomenon: Soldiers from other countries had the same reluctance to kill their fellow man. Grossman says we can trace the resistance to kill throughout history.

When a combat soldier does kill, it is not driven by political ideology, vengeance, or fear—it's driven by the attachment bond to one's "band of brothers." Soldiers don't relish the thought of having to kill another human being, but they loathe failing their beloved comrades more. Protecting and preserving the survival of the group is primary.

Jeff agreed that when he was ordered to kill the young boy, he was only focused on completing his mission and protecting his brothers. But, he remembered feeling "pumped up and almost high" after the mission and was ashamed he could feel elated after people died.

Grossman reports that feeling exalted after killing an enemy in combat is not unusual and is one of the five stages of killing. The stages he's observed are: 1) concern about killing; 2) the act of killing; 3) exhilaration after killing; 4) remorse over killing; and 5) rationalization and acceptance. During the concern stage, soldiers wonder if they will actually be able to kill the enemy and fear they may let their comrades down. Soldiers enter Stage 2 when they are actually confronted with the demand to fire on the enemy. For the properly conditioned soldier, Grossman says the act of killing is usually done reflexively and is over very quickly. Because of the rush of adrenaline needed to survive combat, soldiers can feel a sense of exhilaration shortly after completing a kill, or mission. This is usually followed by feelings of remorse, revulsion, and even nausea. Close-range killing in which the enemy is no longer a distant, abstract target, but a warm-blooded human being whom the soldier can see, smell, hear, and touch, creates the most contrition. The final stage, rationalization and acceptance, can be a lifelong process as the soldier attempts to reconcile the moral injuries of war with his sense of duty to his comrades and country.

When I reviewed these stages of killing with Jeff, he expressed relief. "I'm glad to hear that's normal, I was worried I might be a psychopath or something."

To reconsolidate the memory of this incident, Jeff and I explored what he'd like to believe about himself. He said, "I'd like to believe that if there was another way we could have carried out the mission, we would have. But I feel sorry for that kid. I know he was just doing what he thought was right for his country. Or maybe he didn't have a choice. Maybe he didn't want to be a Taliban fighter, but had to do it to escape poverty or something."

"Tell me more about the nightmares you've been having," I encouraged. "I want to fully understand what you are experiencing and what the dream means to you."

Jeff said the dream is very similar to the actual event where he killed the sentry. He explained that his unit was planning to raid a compound where a high-value target was hiding. Jeff was ordered to take out a sentry who was guarding one of the passageways. He estimated that the sentry was about six feet tall, but he couldn't make out the man's face at first since it was nighttime. Jack sneaked up on the man from behind and stabbed him in his lower back through the kidney. As the man fell back into Jeff's arms, he saw young man's face and realized he'd killed a teenage boy. In the dream, the boy looks at Jeff and asks, "Why did you kill me? I'm on your side." Jeff said he's so shocked he can't say anything to the boy in the dream. The boy dies, then Jeff wakes up in a cold sweat.

Compassionately, I asked, "What would you like to say to him?"

Jeff shook his head, "I don't know. I guess I want to tell him I'm sorry."

"Okay. What does it mean to you in the dream when he says he's on your side?" I asked.

Jeff answered, "I think it means that we're both caught up in a game we didn't want to play. He's doing what he thought was right for his country, just like I'm doing what I think is right for mine."

I invited Jeff to rescript the nightmare by telling the boy what he wanted to say.

He closed his eyes and moaned, "I'm sorry, kid. I didn't want to have to do this. I know you're fighting for your brothers like I'm fighting for mine. I don't hate you. I'm sorry for whatever happened that got you in this mess. May you be at peace. May you go with God, or Allah, or whatever you believe in."

I suggested Jeff imagine what the boy would say back to him, having a broader perspective of the war now, and speaking to him from a place of compassion and understanding. Jeff was silent for a few moments, then said, "I'm imagining being able to stay with him and comfort him until he passes. As he is taking his last breath, he looks relieved, and I feel like he is telling me that 'he's free now.' Maybe I'm just imagining that to make myself feel better."

"Well, check it out," I offered. Run back through the dream again and imagine him cussing you out or something. See how it plays out, or if there is anything else you want say." Jeff closed his eyes and ran back through the dream in his mind again. His face flushed and his chin began to tremble as he cried, "No. It's strange but I feel like he understands that I wish I didn't have to take his life. I'm sorry, kid. I know you were just doing what you thought was right for your country. I hope you find peace."

I leaned in and offered softly, "Now hear him say back to you: *"And I know that you were doing what you thought was right for your country. It's okay. I'm free. May you be at peace."*

Jeff took a deep breath as he listened to my words, then let out a slow exhalation. He wiped his eyes with his hands and nodded, "Thank you. I don't know how it all works in the afterlife, but I hope he is free and at peace."

I looked deeply into Jeff's eyes and said, "Sounds like your experience caused you to value life even more than before you went to war. And that you understand how someone could become misguided and think terrorism is a way to fight for their country. You didn't murder this man. You were charged with protecting innocent lives from misguided violence. It's an admirable duty and not one that many could carry out. I sincerely thank you for your service."

Jeff nodded, "Thank you. That's all we want to hear as veterans. We don't want to tell everyone the details of the horrors we see in war. We just want people to appreciate our efforts to lay our lives on the line to protect yours."

While I hate war and don't always agree with the decisions our government makes, I think it is important to convey our appreciation for these women and men in uniform who courageously risked their lives. Our recognition and appreciation for their service helps veterans integrate back into a society that seems oblivious to their plight.

Morris (2016) confessed he struggled with a "palpable sense of not belonging," more than he struggled with his traumatic memories. Not only did he feel separated from his fellow troops, who he'd come to love like brothers, but he also had difficulty relating to civilians. He felt angry that no one seemed to care or be concerned about the war. He states, *"Part of me needed to be reminded that the war had been real, not just something I saw when I closed my eyes. I needed to know that the experience had meaning and that the death I had seen really mattered."*

As I mentioned earlier, Morris achieved this by connecting to others who had been through similar experiences in his cognitive processing therapy (CPT) group. But, Morris writes that he experienced another level of healing through writing his book and stumbling across post-traumatic growth research by Calhoun and Tedeschi (2008). Contemplating how he could grow from his war experience helped him clarify his priorities and gave him renewed appreciation of life. I'll discuss the characteristics of post-traumatic growth next in Chapter 14, and how you can lead your clients toward it.

PHASE III

Facilitate Post-Traumatic Growth

14

Post-Traumatic Growth

C an trauma have a positive impact on people? It seems so. Groundbreaking research by psychologists Calhoun and Tedeschi (2008) revealed more than half of trauma survivors believed their adverse experiences prompted them to create better lives for themselves. Tedeschi and Calhoun began their studies interviewing widows between the ages of 50 and 80 years old, then interviewed people who had disabilities or debilitating illnesses, and then studied people who had been in combat, raped, abused, tortured, or survived natural disasters. The results were consistent: at least 30 to 90 percent of the thousands of people they interviewed reported positive changes that occurred in their lives after trauma.

Calhoun and Tedeschi coined the term *post-traumatic growth* (PTG) to describe this type of personal development, and they weren't the only researchers observing this phenomenon. In 1976, William Sledge, a military psychiatrist who is now a Yale professor, was deeply moved by the frequency that former prisoners of war (POWs) told him they treasured life more because of their captivity experience. These POWs didn't deny their pain, but focused on how they were using their experience to make their lives better. Similarly, positive psychology researchers Martin Seligman (2011) and Stephen Joseph (2011) were studying people who seemed stronger after facing adversity. Seligman and Joseph both noticed that people who experienced PTG engaged in approach-focused coping rather than avoidance-focused coping. In other words they intentionally sought out opportunities to make positive changes in their lives.

So, while the PTG research is encouraging, researchers like Mancini (2016) suggest we need to be cautious in our interpretation of the data. He critiques the fact that PTG research is based on a person's self-report, not necessarily observable behaviors in a person's life. Moreover he's observed that PTG usually doesn't occur until one to two years after the event. Calhoun and Tedeschi (2008) agree, and emphasize that PTG results from the *struggle* to redefine our beliefs, and rebuild our lives, after trauma. It's through the struggle that we forge new strengths and skills.

That said, PTG should not be pushed as a goal of treatment. We need to be sensitive to the pain of our clients and avoid prematurely suggesting silver linings. Our role is to walk supportively alongside our clients and gently plant seeds along the way to nurture their growth. Identifying your client's desired beliefs during the process of memory reconsolidation is one way you may have already planted seeds for growth. In this chapter, I'll share additional ways to recognize and nurture positive change in your clients after trauma.

FIVE CHARACTERISTICS OF POST-TRAUMATIC GROWTH

Calhoun and Tedeschi (2008) identified five areas where survivors reported positive changes in their lives after trauma: 1) greater sense of personal strength; 2) openness to new possibilities; 3) greater appreciation for life; 4) spiritual development; and 5) enhanced relationships. It's good to notice when your clients are displaying these positive changes and applaud them for it. They may not recognize these changes, and it bolsters their sense of hope and confidence to hear you point them out. To avoid minimizing their pain, I usually say something like, "I realize that going through that traumatic event is not the way you wanted to get that (strength, appreciation, spiritual insight, and so on), but you got it, and that is to your credit."

Greater sense of personal strength

Surviving trauma requires personal strength in and of itself. But, when clients come to treatment, they're so overwhelmed with feelings of helplessness, anxiety, and distress that they have trouble recognizing their inner resources. Even if your client doesn't feel strong, you can point out that it takes a lot of strength to go on living when you are feeling tired and defeated.

Clients certainly feel more vulnerable after trauma. But Calhoun and Tedeschi (2008) found the struggle to accept their vulnerability paradoxically helps clients develop more courage and endurance. Over time, survivors report a greater sense of confidence in their ability to handle life's difficulties. Prior problems can seem like minor annoyances after surviving a crisis. For example, a study by Mancini, Littleton, and Grills (2015) reported that 13 percent of survivors of the 2007 Virginia Tech mass shooting actually found they felt less anxious and depressed than they did before the shooting. As horrific as the shooting was, it helped them put things in perspective. To help your client identify strengths they forged through adversity, Tedeschi and Moore (2016) recommend asking the following questions:

1. What did you do to survive your experience? How did you cope?
2. What were some things that seemed difficult before the trauma that now seem easier for you, or seem easier for you to handle than people who haven't gone through trauma?
3. What advice would you give to others facing a similar situation?

Positive psychology researchers Chris Peterson and Martin Seligman (2004) developed another tool you can use to help your clients identify their inner assets called the VIA Survey of Character Strengths. This survey assesses 24 character strengths across 6 areas: 1) wisdom and knowledge; 2) courage; 3) humanity and love; 4) justice; 5) temperance; and 6) transcendence. You can invite your client to complete the full or brief version of the VIA character strengths survey at Martin Seligman's website: http://authentichappiness.org. In his book *Flourish*, Seligman (2011) asserts that when a person recognizes these innate strengths, they can use them more intentionally to overcome challenges and find more fulfillment in life.

To share an example of how exploring your client's hidden strengths can improve self-worth, I'll refer back to my client Pamela, whose story I shared in Chapter 10, Childhood Physical Abuse. Although Pamela's personal life had been fraught with chaos, she was very effective in her job as a lead engineer and managed a small group of employees at her company. After taking the VIA Survey of Character Strengths, Pamela, discovered her top five strengths included: 1) genuineness and honesty; 2) fairness and equity; 3) leadership; 4) critical thinking and open-mindedness; and 5) prudence and discretion.

When I asked Pamela how she thought she developed these strengths, she realized they grew partially from being the oldest sibling in an abusive home. Her younger siblings looked to her as their leader, nurturer, and protector. She viewed her leadership role with her employees somewhat as she did her role with her siblings. Determined not to use her authority to control and manipulate others, Pamela was fair-minded, open to her employees' ideas, and used positive reinforcement to motivate them. As a result, her team was very productive and demonstrated respect for her. Pamela also realized her abuse experience caused her to be very cognizant of safety and to make decisions carefully, rather than impulsively. These skills ensured her engineering designs were safe, compliant with building codes, and structurally sound.

I commended Pamela for developing these leadership and critical thinking skills, stating: "You created something good out of something that was so horrible. That is to your credit." Looking at the strengths she developed in spite of her abuse experience helped her feel more competent. As Pamela began to embrace these qualities, her tendency to see herself as a powerless victim began to shift toward an identity of empowered survivor.

Openness to new possibilities

When the world as you knew it was destroyed, it opens the door for new possibilities. Traumatized clients may feel depressed because prior life goals have been derailed by the trauma, or activities they once found pleasurable no longer have appeal. While we must validate our client's feelings of disappointment, we can gently lead them to look for other opportunities life might hold for them. When exploring other options for clients, I ask them to look at the way trauma changed their priorities and values first. I notice which issues and topics bring up the most energy for them—either in a way that excites them, or even in a way that angers them. Bill O'Hanlon (2013) suggests people will find their passion when they examine where they feel "blissed or pissed." Interests that "bliss you out" include anything that fascinates you, gives you energy, or uplifts your heart and soul. Issues that "piss you off" signal injustices in the world that you feel compelled to address or correct. To help your clients explore new possibilities, passions, or missions, ask:

1. Are there any goals, activities, or interests that have lost their appeal since the traumatic event? If, so why do you think they aren't as satisfying to you?
2. What new interests, values, or priorities have you noticed as a result of surviving your experience? Is there a way you could make time or space in your life for these things now?

Dixon, my client who struggled with road rage and whom I discussed in Chapters 1 and 12, felt bitter after his sister's death. He noticed more negative aspects of life than good, and seemed angry at the world. Instead of treating Dixon's anger as a shameful symptom, I suggested his anger indicated that he had more appreciation for life than most people. I offered, "Your anger seems to be your attempt to get people to slow down, drive more carefully, and not take their lives or their families for granted." Dixon agreed and welcomed my redeeming interpretation of his highway outbursts.

"I wonder if there is a more constructive way to fight for your cause?" I posited. "Candace Lightner created Mothers Against Drunk Driving (MADD) after her daughter was killed by a drunk driver. I wonder if it would be worthwhile to share your story with the students whom you teach? I think they would listen to you, and you might actually save some lives." Dixon balked at my suggestion, stating he preferred to keep his personal life private from his students.

When he returned for our next session, Dixon sheepishly confessed that he shared his story with his students, but not in a way that was constructive. Several students in his class had been bragging about "getting wasted" and then driving around town. In response, he yelled: "You idiots! You could've killed somebody!" Then he ripped his shirt open to show them his scars and asked if they wanted to look like him.

Oh no, I thought, *I've pushed him too far.* "My gosh," I replied, struggling to project calm. "I can understand why that upset you. Do you think it made an impression on them?"

"Well, yeah," he said. "Everyone just fell silent and looked at me like I was crazy. Now I feel like I have to tell them my story so they don't think I'm a nut job. I talked to the principal this afternoon, and he's all for it."

Over the next few weeks, Dixon scripted his talk and practiced giving it in our sessions. Initially, he presented his talk only to the students in his classrooms and was surprised how respectful and appreciative they were. Many thanked him for sharing his story, and several pledged that they'd never drink and drive again. His principal commented that his passion for his topic, dry wit, and ability to relate to young people made him a compelling speaker. This gave Dixon the confidence to speak to the entire school at a general assembly meeting.

He gave his presentation TED talk style and included pictures of his sister, the burned car, and photos of his debriding treatments. He even flashed a setup shot of himself screaming out his window at another driver and said, "At first I tried to educate the world about drunk driving through my road rage. Then I realized the reason I'm mad is because I care." He gripped the podium and looked out at his young audience. "I care about all of you. And I don't want you to end up losing *your* sister or brother, or living with horrible scars like I do."

When he finished, the students shot up from their seats to applaud him. Word spread fast as they told others what an enormous impact his talk had had on them. He received scores of emails and letters from students and parents. Before he knew it, he was getting invited to speak at other schools and organizations. Channeling his pleas for safe, sober driving into these talks not only decreased his outbursts on the road, but it also gave him a renewed sense of purpose in his life.

Of course, pursuing new paths after trauma doesn't require this big an action. Your clients may find small ways to make time for activities that reflect renewed priorities and a greater appreciation for life, as I discuss in the following section.

Greater appreciation for life

Surviving loss causes many people to slow down and appreciate what they have more. Having been confronted with pain and grief, they are better able to savor small moments of joy, beauty, love, or peace. With stark awareness of life's fragility, they stopped putting dreams on hold and made more time to pursue pleasurable interests and pastimes. After one of my aunts was diagnosed with terminal cancer and told she only had six months to live, she took a cross-country trip to visit parts of the United States that she'd never seen. Interestingly, her health improved after her trip, and her doctor encouraged her to keep traveling. She had some of the best times of her life on these trips and believed these joyful experiences extended her life several more years.

Similarly, one of my clients cultivated an appreciation of nature after she survived a tornado. She made a point to enjoy being outside when the weather was nice, and expressed wonder at the ability of nature to revitalize itself after disaster. She appreciated her neighbors more and found a deeper sense of community in the process of rebuilding their neighborhood. To help your clients explore areas where they may have developed a deeper sense of appreciation, simply ask:

1. Is there anything that you value more because of what you have been through?
2. How can you make more time to attend to this value or interest now?

Patrick, one of the combat veterans I discussed in Chapter 13, felt ruined when PTSD and a mild traumatic brain injury (TBI) ended his military career. He felt encouraged when his PTSD symptoms remitted and he entered a cognitive rehabilitation program to redress impairments caused by the TBI. He'd hoped to find a civilian job after finishing his rehabilitation program, but employment opportunities were scarce in his community.

Patrick was beginning to lose hope when his wife suggested he be a stay-at-home dad. She had a good job and thought it would take a good deal of stress off her if he could tend to their two children and the household responsibilities. At first, Patrick refused. The thought of not being the provider of his family made him feel weak. But, his psychologist at the Department of Veterans Affairs encouraged him, pointing out that raising children was not for "sissies." Patrick contacted me months later to let me know he was actually enjoying being a stay-at-home dad. He was surprised how busy his new role kept him and cherished the time with his daughters. Being gone for two tours of duty in the military, he'd missed a few years of their lives. Before his trauma, he would have never considered this option.

Inviting clients to notice three things each day for which they feel grateful can instill hope and decrease despair after trauma too. Studies have shown that keeping gratitude journals or writing gratitude letters improves or reduces depression and anxiety, not just during the moment of writing, but for several weeks after recording one's gratitude (Sheldon & Lyubomirsky, 2006; Wong et al., 2018). Furthermore, studies have found that expressing appreciation or receiving gratitude from others increases positive brain activity in the anterior cingulate cortex and medial prefrontal cortex (Hoffman, 2015; Wong et al., 2018).

When suggesting a gratitude activity, I present it as a way for clients to comfort themselves, instill hope, and decrease feelings of despair. So clients don't feel as though I'm minimizing their pain by suggesting they be grateful, I recommend they divide their journal into two columns with the headings: "What was difficult today" and "What went well today." This way they can give voice to their struggles and simultaneously recognize where they are making progress. For clients who feel angry, I might call the gratitude activity a "fighting back" activity, suggesting it's a way to turn the tables on trauma, reclaim their power, and affirm their lives are still worthwhile.

Jenny Lawson (2015) humorously demonstrates this concept in her book *Furiously Happy*. She became so angry at her anxiety and depression that she decided she was going to be *furiously happy* to spite it. Her book is about accepting her mental illness and going out of her way to do joyful, humorous, and eccentric activities. She states, "It's not a cure for mental illness . . . it's a weapon, designed to counter it. It's a way to take back some of the joy that's robbed from you when you're crazy" (p. 6). If you haven't read *Furiously Happy*, I highly recommend it. Lawson's hilarious stories and spunky attitude have inspired my clients as much as any serious self-help book.

Spiritual development

Many survivors cope with trauma by strengthening their religious faith. Even when trauma causes someone to question their spiritual beliefs, over time they may find the experience helps them cultivate deeper spiritual insights and maturity. In his book, *When Bad Things Happen to Good People*, Rabbi Harold Kushner (1981) wrote that the death of his 13-year-old son compelled him to find an explanation for suffering. Before his son became ill, Kushner thought God protected faithful people from certain tragedies. But, after his son died, Kushner questioned his beliefs. He couldn't understand why God failed to protect his family, especially after he'd dedicated his life to Him. After months of soul-searching, Kushner concluded that God doesn't cause tragedy—living in a random universe where people are given free will leads to accidents, illness, and suffering. Kushner surmised that God offers us His divine love and compassion as ways to cope with the inevitable pain and loss we will experience as human beings.

My client Craig came to a similar conclusion, but through a different spiritual path. He is the client whom I discussed in Chapter 11, Relational and Attachment Trauma. If you recall, Craig's father abused him, his mother died of cancer, and his oldest son died in a tragic accident. After these losses, he abandoned his Christian faith and identified himself as an atheist. He didn't believe a "just and benevolent God" would reward "cruel" people like his father and prematurely end the lives of "good" people like his mother and son.

Craig, however, did find solace in practicing meditation and became interested in Buddhist philosophy. He began listening to podcasts on Buddhist thought and voraciously read books on mindfulness practices. In one of our sessions, he commented, "As a child I was taught in church that if you're a good person, then life will be good to you. But that's just not how it works. The Buddhists understand that suffering is a part of life. It's universal, it's not personal."

The other Buddhist tenet that Craig found helpful was the concept of impermanence. If he was having a bad day, or experiencing physical pain, he would remind himself that it would eventually shift and change. Likewise, this belief helped him notice and appreciate good moments in his life more. He came to accept loss as a part of life, stating, "We're not guaranteed how long we're going to have someone in our lives. Instead of feeling resentful, I am learning how to feel grateful for the time I had with my mother and my son."

Witnessing these changes in Craig was amazing because he seemed so cynical when we began working together. But these changes took time. As we explored existential and spiritual questions together, I mostly served as a sounding board and let him work out his own beliefs. Ultimately, it is your client's decision to forge a belief system that makes sense for him. As long as a client's beliefs aren't causing harm, I don't interfere too much with their process. In *The Posttraumatic Growth Workbook*, Tedeschi and Moore (2016) echo this sentiment, advising, "The key is to seek your own truth for how to live life well."

Enhanced relationships

Trauma can bring people closer to one another. Although Craig had an avoidant attachment style, the loss of his oldest son, estrangement from his daughter, and the months when his youngest son was missing helped him value his relationships more. When they located his youngest son, he was admitted to a substance abuse treatment center. Family meetings at the treatment center gave Craig a new opportunity to get closer to his surviving children. Too grief-stricken to control his emotions, he began to express his fears and feelings to his family more honestly. His willingness to drop his guard was the first step in healing these relationships.

Trauma may also lead clients to develop new relationships they wouldn't have considered previously. After her son died from suicide, Lydia, the client I discussed in Chapter 12, Traumatic Grief and Loss, became closer to her daughter and her son's partner. Before Logan died, Lydia's daughter had distanced from her. She felt like Lydia was always enabling Logan and resented her. After Logan died, Lydia made more effort to understand her daughter's feelings and work out their conflicts, and they became closer. Lydia also found her son's partner to be a wonderful support and friend. He could understand her grief in a way her other friends could not, had a great sense of humor, and enjoyed going to plays and concerts with her. She was delighted to have him as a new close friend.

Trauma can help clients enhance relationships by teaching them how to accept help from others, or feel fulfilled by helping other people. Cindy, the client with dissociative amnesia whom I discussed in Chapter 12, became more involved in her church after recovering her memory. Before the trauma, she'd lost interest in church activities and had begun to experiment with drugs and alcohol. After the trauma, she realized how dangerous the people she'd been hanging around really were. Her old friends from church came by regularly to encourage her and support the family. The church was taking steps to address the violence in the community and help young people get out of gangs, or avoid getting into gangs in the first place. Cindy and her family became very involved in this program and found it empowering to join with others to make their community safer.

The therapy relationship itself helps clients improve relationships outside the therapy room. Being with someone with whom they can confess their shame, guilt, fear, and anger without judgment can help clients gather the courage to be more open with others. But, what do you do with clients whose attachment trauma makes it difficult for them to develop healthy relationships? Even if you are able to heal memories of past attachment traumas, these clients still seek relationship guidance because they weren't taught healthy interpersonal skills. I'll address ways you can help your clients build healthy relationships next, in Chapter 15.

15

Healthy Relationship Skills

Even when clients understand how traumatic experiences shaped their beliefs about themselves and other people, they still need help implementing healthy relationship skills. Recognizing healthy boundaries, asserting themselves, and managing interpersonal conflicts can still be a challenge because these skills weren't modeled or taught in their families of origin. Moreover, the people in our client's lives may not be receptive to their new insights and behaviors. As psychologist Harriet Lerner (2014) warns in her book, *The Dance of Anger*, when one member attempts to change the "dance steps" in a relationship, it threatens established attachment bonds and creates tremendous anxiety. Uncertain of the consequences of this new dance, family members often pressure clients to "change back" to their old moves. In this chapter, I'll discuss how to help your clients develop healthier relationship skills and how they can manage inner and outer conflicts as they implement change.

MENTALIZATION AND MINDFUL
REFLECTION SKILLS

Mentalizing is the ability to understand the mental and emotional state of oneself, as well as the mental and emotional states of others (Bateman & Fonagy, 2010). Psychologist Peter Fonagy coined the term while studying people diagnosed with borderline personality disorder (BPD). He believed the interpersonal difficulties of BPD were related to attachment trauma. Without a caregiver who could accurately respond to their emotions, or help them make sense of the emotions of others, people with BPD continue to interpret interpersonal situations through the eyes of a child. Fonagy's studies demonstrated that teaching mentalization skills helped people with BPD better regulate their emotions and more accurately interpret the intentions of others (Lorenzini & Fonagy, 2013).

Mentalization is essentially a mindfulness skill. It's the ability to observe one's emotions with an open-minded, nonjudgmental attitude and express compassionate curiosity about the emotions of others. These mindful reflection skills help clients with anxious attachment be less reactive, and help clients with avoidant and disorganized attachment gently face their feelings instead of avoiding them. For example, my client Craig often changed the subject when I attempted to explore his emotions. I let this go during our first few sessions because we were still developing rapport and I wanted him to feel safe with me. Once our therapeutic alliance was stronger, I began to invite him into mindful reflection of his feelings like this:

"Craig, I noticed you changed the subject when I asked how you felt when your father criticized you. I realize that's probably an old coping pattern that served you in the past. But would it be okay for us to look at it for a moment? What did you notice inside when I asked how you felt? If you can't describe the emotion, maybe you can just notice where you felt a sensation in your body and describe that."

To help a client stay within his window of tolerance while exploring strong emotions, guide him to do it in small doses. For example, you could invite a client to stop and notice his feelings for 5 to 10 seconds, then do grounding activity or talk about something lighter for a minute. Then, you can invite him to attune to his feelings again for 10 seconds, and so on. Facing discomfort in small increments makes the experience more manageable and helps your client build confidence in this ability.

As Craig became more comfortable with mindfully reflecting on his emotions, he became more aware of times he shut down emotionally, too. He realized he felt uncomfortable when his wife wanted him to sit with her and hold hands while watching television. He couldn't identify a specific emotion to describe his feelings, so I invited him to tell me what he noticed in his body when he reflected on this experience with his wife.

Craig: I feel weird in my stomach. My jaw is clenching. I want to run away.

Therapist: Mm-hmm. To understand what may be triggering this response, see what comes to mind when you say these words to yourself, *"If I sit close to her and hold her hand, then she will want _____ , or it will mean I am _____ ."*

Craig: I'm afraid she'll keep wanting more from me and I'll never be able to please her. Another part of me feels sappy for holding a girl's hand.

Therapist: Aha! Now follow that feeling back to an earlier time in your life and tell me if it reminds you of how you felt with anyone else.

Craig: My father. I could never please him and he told me I was weak if I showed emotion. But we already reprocessed those memories about him. Why am I still feeling this way?

Sometimes a longstanding emotional pattern isn't completely eradicated with memory reconsolidation because it has been reinforced for many, many years (Beckers & Kindt, 2017). Or there are other relational factors reinforcing the old pattern. As it turned out, Craig's wife had anxious attachment tendencies. His distancing triggered her fears of abandonment, causing her to cling to him or criticize him, which made him distance more. He brought her to a few sessions so I could help them understand and talk about this dynamic together. To his surprise, opening up to his wife caused her to feel more secure in their relationship. She could better tolerate giving him space, and he began to feel more comfortable opening up to her.

ASSERTIVENESS AND BOUNDARIES

Boundaries can be a real challenge for people with insecure attachment because they've had to set very rigid or very loose boundaries to survive in their families. Flexing boundaries can make clients with avoidant attachment extremely anxious. They got the message, "If I let people get close they will exploit, criticize, or reject me." In contrast, survivors with anxious and disorganized attachment got the message, "If you really loved me, you'd give up your feelings to accommodate my feelings." These clients may feel the only way they can set boundaries is to act sick, incompetent, or helpless. Or they encroach on other people's boundaries with excessive caregiving or extreme expectations of loved ones.

This was an issue with my client Mallory, whom I discussed in Chapters 4 and 10. If you recall, Mallory and her husband had grown distant in their marriage due to the demands of their children and careers. One day she was furious because her husband did not accept a phone call from her at work when she was worried about one of their children. First, I used mentalizing to help her consider alternative reasons for her husband's behavior.

Mallory: Our son Ryan was sent home because he started a food fight at school. I called my husband at work for help, and he refused to talk to me!

Therapist: Oh my goodness! I can understand why that upset you and am sorry he was not responsive in the moment. Why else do you think he wouldn't take your call?

Mallory: He doesn't care if our son flunks out of school and expects me to do all the discipline.

Therapist: Well, that's one possibility. Did he give you another explanation?

Mallory: He said he was in an "important" meeting and felt like he could address it when he got home. I told him his kids were important and he needed to rethink his priorities!

Therapist: Yes, your kids are important. I know you probably would've excused yourself from a meeting to take his call. But perhaps you are better at juggling multiple priorities than your husband is. As much as I wish he could've understood your sense of urgency, was there any advantage to waiting until he got home so he could give you his full attention?

Mallory: Yeah, I guess if he'd taken my call at work, he'd only be half listening. He did want to talk about it when he got home. But I was still angry that he blew me off, so we fought more about that than figuring out what to do with Ryan.

Assertive communication skills

Assertiveness is the ability stand up for your own needs and feelings, while respecting the needs and feelings of others. In households where children had to deny their needs or angrily act out to be recognized, assertiveness may seem like a foreign concept. While being sensitive to Mallory's feelings, I suggested we explore ways she could communicate with her husband more effectively. I use Worksheet 15.1, Communication Tips for Resolving Conflicts, to help my clients with assertiveness skills, and have included it at the end of this chapter for your use, too.

When teaching clients assertiveness skills, the general principles are to objectively describe the behavior of the other person, use "I" statements to express one's feelings, and describe our interpretation of the other person's behavior as an impression, not a fact. Additionally, it's wise to to propose a solution to the problem, otherwise the other person is likely to get defensive, or lob their own complaint back toward the client. The basic assertiveness statement I teach clients is:

"When you _____ , I feel _____ , because it gives me the impression that _____ . To avoid this misunderstanding in the future, can we _____ ?"

Mallory applied the formula this way: "When you *refuse my call at work*, I feel *angry*, because it gives me the impression *that our family is not as important as your job.* To avoid this misunderstanding in the future *can you or your secretary give me a time when you will be free to talk? That way I'll know my call is important to you.*"

Once Mallory worked out what she wanted to say to her husband, we used role-plays to practice assertiveness skills in our session. Remember—the emotional brain only learns through experience and repetition! First I played her role, while she played her husband. That way, she got the sense of how he might respond to her when she used this statement instead of accusing him of not thinking his kids were important. Then, we reversed roles, so she could rehearse her statement and get more comfortable communicating her feelings this way. At first she was skeptical and didn't think assertive communication would make any difference in her relationship. I acknowledged she could be right, but asked if she'd be willing to experiment with it for a few weeks. To her surprise, her husband was more responsive to her when she made an effort to communicate to him this way. But she also gave him Worksheet 15.1 so he could communicate more clearly and respectfully to her!

Fortunately, Mallory's husband was receptive, but some clients' family members may resist their attempts to assert themselves. Explore the risks associated with your client asserting themselves or setting new boundaries first. This way you can help them prepare for countermoves, or determine if there is a more effective way to handle a relationship problem. For example, if a client is in a physically abusive relationship, speaking up may get her hurt. Making a safety plan may be more effective than encouraging assertiveness. For clients with complex family dynamics, I recommend couples and family therapy in addition to individual therapy. I don't provide couples therapy for clients whom I am seeing individually. Traumatized clients need to feel completely safe in our therapeutic relationship, and I'm very protective of those boundaries. I am open to clients bringing a partner or family member to a session so I can provide education or get a better understanding of their dynamics. As long as they realize I can only attempt to facilitate understanding, not mediate their conflicts, then these types of family sessions can be helpful.

RESOLVE INNER CONFLICTS WITH PARTS WORK

Conceptualizing inner conflicts as a disagreement between two or more "parts" of ourselves can be useful. Most people understand the concept of parts because we use this term in our everyday language. For instance, you might say, "A part of me wants pizza for lunch, but another part of me knows it's better to have a salad." Or, we commonly hear clients say, "A part of me wants stay in this relationship, but another part wants to leave." Parts work can be used with any client, but it is especially useful for clients with disorganized attachment.

People with disorganized attachment are fraught with inner conflict in relationships. When they were children, the people they looked to for safety were the people who posed the most threat. Subsequently, their drive to attach competes with their instinct to fight, flee, freeze, or submit when they get close to people. Not only does this make their personal relationships chaotic and confusing, but it also makes securing the therapeutic relationship challenging. You can feel like you're in a constant push-pull dynamic as they alternate between vying for your attention and pushing you away, withdrawing, or becoming angry. It's tempting to write these maneuvers off as resistance, manipulation, or a personality disorder. But recognizing these behaviors as adaptive strategies that helped them cope in their families is more useful. Trauma expert Janina Fisher (2017) suggests thinking of parts as manifestations of the following survival responses:

1) *Adult parts* attend to daily self-care and work responsibilities.

2) *Attach parts* seek connection and care.

3) *Flight parts* distance or engage in escape behaviors, like addiction.

4) *Fight parts* defend, protect, but can be mistrustful, violent, or self-destructive.

5) *Freeze parts* panic, feel paralyzed, or want to hide, disappear, become invisible.

6) *Submit parts* cope by people pleasing, self-sacrificing, or becoming depressed.

I recognized all six of these parts in my client Pamela who survived severe child abuse. She did not have dissociative identity disorder, but had extreme emotional responses that could look like different personas. The part of her that went to work was an adult part who was very high-functioning and logical. Her attach part brought her to therapy seeking connection, support, and care. But when I responded warmly to her attach part, her fears of being abandoned or abused could get triggered. Her flight part reacted by distancing from me and cancelling appointments. Or a fight part would show up expressing anger, mistrust, and suspicion of my motives. Then, there were times she felt frozen, unable to make decisions or think clearly. And sometimes she exhibited submit behaviors, superficially complying with my suggestions or telling me what she thought I wanted to hear.

When one of these parts manifested in our sessions, it didn't feel like a part to Pamela. To her, it felt like a totally reasonable response based on how she was perceiving the situation at the moment. One day she began our session by lying down on the couch instead of sitting in her usual chair. She sighed, "I'm in poor girl status today. I'm probably not going to be very talkative." Then she turned away from me, covered herself with a blanket, and closed her eyes. The attach part of her was asking for my care and compassion, but another part of her was obviously shutting me out.

To navigate this dilemma I said, " I'm glad you came. But, it seems like one part of you wants to be here and another part doesn't. I'm not sure what to do. Part of me wants to understand what's bothering you, while another part gets the sense you want to be left alone. Can you help me out here?"

Pamela mumbled, "I'm sorry. I'm in poor girl status. I don't feel like talking."

My fight part wanted to confront her and wasn't in the mood for this gamey behavior. But, my therapist part realized she was exhibiting a survival strategy that probably worked for her as a child. I silently asked my fight part to be patient as I attempted to connect with Pamela again, "Okay. If you want to use our session to rest, I'll honor that today. But, when you feel like talking I want to understand what you mean by 'poor girl status,' so I know how to support you."

Pamela snapped, "Leave me alone! I told you I don't want to talk today!"

Now I was encountering *her* fight part. I imagined it's role was to protect the "poor girl" and get people off her back. I did a little mindful breathing to keep my own parts from freaking out and nervously doodled on my notepad, trying to think of what to do next.

After a few minutes of silence, Pamela rolled over and said, "I call it poor girl status because I want people to say 'Poor girl, she's having a hard time' when I feel like this. I don't want pity. I want people to realize I'm hurting so they don't expect anything from me."

Grateful she was at least willing to explore this experience, I replied "So poor girl status sounds like a way to cope when you need to step back from demands and get people to treat you with care and empathy. Am I understanding that right?"

"Yeah, but there's nobody to give me care so I want people to go away," she groaned.

"Okay, so one part wants care, but another part of you seems angry. Is the angry part's role is to protect Poor Girl from people who don't seem to care about her needs?"

Pamela nodded, "Yeah. My Poor Girl is like an orphan. But, like little orphan Annie, she has a guard dog who growls when people try to get too close. She doesn't trust people. When people get close, it's because they want something from her."

"I see. How old is this poor girl? I want to understand the best way to support her and make sure she knows I don't have any expectations of her right now. I just want to make sure she is okay," I reassured.

Pam mulled, "She feels about 7 years old. She doesn't know what she wants. She knows you want to help, but she wants you to stop asking her questions. It feels demanding."

"Okay, I can understand how questions might be annoying her. Is there another part of you that could comfort her right now? Perhaps the part of you who knew how to comfort your siblings. Could that part of you offer care and comfort to this poor girl?" Janina Fisher (2017) and Richard Schwartz (2013) both recommend guiding the client to recruit her own adult parts or inner helper parts to teach the client to self-soothe and regulate affect.

Pamela closed her eyes and said, "I see the dolphins again. I see a little dolphin who is hurt and a mama dolphin who is tending to it while the daddy dolphin protects them and makes sure nobody comes into the pod to bother them."

"I'm so glad. Feel free to explore that imagery as long as you like, Pamela. I'm right here. Let me know if there is anything I can do to support you. I'm glad you can call on these inner helpers, too. That Poor Girl sounds like she needs their understanding and care right now."

Pamela began to sob. I asked if there was something I could say or do to comfort her. She shook her head, "No. Poor Girl just needs to cry. The dolphins are helping her."

Pamela sank deeper into her imagery experience. Although it seemed to be helping her, I felt uncertain about whether this was the right thing to do. Was she at risk of dissociating? Should I be attempting to ground her and orient her to the present moment? Was this a way of avoiding other issues we should be talking about? I kept checking in every few minutes, saying gently, "Hi Pamela, I just want to check in. Let me know if this is still feeling helpful to you, or if there is anything you want me to understand about what you're experiencing right now."

She was responsive to my checking in. With her eyes still closed, she described what the dolphins were doing and how her younger self was responding positively to them. After 10 minutes, Pamela let out a long exhalation, wiped her face with her hands, and slowly sat up.

"How are you doing?" I asked.

"All right. Imagining dolphins taking care of me helped. I've never known what to do for myself when I was feeling like Poor Girl. I'd either cry myself to sleep or binge on ice cream." Then she looked at me and teased, "Are you okay? You look like you've seen a ghost!" Relieved her adult self was back, I sighed nervously, "Yeah! I wasn't quite sure what you needed from me, but I was hopeful we could figure it out while you were here."

She nodded, "Me too. I'm glad I came. But I'm tired. This Poor Girl needs some sleep!"

We continued to use the language of parts to help Pamela understand and manage her feelings in personal relationships. Cultivating compassionate curiosity toward her parts, and the parts of others, gave her the courage to work through conflicts and express her feelings. In all, we worked together for 10 years. Healing from her tortuous past and implementing new skills took time. But, during the last year of our therapy, she successfully established healthy new friendships and felt hopeful she could have a healthy romantic relationship someday, too.

Working with complex trauma survivors like Pam, Craig, and Mallory is extremely rewarding, but it is intense and can drain you if you're not careful. To sustain the stamina to do this challenging and important work, you have to take good care of yourself. In Chapter 16, I'll talk about how to counter compassion fatigue.

I. When you have a complaint about something in your relationship:

A. Appreciate: Tell your partner one thing you like or appreciate about them first (This is hard when you're angry, but people are more open to listen when they feel appreciated.)

Example: I really enjoy spending time with you. But I notice we keep getting into conflicts around something. I'd like to figure out how we can resolve it or make it better.

B. Behavior: Make the complaint about the behavior, not the person. Use the following script:

When you do (or don't do) _____ , then I feel _____, because it gives me the impression that _____.

Example: When I text you and you don't respond for several hours, then I feel hurt and angry because it gives me the impression I'm not important to you.

C. Consider a solution. If you don't invite discussion about a potential solution, the argument will go nowhere. Focus on things you both could do differently to solve the problem.

Example: Could we agree on a time frame that we'll reply to calls or texts, so I don't feel ignored and you don't feel so pressured?

II. When you're the one being criticized:

A. Acknowledge that you can understand the person's feelings based on this script:

I understand you felt _____ *when*
I did (or didn't do) _____ *because*
it gave you the impression that (or seemed like I)

_____.

> *Example: I understand you felt hurt and angry because it seemed like I was blowing you off.*

B. Reassure your partner you care, then share your explanation of why you did or didn't do whatever it is that upset them.

> *Example: You are important to me, but when I'm working I can't reply right away and I want a minute to think about what I'm saying before I reply so it makes sense.*

C. Compromise: propose a potential solution you can both live with.

> *Example: If we can agree that I'll reply to you within an hour of my getting off work, would that be okay? Then you'll know when to expect a reply, and I can be more thoughtful in my response.*

16

Counter Compassion Fatigue

C ompassion fatigue can be a natural consequence of listening to stories of traumatic events, especially for those who have an enormous capacity for empathy and the desire to help others. (Figley, 1995). In their book *The Resilient Practitioner: Burnout and Compassion Fatigue Self-Care Strategies*, Skovholt and Trotter-Mathison (2016) note that the best therapists are the ones who are compassionate, emotionally attuned, and fully engaged with clients, but these interpersonal strengths can also be risk factors for burnout. We're caught in the constant struggle of balancing our own needs with the needs of others. Full therapeutic engagement takes a great deal of energy and can leave you feeling depleted, with little left for yourself or loved ones. In this chapter you'll learn how to recognize the signs of burnout and compassion fatigue, as well as what you can do to counter it.

Signs of burnout, secondary trauma, and compassion fatigue

Burnout results from prolonged work stress. Signs of burnout include exhaustion, irritability, cynicism, and a reduced sense of effectiveness in your work. Burnout experts Maslach & Leiter (1997) opine burnout can result from problems in the work environment, too. Environmental risk factors for burnout include high caseloads, lack of control, unfair treatment, insufficient rewards, value conflicts, and lack of support in the workplace.

Compassion fatigue is a bit different from burnout in that it involves elements of secondary traumatization caused by repeated exposure to stories of trauma and human suffering. For example, a person with compassion fatigue may have intrusive images and thoughts about clients' stories, or find themselves preoccupied with traumatized clients. Having more awareness of the dangers in the world, therapists who treat trauma could feel more anxious, vigilant, or depressed. Working with sexual trauma survivors made me more wary of my surroundings. After a while, I also stopped watching one of my favorite television shows, *Law and Order: Special Victims Unit*, a classic "whodunnit" crime show. I used to enjoy attempting to solve each episode's mysterious crime. But I heard so many real stories about rape and murder at my office that I couldn't spend my free time exposing myself to any more stories about human suffering. I had to go out of my way to balance my life with positive activities and actively initiate self-care.

ASSERTIVE SELF-CARE

When most of us think of self-care, we think, "Eat right. Exercise. Get enough sleep. Meditate. But how do I do that when I work 8 to 10 hours a day and take care of a family?"

I learned the hard way that you cannot wait until you have a free moment to do self-care, you have to practice what Skovholt and Trotter-Mathison (2016) call *assertive self-care*. Thinking of self-care as something I needed to assert emboldened me to make it a priority. Self-care can be done in small ways. For example, I asked my family to give me 30 minutes of quiet time after I get home from work so I could decompress before engaging with them. I hired a virtual assistant to do my billing and answer my phone calls and emails. I gave myself longer breaks between clients. All these shifts made a big difference in my well-being.

Simple self-care practices

In her book *Simple Self-Care for Therapists*, author and social worker Ashley Davis Bush (2015) suggests micro self-care activities that only take a few minutes. She divides self-care activities into three categories: grounding, energizing, and relaxing. An example of a grounding activity she shares is a self-compassion practice. She recommends starting your day by placing a hand on your cheek or heart and saying to yourself, *"May I be at ease. May I accept myself. May I know deep peace. May I be kind to myself"* (p. 91). I also end my day with this practice by briefly recalling each client who was on my schedule and mentally saying, *"May you be at ease. May you accept yourself. May you know deep peace. May you be kind to yourself."* This ritual helps me avoid worrying about clients and affirms my belief in their ability to heal.

Similarly, you can use any of the tools I shared in Chapter 5, Tools for Grounding, Calming, and Soothing and Chapter 7, Instill Hope and Empowerment for yourself. I use the grounding and movement practices I shared in Chapter 5 to discharge emotional energy between sessions and keep myself energized throughout the day. I use the Breath-Symbol Imagery exercise I shared in Chapter 7 to help me embody strength, fortitude, patience, and calm. Additionally, I use the 4-Point Daily Stress Shield activity I shared in Chapter 6, How to Work with Dissociation, when I need to feel safe, grounded, and protective of my boundaries.

Seek out positive experiences

Because we hear so many negative stories every day, we have to go out of our way to attend to positive moments in our lives. In his book *Hardwiring Happiness*, Rick Hanson (2013) states, ". . . the brain evolved with a negativity bias that makes it like Velcro for bad experiences, but

Teflon for good ones" (p. 2). In order to make good experiences stick and balance our emotional states, Hanson says we have to notice positive moments and take them in deeply for at least ten to twenty seconds to install them into our neural networks. He uses the acronym HEAL to describe the steps for installing positive experiences into your brain:

1. **H**ave a positive experience.
2. **E**nrich it by intensifying it, valuing it, and lengthen for 10 to 20 seconds. This helps new neurons wire together.
3. **A**bsorb it by intending to receive it and let it reward you with a sense of appreciation, pleasure, reassurance, or joy. This stimulates reward neurochemicals in the brain.
4. **L**ink positive and negative material (optional). Hold the positive experience as you recall a negative experience. Let the positive experience be more prominent so it can penetrate and influence the negative material with a new meaning.

To apply this in your day, you may take a moment to savor the satisfaction of a good session. You may eat your lunch in a mindful way, relishing each bite. You may notice a moment of quiet and take a few moments to rest peacefully in it.

The "Link" step in the Hanson's HEAL sequence is essentially the process of memory reconsolidation. Hanson's suggestion to focus on a positive experience before linking to a negative experience is another reason that I suggest you connect your clients to positive new meaning experiences in the RECON protocol *before* you have them revisit the traumatic memory in detail. Likewise, it is useful for you to focus on the positive experiences you've had in your day before reflecting on negative experiences with clients. Focusing on the positive first helps you get perspective, expands your vision, and actually helps you solve problems better.

Positive psychology researcher Barbara Fredrickson (2009) found that focusing on positive emotions broadens people's awareness of creative solutions and fosters resilience in the face of adversity. Specifically, she discovered that people who felt more satisfied in their lives actively practiced acknowledging at least three positive experiences to every one negative moment. She calls this the "positivity ratio" and found this 3:1 proportion to be the "tipping point" for promoting a higher state of well-being. Fredrickson clarifies she's not suggesting positive thinking, it's more about letting ourselves take the time to *notice and experience positive emotions*. Welcome moments of hope, inspiration, joy, love, humor, and serenity in spite of negative experiences. Fredrickson found the mindset of being open, curious, kind, appreciative, and real gives us more access to positive emotions. This is the mental stance most of us practice when sitting with our clients, so you're already doing it. Just be sure to do it for yourself.

REALISTIC EXPECTATIONS

As therapists we tend to be idealistic, but we have to be realistic about what we can do with the time and resources we have. If you work in a hospital or at an agency with high caseloads and few resources, your employer may not be realistic about what you can accomplish in an eight-hour day, but you have to be realistic about it. You may only have time to stabilize the client's current crisis without getting a chance to do deeper work with them. You may only have an opportunity to teach clients a few stress management or interpersonal skills, and not have a chance to reconsolidate traumatic memories. Fortunately, research by Cloitre et al. (2010) affirmed trauma symptoms can improve from learning emotional regulation and interpersonal skills alone. Prioritize the client's needs and do what you can in the time that you have.

If you work in private practice, you do not have to see clients back to back, as I used to do. I've seen so many private practitioners routinely skip lunch and avoid taking breaks. That's not good for you or your clients. Rethink your schedule and make sure you give yourself enough time to eat, do your paperwork, and take breaks. Because I do so much trauma work, I schedule clients every 90 minutes, instead of on the hour. This way I have time to handle any unexpected crises that may arise in a session, or have time to do a full memory reconsolidation protocol when needed. For sessions that don't require 90 minutes, I use the additional 30 minutes between sessions to do paperwork, chat with colleagues, meditate, or go for a walk.

If you have control over your caseload, limit the number of traumatized clients that you take. I take only one dissociative identity disorder client at a time, and limit high crisis or suicidal clients to 10 percent of my caseload when I can. I also had to get realistic about the length of time it takes for clients with complex trauma to heal. When I learned techniques that produced rapid memory reconsolidation like eye movement desensitization and reprocessing, coherence therapy, and trauma-informed hypnotherapy, I got excited. Memory reconsolidation reduced the acute symptoms of PTSD, anxiety, and depression quickly. But clients still needed ongoing guidance and support for current relationship, work, or family problems. You're not meant to be a miracle worker, you're meant to be an expert companion guiding and supporting clients on their healing journey. Ultimately, the client can and will be responsible for their own healing.

RECOGNIZE ENACTMENTS AND HANDLE ACCORDINGLY

Enactments are those transference/countertransference moments when you and the client trigger each other. The client's unconscious material stimulates your unconscious material, and you both play out relational patterns from your histories. It's going to happen and it's nothing to be ashamed of. You just need to recognize when it's happening and have the courage to address it. Doing so can be a wonderful growing experience for both you and your clients. When we are able to admit to and repair empathic failures, misunderstandings, and mistakes, it usually strengthens the relationship and deepens the client's trust.

In their book chapter, *Preventing Compassion Fatigue: A Team Treatment Model*, Munroe et al. (1995) observed that compassion fatigue can result from the following enactments:

Exploiter/exploited: Client may feel exploited and accuse therapist of being like all the others who used her, or exploit therapist by pushing boundaries.

Allies/enemies: Client believes you are either friend or foe; therapist afraid of becoming "enemy" may avoid challenging client appropriately, or setting limits.

Aggressor/attacked: Client may manipulate therapist with threats; client may feel attacked if therapist doesn't give him/her choices about therapy process.

Rescuer/rescued: Therapeutic relationship revolves around crisis—usually client seeking for therapist to rescue her, but client could also attempt to "rescue" therapist.

Enactments often come up around boundary issues such as: no-shows or arriving late to sessions; running over the time limit for a session; bringing a partner, child, or pet to a session without asking you in advance; or coming to a session high or drunk. It's very stressful to confront clients about these issues, but better to do it sooner rather than later. If you don't address it early on, it becomes more difficult to resolve. When you're addressing these issues, use empathic confrontation, compassionate curiosity, and appropriate self-disclosure about your feelings. Don't take their behavior personally—they are acting out patterns from their past.

For example, when a 37-year-old alcoholic client came to a session drunk, I didn't scold her. I understood that drinking was how she'd learned to cope with emotional pain and stress. But she was too intoxicated for us to have a productive therapy session and too drunk to drive home. To address the issue, I said compassionately, "Corinne, it's good to see you. But I can tell you've had a few drinks. Did something happen today to cause you to drink in the middle of the afternoon?"

Corrine shook her head and slurred, "Nah. Just the usual flusteration." (Not a typo—that's how she said it.)

Relieved she didn't have any other crises, I said warmly, but firmly,

"Unfortunately, we can't work together while you're drunk. You have to be able to think clearly, and I'm not seeing signs of that at the moment."

Corinne looked down at her feet in shame and mumbled, "Are you going to fire me?"

I answered, "No. I'd like to reschedule this appointment and call you a cab so you get home safely."

Corinne opened her eyes wide and exclaimed, "Call me a cab? No! I only live five minutes away. I can drive home!"

Shaking my head, I said, "No, Corinne. I care about you. If I think you could be a danger to yourself or others, I have to take action to ensure your safety. I'm not mad at you, but I insist that you call a friend to come get you or take a cab home. I can't let you drive home drunk."

To make a long story short, she reluctantly called a cab to come get her at my office. At her next session, she apologized and didn't want to talk about the incident further.

"I know it's uncomfortable, but *I really need to talk about it*," I said. "I want to understand what was going on for you that day and what our interaction was like for you. And I'll share what it was like for me, if you're interested. I felt weird and awkward too."

Corinne covered her face, "Ugh! I'm so embarrassed. You felt weird and awkward too?"

Revealing my vulnerability and feelings first seemed to help Corinne open up and feel less ashamed about sharing hers. Although I was nervous starting this conversation, we were both relieved after we had a chance to process it. She feared I would shame and punish her for being drunk, like her mother, and was touched by how respectfully I treated her that day. But she was hurt and confused that I didn't call later to check on her—something her mother does after one of her drinking binges. I told her I didn't call because I thought she was an intelligent adult who was capable of taking care of herself. My faith in her ability to take care of herself sparked an "Aha!" insight for her. She'd perceived herself to be an incompetent person who couldn't get her life together. Suddenly it occurred to her that she could function independently and was competent enough to run her own life. You never know the insights that processing an enactment will produce, but they're usually profound.

Know your triggers

There are no hard and fast rules for addressing enactments because it's a relational issue, and every relationship is different. But, it does help to know which issues trigger strong feelings for you so you can prepare yourself. One way to know your vulnerabilities is to assess your attachment style. I've listed several tools you can use in Chapter 3, Relationships Change the Brain. If you have anxious-preoccupied tendencies, you may be vulnerable to pleasing or rescuing clients, tying your self-worth to client progress, overworking, over-empathizing, or over-flexing boundaries. If you have avoidant-dismissive tendencies, you may feel uncomfortable exploring deeper emotional issues with clients; feel annoyed or overwhelmed with clients who seem needy or helpless; or misattune to clients by providing overly rational responses instead of warm, empathic responses. If you have a history of disorganized attachment, you may fluctuate between anxious and avoidant attachment behaviors, depending on the relational dynamic with each client.

When you find your issues getting triggered, the best thing to do is to get your own therapy! I've been a therapist for 20 years, and I still go to therapy. I don't go every week, but I have a longstanding relationship with a therapist I see when life throws me curveballs or I have a challenging client caseload. To me, psychotherapy isn't just about mental health, it's about personal growth, human development, and well-being. Each developmental stage of life has new challenges, insights, and experiences to process. If you don't have the time or money for therapy, at least seek consultation and peer support.

Consultation and peer support

If there is one mistake I see therapists make over and over, it's failing to ask for help. When you are working with traumatized clients, it's important for you to get support. This is hard work, and you don't have to do it alone! Consultation and supervision are not just for beginning therapists. We can use it throughout our careers. Find a therapist you respect and ask if he or she is open to offering consultation or supervision. Or find a peer consultation group you can join. I offer monthly video consultation groups, as do many other trauma therapists across the country. Consultation helps you feel less isolated and gives you fresh perspectives, encouragement, and confidence.

In case of emergency, remember this story

Sometimes you just need reassurance that you're doing enough. Brain science is finally validating what we've intuitively known as therapists: People heal through feeling cared for by others. Study after study shows that a caring, compassionate relationship with another human being promotes healing more than any single therapy technique or medication.

I witnessed the power of this principle firsthand when I worked with Vanessa, a victim of the 2012 movie theater massacre in Aurora, Colorado. Vanessa wasn't in the *Batman* movie where the shooting happened, but in a showing of another movie next door. The film had just started when the overhead lights suddenly came on and ushers hurriedly evacuated the audience, including Vanessa and her sister, out of the theater.

Vanessa stepped out of a comfortable, air-conditioned movie theater into a parking lot of pandemonium, bloodshed, sirens, and tears. She tried to find her way through the chaos and almost stumbled over a woman whose pants were covered in blood. The woman had been shot in the leg. Vanessa panicked. She and her sister still didn't know what had happened. They feared they were in the middle of a gang war and needed to find shelter as soon as possible, or risk getting shot themselves. Yet they knew this woman needed help and didn't feel right about leaving her to bleed alone in the street.

Vanessa's sister agreed to find a first responder who could help them while Vanessa knelt down, held the injured woman's hand, and let her know her sister was going to get help. The woman squeezed Vanessa's hand and asked with a weak, raspy voice, "Can you please call my mother?"

The woman began to call out her mother's phone number as Vanessa fumbled through her purse as fast as she could to find her phone. She managed to get the number punched into her phone and held it up to the injured woman's ear so she could hear her mother's voice. Vanessa continued to hold the woman's hand until the medical team could get to her and thought she would never see or hear from this woman again.

Seven months later, when Vanessa came to me for trauma therapy, she wasn't as troubled by post-traumatic stress as she was by survivor's guilt. Vanessa, an occupational therapist, buried her face in her hands and cried, "All I could think to do for the gunshot victim was to sit there and hold her hand. I am in the healthcare field, and I felt completely incompetent."

I put a hand on her shoulder and replied, "Vanessa, you did the perfect thing. You showed her care and compassion in the midst of tragedy, and you connected her to her mother."

Without realizing it, Vanessa instinctively activated the first two conditions of psychological first aid: 1) Recreate a sense of safety; and 2) establish meaningful social connections and reconnect victims with loved ones. These conditions were established after a landmark study published by Hobfoll et al. (2004) that identified five essential elements that helped disaster victims overcome traumatic stress reactions: safety, calming, connectedness, self-efficacy, and hope.

Sharing this information with Vanessa lifted her spirits a little, but it didn't alleviate her guilt. What I needed to do was create an *experience* in our session that would help her realize that the way she demonstrated care toward this woman was extremely valuable.

To accomplish this, I asked Vanessa to retell the story of what happened that day in Aurora as I *held her hand* and assisted her in remaining emotionally present with me. She noticed that my holding her hand as she revisited this memory was very reassuring and comforting and said, "Maybe I was more helpful to her than I thought. I hope she's okay."

A few months later, Vanessa went back to Colorado for a hearing in the case. She was elated when she ran into the woman she had comforted in the parking lot the night of the tragedy. As soon as she saw Vanessa, the woman ran to her and hugged her neck. As they talked about how they'd been doing since the shooting, Vanessa lamented, "I have post-traumatic stress and I wasn't even shot. I can't imagine how you're doing."

The woman grabbed Vanessa's hand and professed, "Vanessa, I'm surprisingly okay. I've had a few nightmares, and my leg still hurts at times. While I'm not planning on going to movie theaters any time soon, I don't dwell on the incident itself. Do you know what replays in my mind instead?"

"What?" Vanessa asked.

Looking tearfully into Vanessa's eyes, she squeezed her hand and cried, *"The kindness of a stranger who held my hand through all that horror. That's what stands out for me, Vanessa."*

Hearing those caring words from the shooting victim herself was the final experience that released Vanessa from her survivor's guilt and allowed her to move forward with her life.

Demonstrating care toward someone who is in distress is not just a kind thing to do; care is the very thing that can heal them.

As Vanessa experienced, it's not about knowing the perfect words to say, or finding an instant solution to the person's problem. Simply being able to sit compassionately with a person as they make sense of their experience lightens the darkness and dissolves the walls of despair and isolation. Remember this on those days you are doubting yourself, feeling overwhelmed, or wondering if you need more training. Your most powerful skill comes from the softest, humblest place you already possess—the bottom of your own heart.

References

Ainsworth, M. D. S., Blehar, M. C., Waters, E., & Wall, S. N. (2015). *Patterns of attachment: A psychological study of the strange situation*. New York: Psychology Press.

Allison, R. B. (1999). *Minds in many pieces: Revealing the spiritual side of multiple personality disorder* (2nd ed.). Paso Robles, CA: CIE Publishing.

American Psychiatric Association. (1980). *Diagnostic and statistical manual of mental health disorders* (3rd ed.). Washington, D.C.: American Psychiatric Publishing.

American Psychiatric Association. (2013). *Diagnostic and statistical manual of mental disorders* (5th ed.). Arlington, VA: American Psychiatric Publishing.

Andersen, S. L., Tomada, A., Vincow, E. S., Valente, E., Polcari, A., & Teicher, M. H. (2008). Preliminary evidence for sensitive periods in the effect of childhood sexual abuse on regional brain development. *Journal of Neuropsychiatry and Clinical Neuroscience, 20*(3), 292–301.

Armstrong, C. (2011). *Transforming traumatic grief: Six steps to move from grief to peace*. Chattanooga, TN: Author.

Armstrong, C. (2015). *The therapeutic aha!: Ten strategies for getting your clients unstuck*. New York: W. W. Norton & Company.

Badenoch, B. (2017). *The heart of trauma: Healing the embodied brain in the context of relationships*. New York: W. W. Norton & Company.

Bandler, R. & Grinder, J. (1982). *Reframing: Neurolinguistic programming and the transformation of meaning*. Boulder, CO: Real People Press.

Bateman, A. & Fonagy, P. (2010) Mentalization based treatment for borderline personality disorder. *World Psychiatry, 9*(1), 11–15.

Beckers, T., & Kindt, M. (2017). Memory reconsolidation interference as an emerging treatment for emotional disorders: Strengths, limitations, challenges and opportunities. *Annual Review of Clinical Psychology, 13*, 99–121.

Bonanno, G. (2009). *The other side of sadness: What the new science of bereavement tells us about life after loss*. New York: Basic Books.

Blige, M. J., Garrett, S., Douthit, P., Aries, R., Jackson, F., Morgan, M. (2005). Good woman down. (Recording by Mary J. Blige). In *The Breakthrough* (CD). Santa Monica, CA: Geffen Records.

Boon, S., Steele, K., & van der Hart, O. (2011). *Coping with trauma-related dissociation: Skills training for patients and therapists.* New York: W. W. Norton & Company.

Bowlby, J. (1980). *Attachment and loss* (Vol. 3): *Loss, sadness, and depression.* New York: Basic Books.

Bowlby, J. (1988) *A secure base: Parent-child attachment and healthy human development* (Reprint ed.). New York: Basic Books.

Bremner, J. D., Elzina, B., Schmahl, C., & Vermetten, E. (2008). Structural and functional plasticity of the human brain in posttraumatic stress disorder. *Progress in Brain Research 167*, 171–186.

Bryant, R. A. (2016). Social attachments and traumatic stress. *European Journal of Psychotraumatology 7.* https://doi.org/10.3402/ejpt.v7.29065.

Bush, A. D. (2015). *Simple self-care for therapists.* New York: W. W. Norton & Company.

Carlson, E. B. & Putnam, F. W. (1993). An update on the Dissociative Experiences Scale. *Dissociation: Progress in the Dissociative Disorders, 6*(1), 16–27.

Calhoun, L. G. & Tedeschi, R. G. (2008). *Facilitating posttraumatic growth: A clinician's guide* (Kindle Edition). New York: Taylor & Francis.

Carrion, V. G., Weems, C. F., & Reiss, A. L. (2007). Stress predicts brain changes in children: A pilot longitudinal study on youth stress, posttraumatic stress disorder, and the hippocampus. *Pediatrics, 119*(3), 509–516.

Charney, D. S., Deutch, A. Y., Krystal, J. H., Southwick, S. M., & Davis, M. (1993). Psychobiologic mechanisms of posttraumatic stress disorder. *Archives of General Psychiatry, 50*(4), 295–305.

Charuvastra, A. & Cloitre, M. (2008). Social bonds and post-traumatic stress disorder. *Annual Review of Psychology 59*, 301–328.

Cloitre, M., Stovall-McClough, K., Miranda, R., & Chemtob, C. (2004). Therapeutic alliance, negative mood regulation, and treatment outcome in child abuse-related posttraumatic stress disorder. *Journal of Consulting and Clinical Psychology, 72*(3), 410–416.

Cloitre, M., Stovall-McClough, K., Nooner, K., Zorbas, P., Cherry, S., Jackson, C., Gan, W., & Petkova, E. (2010). Treatment for PTSD related to childhood abuse: A randomized controlled trial. *American Journal of Psychiatry, 167*, 915–924.

Coan, J. A., Schaefer H. S., & Davidson R. J. (2006). Lending a hand: Social regulation of the neural response to threat. *Psychological Science 17*(12), 1032–1039.

Cohen-Posey, K. (2016). *Brain change cards.* Lakeland, FL: Author.

Collins, N. L. (1996). *Revised adult attachment scale.* Author: Santa Barbara, CA.

Connelly, J. (2014). *Rapid resolution therapy level I manual.* Tampa, FL: Author.

Cozolino, L. (2015). *Why therapy works: Using our minds to change our brains.* New York: W. W. Norton & Company.

DeBellis, M. D. & Zisk, A. (2014). The biological effects of childhood trauma. *Child and Adolescent Psychiatry Clinics of North America, 23*(2), 185–222.

Diamond, D. M., Fleshner, M., Rose, G. M., & Ingersoll, N. (1996). Psychological stress impairs spatial working memory: Relevance to electrophysiological studies of hippocampal function. *Behavioral Neuroscience, 110*(4), 661–672.

Doidge, N. (2016). *The brain's way of healing: Remarkable discoveries and recoveries from the frontiers of neuroplasticity.* New York: Penguin Books.

Ecker, B., Ticic, R., & Hulley, L. (2012). *Unlocking the emotional brain: Eliminating symptoms at their roots using memory reconsolidation.* New York: Routledge.

Engdahl, B., Leuthold, A. C., Tan, H.-R. M., Lewis, S. M., Winskowski, A. M., Dike, T. N., & Georgopoulos, A. P. (2010). Post-traumatic stress disorder: A right temporal lobe syndrome? *Journal of Neural Engineering* 7(6), https://doi.org/1088/1741-2560/7/6/066005.

Felitti, V. J., Anda, R. F., Nordenberg, D., Williamson, D. F., Spitz, A. M., Edwards, V., Koss, M. P., & Marks, J. S. (1998). Relationship of childhood abuse and household dysfunction to many of the leading causes of death in adults. The Adverse Childhood Experiences (ACE) Study. *American Journal of Preventative Medicine, 14*(4), 245–258.

Ferentz, L. (2015). *Treating self-destructive behaviors in trauma survivors: A clinician's guide* (2nd ed.). New York: Routledge.

Fielding, L. (2015, October 20). Listening to your authentic self: The purpose of emotions. *Huffington Post,* Retrieved from https://www.huffingtonpost.com.

Figley, C. R. (Ed.) (1995). *Compassion fatigue: Coping with secondary traumatic stress disorder for those who treat the traumatized.* New York: Taylor & Francis.

Fisher, J. (2017). *Healing the fragmented selves of trauma survivors: Overcoming internal self-alienation.* New York: Routledge.

Foa, E. B. & Kozak, M. J. (1986). Emotional processing of fear: Exposure to corrective information. *Psychological Bulletin, 99*(1), 20–35.

Foa, E. B., Hembree, E. A., & Rothbaum, B. O. (2007). *Prolonged exposure therapy for PTSD: Emotional processing for traumatic experiences.* New York: Oxford University Press.

Fosha, D. (2008). *The transforming power of affect: A model for accelerated change.* New York: Basic Books.

Fraley, R. C., Waller, N. G., & Brennan, K. A. (2000). An item-response theory analysis of self-report measures of adult attachment. *Journal of Personality and Social Psychology, 78,* 350–365.

Frankl, V. (2006). *Man's search for meaning.* Boston, MA: Beacon Press.

Fredrickson, B. L. (2013, July 15). Updated thinking on positivity ratios. *American Psychologist.* advance online publication. http://doi.org/10.1037/a0033584.

George, C., Kaplan, N., & Main, M. (1985). *The adult attachment interview.* Unpublished manuscript, University of California at Berkeley.

Germain, A., Krakow, B., Faucher, B., Zadra, A., Nielsen, T., Hollifield, M., Warner, T., & Koss, M. (2004). Increased mastery elements associated with imagery rehearsal treatment for nightmares in sexual assault survivors with PTSD. *Dreaming, 14*(4), 195–206.

Grossman, D. (2009). *On killing: The psychological cost of learning to kill in war and society* (revised ed.). New York: Back Bay Books.

Hanson, R. (2013). *Hardwiring happiness: The new brain science of contentment, calm, and confidence*. New York: Harmony Books.

Hobfoll, S. E., Watson, P., Bell, C. C., Bryant, R. A., Brymer, M. J., Friedman, M. J., et al. (2007). Five essential elements of immediate and mid-term mass trauma intervention: Empirical evidence. *Psychiatry, 70*(4), 283–315.

Jamieson, J. P., Nock, M. K., & Mendes, W. B. (2012). Mind over matter: Reappraising arousal improves cardiovascular and cognitive responses to stress. *Journal of Experimental Psychology, General, 141*(3), 412–422.

Joseph, S. (2011). *What doesn't kill us. The new psychology of post-traumatic growth.* New York: Basic Books.

Kabat-Zinn, J. (2013). *Full catastrophe living: Using the wisdom of the body and mind to face stress, pain, and illness* (revised ed.). New York: Bantam Books.

Klass, D. & Steffen, E. M. (Eds.). (2018). *Continuing bonds in bereavement: New directions for research and practice.* New York: Routledge.

King, L. A. (2001). The health benefits of writing about life goals. *Personality and Social Psychology Bulletin, 27*(7), 798–807. doi:10.1177/0146167201277003.

Krakauer, S. (2001). *Treating dissociative identity disorder: The power of the collective heart.* New York: Taylor & Francis.

Kunze, A. E., Arntz, A., Morina, N., Kindt, M., & Lancee, J. (2017). Efficacy of imagery rescripting and imaginal exposure for nightmares: A randomized waitlist controlled trial. *Elsevier Behavior Research and Therapy, 97*, 14–25.

Kushner, H. S. (1981). *When bad things happen to good people.* New York: Random House, Inc.

Lanius, R. A., Williamson, P. C., Densmore, M., Boksman K., Neufeld, R.W., Gati, J. S., & Menon, R. S. (2004). The nature of traumatic memories: A 4-T FMRI functional connectivity analysis. *American Journal of Psychiatry 161*(1), 36–44.

Lanius, U. F., Paulsen, S. L., & Corrigan, F. M. (2014). *Neurobiology and treatment of traumatic dissociation: Toward and embodied self.* New York: Springer Publishing.

Lawson, J. (2015). *Furiously happy.* New York: Flatiron Books.

LeDoux, J. (2015). *Anxious: Using the brain to understand and treat fear and anxiety.* New York: Penguin Books.

Lenzi, D., Trentini, C., Tambelli, R., & Pantano, P. (2015). Neural basis of attachment-caregiving systems interaction: Insights from neuroimaging studies. *Frontiers in Psychology 6*, https://doi.org/10.3389/fpsyg.2015.01241.

Lerner, H. (2014). *The dance of anger: A woman's guide to changing the patterns of intimate relationships.* New York: William Morrow and Company.

Levine, P. (2015). *Trauma and memory: Brain and body in search of a living past: A practical guide to understanding and working with traumatic memory*. Berkeley, CA: North Atlantic Books.

Linehan, M. (1993). *Cognitive-behavioral treatment of borderline personality disorder*. New York: Guilford Press.

Loftus, E. F. & Pickrell, J. E. (1995). The formation of false memories. *Psychiatric Annals, 25*(12), 720–725.

Lorenzini, N & Fonagy, P. (2013) Attachment and personality disorders: A short review. *FOCUS: The Journal of Lifelong Learning in Psychiatry, 11*(2) 155–166. http://doi.org/10.1176/appi.focus.11.2.155.

MacLean, P. (1990). *The triune brain in evolution: Role in paleocerebral functions*. New York: Springer Publishing.

Main, M. & Solomon, J. (1990). Procedures for identifying infants as disorganized/disoriented during the Ainsworth Strange Situation. In M. Greenberg, D. Cicchetti, & E. M. Cummings (Eds.), *Attachment in the preschool years: Theory, research, and intervention* (pp. 121–160.) Chicago: University of Chicago Press.

Mancini, A. Littleton, H. & Grills, A. (2015). Can people benefit from acute stress? Social support, psychological improvement, and resilience after the Virginia Tech campus shootings. *Clinical Psychological Science*, https://doi.org/10.1177/2167702615601001.

Mancini, A. (2016, June 1). *The trouble with post-traumatic growth*. (blog post]. Retrieved from https://www.psychologytoday.com/us/blog/rethinking-trauma/201606/the-trouble-post-traumatic-growth.

Maslach, C., & Leiter, M. P. (1997). *The truth about burnout*. San Francisco, CA: Jossey-Bass.

McCraty, R. & Childre, D. (2002). *The appreciative heart: The psychophysiology of positive emotions and optimal functioning*. Boulder Creek, CA: Institute of HeartMath.

Mitchell, C. W. (2007). *Effective techniques for dealing with highly resistant clients* (2nd ed.). Johnson City, TN: Author.

Morris, D. J. (2016). *The evil hours: A biography of post-traumatic stress disorder*. New York: First Mariner Books.

Munroe, J., Shay, J., Fisher, L., Makary, C., Rapperport, K., Zimering, R. (1995). Preventing compassion fatigue: A team treatment model. In C. R. Figley, (Ed.) *Compassion Fatigue: Coping With Secondary Traumatic Stress Disorder In Those Who Treat The Traumatized* (pp. 207–229). New York: Taylor & Francis.

Murphy, D. & Joseph, S. (Eds.). (2013). *Trauma and the therapeutic relationship: Approaches to process and practice*. New York: Palgrave Macmillan.

Myss, C. (2003). *Archetype cards*. Carlsbad, CA: Hay House.

Nader, K., Schafe, G. E., & LeDoux, J. E. (2000). Fear memories require protein synthesis in the amygdala for reconsolidation after retrieval. *Nature, 406*, 722–726.

Najavits, L. M. (2015). The problem of dropout from 'gold standard' PTSD therapies. *F1000Prime Reports 7*(43), http://doi.org/10.12703/P7-43.

Nhất Hahn, T. (1995). *Living Buddha, living Christ*. New York: Riverhead Books.

National Institute for the Clinical Application of Behavioral Medicine [NICABM] (2017, June 2). *Two simple techniques that can help trauma patients feel safe with Peter Levine*. [Video file]. Retrieved from https://www.youtube.com/watch?v=G7zAseaIyFA.

Norcross, J. C. & Wampold, B. (2011). Evidence-based therapy relationships: Research conclusions and clinical practices. *Psychotherapy* 48(1), 98–102.

Ogden, P. & Fisher, J. (2015). *Sensorimotor psychotherapy: Interventions for trauma and attachment*. New York: W. W. Norton & Company.

O'Hanlon, B. (2014). *Out of the blue: Six non-medication ways to relieve depression*. New York: W. W. Norton & Company.

O'Hanlon, B. (2013). *Becoming a published therapist. A step-by-step guide to writing your book*. New York: W. W. Norton & Company.

O'Hanlon, B. (2011). *Quick steps to resolving trauma*. New York: W. W. Norton & Company.

Panksepp, J. & Biven, L. (2012). *The archeology of mind: Neuroevolutionary origins of human emotions*. New York: W. W. Norton & Company.

Peper, E., Lin, I. M., Harvey, R., & Perez, J. (2017). How posture affects memory recall and mood. *Biofeedback* 45(2), 36–41.

Pessoa, L. (2013). *The cognitive-emotional brain: From interactions to integration*. Cambridge, MA: The MIT Press.

Peterson, C. & Seligman, M. E. P. (2004). *Character strengths and virtues: A handbook and classification*. New York: Oxford University Press, and Washington, D.C.: American Psychological Association.

Peterson, C., Park, N., Pole, N., D'Andrea, W., & Seligman, M. E. P. (2008). Strengths of character and posttraumatic growth. *Journal of Traumatic Stress, 21*, 214–217.

Philippot, P., Chapelle, G., & Blairy, S. (2002). Respiratory feedback in the generation of emotion. *Journal of Cognition and Emotion, 16*(5), 605–627. https://doi.org/10.1080/02699930143000392

Porges, S. W. (2011). *The polyvagal theory: Neurophysiological foundations of emotions, attachment, communication, and self-regulation*. New York: W. W. Norton & Company.

Resick, P. A., Monson, C. M., & Chard, K. M. (2017). *Cognitive-processing therapy for PTSD: A comprehensive manual*. New York: Guilford Press.

Russell, M. C., Schaubel, S. R., & Figley, C. R. (2018). The darker side of military mental healthcare part one: Understanding the military's mental health dilemma. *Psychological Injury and Law, 11*, 22–36.

Sams, J. & Carson, D. (1999). *Medicine cards: The discovery of power through the way of animals*. New York: St. Martin's Press.

Schore, A. N. (2012). *The science of the art of psychotherapy*. New York: W. W. Norton & Company.

Schwartz, R. C. (2013). *Internal family systems therapy*. New York: Guilford Press.

Seligman, M. E. P. (2011). *Flourish: A visionary new understanding of happiness and well-being.* New York: Free Press.

Shafir, T., Tsachor, R., & Welch, K. (2016). Emotion regulation through movement: Unique sets of movement characteristics are associated with and enhance basic emotions. *Frontiers in Psychology, 6,* 2030. https://doi.org/10.3389/fpsyg.2015.02030.

Shapiro, F. (2017). *Eye movement desensitization and reprocessing therapy: Basic principles, protocols, and procedures* (3rd ed.). New York: Guilford Press.

Shapiro, R. (2016). *Easy ego state interventions: Strategies for working with parts.* New York: W. W. Norton & Company.

Sheldon, K. M. & Lyubomirsky, S. (2006). How to increase and sustain positive emotion: The effects of expressing gratitude and visualizing best possible selves. *The Journal of Positive Psychology, 1*(2), 73–82. http://doi.org/10.1080/17439760500510676.

Shear, K., Frank, E., Houck, P. R., & Reynolds, C. F. (2005). Treatment of complicated grief: A randomized controlled trial. *Journal of the American Medical Association, 293*(21), 2601–2608.

Shear, K. (2010). Complicated grief treatment: The theory, practice, and outcomes. *Bereavement Care, 29*(3), 10–14.

Sherrin, J. E. & Nemeroff, C. B. (2011). Post-traumatic stress disorder: The neurobiological impact of psychological trauma. *Dialogues in Clinical Neuroscience, 13*(3), 263–278.

Siegel, D. J. (1999). *The developing mind: How relationships and the brain interact to shape who we are.* New York: Guilford Press.

Siegel, D. J. (2010). *The mindful therapist: A clinician's guide to mindsight and neural integration.* New York: W. W. Norton & Company.

Siegel, D. J. (2011). *Mindsight: Transform your brain with the new science of empathy.* New York: Bantam Books.

Simeon, D. & Abugel, J. (2006). *Feeling unreal: Depersonalization disorder and the loss of self.* New York: Oxford University Press.

Singer, M. (2007). *The untethered soul: The journey beyond yourself.* Oakland, CA: New Harbinger Publications.

Skovholt, T. M. & Trotter-Mathison, M. (2016). *The resilient practitioner: Burnout and compassion fatigue prevention and self-care strategies for helping professionals.* New York: Routledge.

Smucker, M. R. & Dancu, C. V. (1999). *Cognitive-behavioral treatment for adult survivors of childhood trauma.* Lanham, MD: Rowman & Littlefield.

Steffen, P. R., Austin, T., DeBarros, A., & Brown, T. (2017). The impact of resonance frequency breathing on measures of heart rate variability, blood pressure, and mood. *Frontiers in Public Health, 5,* https://doi.org/10.3389/fpubh.2017.00222.

Tedeschi, R. G. & Moore, B. A. (2016). *The posttraumatic growth workbook.* Oakland, CA: New Harbinger Publications.

Teicher, M. (2000). Wounds that time won't heal: The neurobiology of child abuse. *Cerebrum* 4(2), 50–67.

U.S. Department of Veterans Affairs (2018). *How Common is PTSD?* (blog post) Retrieved from https://www.ptsd.va.gov/public/ptsd-overview/basics/how-common-is-ptsd.asp.

van der Hart, O., Nijenhuis, E. R .S., & Steele, K. (2006). *The haunted self: Structural dissociation and the treatment of chronic traumatization.* New York: W. W. Norton & Company.

van der Kolk, B. (2015). *The body keeps the score: Brain, mind, and body in the healing of trauma.* New York: Penguin Books.

Vedder, E. (1993). Rearview mirror. (Recorded by Pearl Jam.) On *Vs.* (CD). Los Angeles: Epic Records.

Watkins, J. G. & Watkins, H. H. (1997). *Ego states: Theory and therapy.* New York: W. W. Norton & Company.

Wong, Y. J., Owen, J., Gabana, N. T., Brown, J. W., McInnis, S., Toth, P., & Gilman, L. (2018) Does gratitude writing improve the mental health of psychotherapy clients? Evidence from a randomized controlled trial, *Psychotherapy Research*, 28(2), 192–202, https://doi.org/10.1080/10503307.2016.1169332.

Xiao, M., Yue, Z-Q., Gong, Z-Q., Zhang, H., Duan, N-Y., Shi, Y-T., Wei, G-X., & Li, Y-F. (2017). The effect of diaphragmatic breathing on attention, negative affect and stress in healthy adults. *Frontiers in Psychology,* 8, https://doi.org/10.3389/fpsyg.2017.00874.

Index

Note: Italicized page locators refer to figures; tables are noted with a *t*.

fear and anxiety regulated through, 56–57

mood and, 56

MPFC. *see* medial prefrontal cortex (MPFC)

multiple personality disorder. *see* dissociative identity disorder (DID)

Munroe, J., 219

murder, 215

music playlists, creating, 88

Myss, C., 88

Name Five Things exercise, 54, 65

National Institute for the Clinical Application of Behavioral Medicine, 67

negative beliefs, reframing, sexual trauma and, 115, 116, 118, 122–23

Neurobiology and Treatment of Traumatic Dissociation (Lanius, Paulsen, & Corrigan), 63

neurolinguistic programming (NLP), 108

neuroplasticity, 18

new meaning experience, 95

creating, 100, 116–17

finishing the story in a new place, 100–101

imaginal conversations and, 104

imagining perpetrators as childlike, immature, and irrational, 104

integrating while objectively describing event, 102–3, 117–21

internal reparenting and, 103–4, 124–25

other trauma therapies and creation of, 107

new possibilities, post-traumatic growth and openness to, 190, 193–95

Nhat Hanh, T., 59

nightmares

after son's suicide, 165–66

of the dead, combat trauma and, 181–85

rescripting, 166–68, 184

Nijenhuis, E. R. S., 69

NLP. *see* neurolinguistic programming (NLP)

Nock, M. K., 76

norepinephrine, 9, 16

nurturing gestures, evoking sense of safety with, 67

Ogden, P., 101, 107

O'Hanlon, Bill, 193

On Killing (Grossman), 176

oppositional defiant disorder, 16

orbitofrontal cortex (OFC)

"Mohawk of self-awareness" and, 19, 21

securely attached mothers and, 22

orienting tools, 54–55

oxytocin, 22, 28

pace of therapy

with anxiously attached clients, 45–46

for clients with abuse history, 143

with disorganized clients, 49

panic/grief, action request, and survival need related to, 51t

Panksepp, J., 51n, 158

parasympathetic nervous system, 10, 22, 23

parts

accepting, 68

angry/protective, 70

child, 69–70

communicating with, 71–74

functional adult, 69

helper, 70–71

inner meeting room and conversing with, 73–74

questions to ask, 72–73

types of, 69–71

working with, 68–74